Justice, Luck & Responsibility in Health Care

LIBRARY OF ETHICS AND APPLIED PHILOSOPHY

VOLUME 30

For further volumes:
http://www.springer.com/series/6230

Yvonne Denier • Chris Gastmans
Antoon Vandevelde
Editors

Justice, Luck & Responsibility in Health Care

Philosophical Background and Ethical Implications for End-of-Life Care

Springer

Editors
Yvonne Denier
Centre for Biomedical Ethics and Law
Catholic University of Leuven
Leuven, Belgium

Chris Gastmans
Centre for Biomedical Ethics and Law
Catholic University of Leuven
Leuven, Belgium

Antoon Vandevelde
Institute of Philosophy
Catholic University of Leuven
Leuven, Belgium

ISBN 978-94-007-5334-1 ISBN 978-94-007-5335-8 (eBook)
DOI 10.1007/978-94-007-5335-8
Springer Dordrecht Heidelberg New York London

Library of Congress Control Number: 2012955999

Printed on acid-free paper

Springer is part of Springer Science+Business Media (www.springer.com)

Acknowledgments

This book is the upshot of a wonderful 2-day conference held at the University of Leuven in May 2011. During this conference, an international group of philosophers, economists, and theologians focused on the relationship between justice, luck, and responsibility in health care, thereby both inquiring into the philosophical background of the theme and into its implications for end-of-life care. We heard many interesting lectures, exchanged inspiring ideas, and had lively discussions, which brought about many suggestions for further reflection and research on the theme. In this volume, we collect those ideas, reflections, and suggestions, thereby offering the basics for further research on the topic.

Having now completed this volume, it is finally our pleasure to thank all those who have, in many ways, contributed to the conference and the book. First of all, we wish to thank all the speakers of the conference for giving high-standard lectures, thereby provoking many reflections and interesting discussions. We also wish to thank the authors who have converted their lectures into excellent essays in contribution to this volume. Not only have they produced high-quality material, they also had to put up with deadlines and editorial comments, which they all did in a magnificent way. We are grateful for such a high-quality and fruitful collaboration.

We especially want to thank Ms. Ann Van Espen, who took up all the practical matters concerning the organization of the conference in an excellent way. We thank Tom Grimonprez for his assistance in the project and during the conference. We are also indebted to Paul Schotsmans and Pieter De Geyter, respective President and Director of the Holy Spirit College in Leuven, for hosting the conference. It was a true pleasure to enjoy the beautiful surroundings of the College and the warm and professional hospitality of the staff.

We would also like to thank the people from Springer, in particular the editorial board of the series Library of Ethics and Applied Philosophy for including this book into the series; and most especially Mr. Christopher Wilby and Ms. Meagan Curtis for their wonderful editorial assistance. We are much obliged to Lode Waelbers for his meticulous copy-editing during the final editorial work, for his assistance in language matters, and for relieving us of all possible IT and lay-out concerns in preparing the manuscript.

We are grateful to the Fund for Scientific Research (Flanders) for financially supporting the project. This project has been the result of an excellent collaboration between three faculties of the KU Leuven, viz., the Faculty of Philosophy, the Faculty of Medicine, and the Faculty of Business and Economics. We are grateful to various colleagues at these faculties for their practical and moral support of the project, the conference, and the book.

Leuven
December 10th 2012

Yvonne Denier, Chris Gastmans and
Antoon Vandevelde

Contents

Chapter 1
Justice and Responsibility in Health Care – An Introduction

Yvonne Denier, Chris Gastmans, and Antoon Vandevelde

The cricket, having sung her song
All summer long,
Found – when the winter winds blew free –
Her cupboard bare as bare could be;
Nothing to greet her hungering eye:
No merest crumb of worm or fly.
She went next door to cry her plight
To neighbor ant, hoping she might
Take pity on her, and befriend her,
Eke out a bit of grain to lend her,
And see her through till spring: "What say you?
On insect's honor, I'll repay you
Well before fall. With interest, too!
Our ant – no willing lender she!
Least of her faults! – replied: "I see!
Tell me, my friend, what did you do
While it was warm?" "Well... Night and Day
I sang my song for all to hear."
"You sang, you say? How nice my dear!
Now go and dance your life away!"

Jean de la Fontaine

Y. Denier • (✉) C. Gastmans
Centre for Biomedical Ethics and Law, Catholic University of Leuven,
Kapucijnenvoer 35, box 7001, 3000 Leuven, Belgium
e-mail: Yvonne.Denier@med.kuleuven.be; Chris.Gastmans@med.kuleuven.be

A. Vandevelde
Institute of Philosophy, Catholic University of Leuven,
Kardinaal Mercierplein 2, box 3200, 3000 Leuven, Belgium
e-mail: antoon.vandevelde@hiw.kuleuven.be

Y. Denier et al. (eds.), *Justice, Luck & Responsibility in Health Care*,
Library of Ethics and Applied Philosophy 30, DOI 10.1007/978-94-007-5335-8_1,

1.1 The Question

Does a human right to health care imply individual obligations to healthy behavior? Can we refuse medical treatment to patients whose bad condition was self-inflicted? For instance, should a drunk driver bear the costs of medical care that he needs after a car accident he has caused? Should there be a difference in health care entitlements between the smoker with a heart attack who is seriously overweight and the 60-year old man who has always taken excellent care of himself and is suddenly stricken by leukemia? And how should we think about the risk-taking behavior of people engaging in extreme sports, going on a skiing holiday or on an exotic hiking trip? What should we think about parents' responsibilities for the health of their children? And how far do our individual responsibilities regarding end-of-life care reach?

These are all examples of topics raised in discussions about the role of personal responsibility in health care. On the one hand, it is most reasonable to hold people responsible for the consequences of their choices and actions. On the other hand, it is not at all clear what this idea implies in the field of health care. To what extent should we allow personal responsibility to play a role in allocating health care services or resources, or in justly distributing the costs of receiving health care?

In this book, we will explore these matters by concentrating on the following philosophical and ethical questions: How should we understand justice in health care? How should we value health? Are health care interests so important that they deserve special protection? What are its functions and do these make it different from other goods? Furthermore, how much equality should there be? Which equalities and inequalities in health and health care are unfair and which are simply unfortunate? Which matters of health belong to the domain of justice, and which to the domain of charity? And what can be a fair position of personal responsibility in these matters? Taken together, is every person to be respected as an autonomous individual in these matters, or should we think of legitimate forms of paternalism in order to promote prudent behavior, responsible decisions and healthy life styles?

As such, this book has a double objective. First, it wants to provide a comprehensive philosophical framework for understanding the concepts of justice, luck and responsibility in health care. What do we mean when using these notions? And how do they relate to each other? Our approach in this is interdisciplinary. The book brings together various lines of reasoning from the disciplines of philosophy, economics, sociology, ethics and medicine.

Secondly, it particularly wants to explore whether these concepts have practical force to guide normative discussions in the field of health care. Are they well-suited to guide us in specific contexts of health care, like the domain of prevention of infectious diseases, or in matters of reproductive technology? Most extensively: how can they help us in reflecting on our responsibilities regarding end-of-life care? What are our rights and duties in this regard? Do the concepts of justice, luck and responsibility indeed have sufficient normative force in these fields, or should we perhaps look for alternative perspectives?

1.2 Justice and Equality: Equality of What?

An important starting point for the discussion is the relationship between justice and the idea of equality. After all, the concept of 'equality' has substantial rhetorical force in the general moral discourse. The basic assumption is that ethics always starts from equality. Equality of treatment has moral priority and any departure from it is morally unacceptable unless it can be shown that it is justified because there are sufficient and good reasons for it. Proposals for equality of treatment, however, are never in need of justification. The burden of proof lies with proposals for unequal treatment. Also in our daily lives, we experience the strong force of equality as default position in ethics. Isaiah Berlin describes it as follows:

> The assumption is that equality needs no reasons, only inequality does so... If I have a cake and there are ten persons among whom I wish to divide it, then I give exactly one tenth to each, this will not, at any rate automatically, call for justification; whereas if I depart from this principle of equal division I am expected to produce a special reason (Berlin 1955–56, p. 132).

Our preference for equal treatment does not seem to need a justification. On the contrary, we generally consider it as a matter of good sense and basic politeness.

When taking a look at contemporary theories of justice, we meet the same assumption – "Equality? Yes!" – and see that the discussion focuses on the question "Equality of What?" Which kind of equality, or which conception of equality would be the best representation of a just society? Let's have a look at some highly influential theories of justice since the 1970s.

The starting point is obvious: John Rawls's *Theory of Justice* (1971). According to Rawls, a society is just when it guarantees equal basic rights and liberties to all. Social and economic inequalities between people are only justified when they are (a) 'to the greatest benefit of the least advantaged' and (b) 'attached to positions and offices open to all under conditions of fair equality of opportunity'.

In his libertarian answer to Rawls's theory, Robert Nozick (1974) poses that each individual has an equal and inalienable right to private property. Individuals have a property right in their own person (their body, talents and skills) and in the goods that they come to have through actions that conform to 'the principle of justice in acquisition' and 'the principle of justice in transfer'. Consequently, Nozick's theory is anti-redistributive: attempts to force anyone to contribute any part of his legitimate holdings to the welfare of others is a violation of that person's property rights, whether it is undertaken by private individuals or by the state. Coerced redistribution would be an unjust redistribution of private property, by illegitimately considering it to be public property.

The controversy between liberals and libertarians is well known. Rawlsians have argued that indeed they want some correction of the social and natural lottery distributing opportunities, talents and handicaps amongst individuals. This does not mean that they want to deny individual property rights over their own personhood. However, they think it to be fair that some of the proceeds of personal' talents should be redistributed to the least advantaged in society.

In 1981, Ronald Dworkin makes an important contribution to the discussion by asking whether we should talk about equality of *welfare* or about equality of *resources*? (Dworkin 1981b, c). In the first case, the object of our egalitarian concerns would be the general welfare that people experience from the resources available to them (income, time, talents and opportunities, etc.). According to Dworkin, this would be an unfavorable interpretation of egalitarianism, since it would imply – when applied to Charles Dickens's *A Christmas Carol* – that the embittered but immensely rich miser Ebenezer Scrooge should be compensated more than Tiny Tim who is crippled but nevertheless always contented. Therefore, Dworkin argues, the question concerning "Equality of What?" should focus on equality of resources. It is not because Tiny Tim has a merry nature and is always cheerful, that he does not need a wheelchair.

If, however, our egalitarian concerns are based on equality of resources, what kind of resources do we talk about? There are, after all, resources that can be allocated or distributed (like rights and liberties, income, education, health care and wheelchairs), as well as resources that cannot be allocated, but nevertheless have an important influence on the lives and opportunities of people (like talents and abilities, health, life history, social environment and cultural background). The first category is often called – in Rawlsian terms – 'primary social goods'. The point is that it is possible to distribute these goods in a just or fair way, but that is much more difficult to reflect on the second category of unalterable resources in terms of justice. In short: inequalities in the first category may be unjust. In the second category they seem to be more a matter of good or bad luck.

Two types of critique have cropped up in the debate about egalitarianism, both of which share the idea that the discussion should not focus too much on distribution of resources.

The first critique was formulated by Amartya Sen and Martha Nussbaum and entails that the debate is not so much about people possessing equal primary social goods, but about what people can *do* and *be* with these goods (Sen 1980, 1985; Nussbaum 2000, 2003). Starting point of their theory is the idea of truly human capabilities, namely what people can *do* and *be* in their lives. For Nussbaum, it is about people's real opportunities for human flourishing (like the human capability to live a good life; to be in good health; to have one's bodily integrity respected; to use one's senses, imagination and thought; to form emotional attachments; to use one's practical reason, etc.). A theory of justice should focus on the way in which people can develop their *capabilities* and are free to transform them into real *functionings*; not only having the formal opportunities, but also the freedom to actually *do* something with them. It would be utterly meaningless for Tiny Tim, for example, should he have the formal possibility to take part in the public life when the public space would not be adjusted to or accessible for wheelchairs.

The second line of critique is known as 'luck-egalitarianism', which is a family of positions associated principally with the works of Ronald Dworkin (1981b, c, 2000), Gerald Cohen (1989, 2000), Richard Arneson (1989, 1997, 1999, 2007, 2011), and John Roemer (1985, 1996, 1998). The critique entails that theories of justice should not disregard a fundamental moral intuition on just inequalities, viz. the intuition that people are responsible for the consequences of their free and conscious choices. This intuition fits in with La Fontaine's fable of the cricket and the ant. Why should the ant, having worked hard all summer long and now enjoying a nice winter stock, help the cricket who sang all summer long but is threatened by starvation during wintertime? Can the cricket make a claim of justice on the ant? According to luck-egalitarian reasoning, he cannot. The ant does not have a duty of justice to help the cricket. Should he help the cricket nevertheless, then it would be out of compassion or charity, but not out of justice.

Put differently, when John Rawls states that social and economic inequalities are justified only when they are 'to the greatest benefit of the least advantaged' and 'attached to positions and offices open to all under conditions of fair equality of opportunity', he is not concerned with the question how it comes that the most advantaged *are* most advantaged, and the least advantaged *are* least advantaged. Holding people responsible for what they choose to do with their talents and opportunities, is an important issue that, according to luck-egalitarian theorists, should be taken into consideration in our reflections on justice.

1.3 Justice and Responsibility in Health Care

In this book, we aim to explore the basic intuition of luck egalitarianism with a particular focus on health care. What is the right thing to do when someone needs a bigger piece of the cake due to special needs that arise from free and consciously made choices? What would we say when Tiny Tim has become crippled due to reckless driving and therefore needs life-long assistance? What should we do when the smoker contracts lung cancer? And what should we do when an elderly person, or a person in the beginning stages of dementia, freely chooses to live his life fully to the end, requiring the necessary care that comes with this decision? Is there a duty to die at a certain moment (Hardwig 1997)? Is there a duty to write an advance directive, thereby curbing the costs of end-of life care (Hersch Nicholas et al. 2011)? And what should happen when a pregnant couple does not wish to abort the severely handicapped fetus but decides to care for the child for as long as it takes (at a considerable cost for themselves, their family and the broader society) (Denier 2010)? Do they have a claim of justice for the necessary support? Or is this only a matter of charity, beneficence or compassion?

In mainstream bioethics, the predominant focus of questions regarding responsibility in health care has not been so much on matters of this kind. Rather, issues in the field of clinical ethics (responsibility for professional care-giving), the ethics of the patient-physician relationship (respecting autonomy, informed consent, etc.), and in the field of research ethics (use of human subjects in experiments) have been the main contexts where matters of professional responsibility (as physicians or as scientists contributing to the well-being of the patient) have been discussed.

However, a specific social focus on the relation between health care and responsibility can be found in the writings of health care ethicists and philosophers like Dan Brock (1993, 1998, 2002, 2004), Allen Buchanan (1985, 2009), Daniel Callahan (1987, 1990, 1993, 1998, 2008, 2009, 2011), Norman Daniels (1981, 1985, 1988, 2008, 2011), Yvonne Denier (2005, 2007, 2008, 2010), Gerald Dworkin (1981a), Ronald Dworkin (1993, 1994, 2000), Susan Hurley (2001, 2007), Thomas Pogge (2004), Jennifer Prah Ruger (2010), Shlomi Segall (2007a, b, 2010a, b, 2012), ter Meulen et al. (2001, 2008), Robert Veatch (1980), and Dan Wikler (1988, 2004a, b).

Taking these views into account, how then, should we think about our personal and social responsibility for health when seen from the viewpoint of social justice? Or put another way, how should we treat people who are voluntarily engaging in risky behavior and making imprudent choices? Are they to be considered as people who should bear the cost of their 'expensive tastes' themselves?

1.3.1 Yes, They Should!

Several arguments support the idea that people who knowingly take health risks should pay additional sums of money to carry health care costs, or should pay higher premiums for their health insurance and fend for themselves with the consequences of their imprudent choices.

1.3.1.1 Antisocial Behavior

The first argument is grounded in the antisocial character of an unhealthy life style. Just as a person can forfeit his or her right to liberty by criminal behavior, one could argue that a person can forfeit his or her right to healthcare by failing to act responsibly. It is unfair that those contributing to the insurance pool pay the extra costs of those who voluntarily engage in risky actions that increase their need for medical services, and it is fair to withhold societal funds from persons whose medical needs result from voluntary risk taking. Free riding cannot be accepted.

At the background is the idea that duties are owed to the state. Society has a right to expect a decent return on the investment it has made in public health measures, medical facilities, nursing schools, funding for biomedical research, hospital subsidies, and many other parts of the system that pertain to healthcare. This sounds reasonable, because society is not a trough filled with services and resources that should always be at our free disposal. Citizens have rights but also duties. In this sense, one could argue that sensible care for oneself and one's health is a moral duty. It is part of what free and adult citizens with a sense of justice may expect of one another.

1.3.1.2 Voluntary Risk Taking

A second, more fundamental argument is based on the idea of moral arbitrariness. This idea refers to what we consider to be relevant or irrelevant in matters of justice. In *A Theory of Justice* John Rawls writes: "The natural distribution is neither just nor unjust. These are simply natural facts. What is just and unjust is the way that institutions deal with these facts." (Rawls 1971, p. 102, 1999, p. 87). Hence, we do not allow biological differences such as gender or race to limit our opportunities for employment and, more generally, our chances in life. We condemn gender or race discrimination because they rely on an irrelevant criterion and because these natural differences are determined by the arbitrariness of fortune. Being black or white is morally arbitrary because it is determined by the whims of nature, randomly and capriciously. One cannot be held responsible for these features, nor can one be rewarded for it. In the same line of reasoning, Ronald Dworkin's argument of the "Responsibility Cut" holds that interpersonal inequalities may be the result of preferences or ambitions but not of endowments (Dworkin 1981c, 2000). In fact, justice is about mitigating the arbitrariness of nature and fate by installing social institutions that assure equal opportunities to everyone, despite all natural and social differences.

Now, when are health inequalities between individuals unjust? At first glance, the answer is simple: when they are avoidable by just and responsible social policy (Daniels 2001; Pogge 2004). Hence, health inequalities due to determinants such as unequal access to clean water, sanitation, adequate shelter, basic education, vaccinations, and prenatal and maternal care are unjust because we believe that these inequalities are *avoidable by just and responsible social policy* that supplies these missing determinants. When health inequalities are rooted in biological differences that we *do not know* how to overcome, the situation is unavoidable, and therefore not an injustice (Buchanan et al. 2001). As such, a fair and just healthcare system mitigates arbitrary health inequalities by providing equal access to a general healthcare framework – safe environment, good quality care, support, and so on – thus contributing to equality of opportunity. If a person needs more health care (requiring hemodialysis, for instance, or a wheelchair) due to unequal bad luck, it would be unfair if society did not try to fulfill these healthcare needs and in that way reinforce unequal opportunity. Morally arbitrary health differences that we *know* how to overcome or mitigate may not determine unequal results.

Society, however, has no moral obligation to mitigate the differences in health for which we are personally responsible. When society provides the general health framework and the opportunity to be healthy, the poorer health status of individuals who *voluntarily* smoke and drink heavily is not unfair because in cases of voluntary risk taking, the differences in healthcare needs are no longer considered to be morally arbitrary. On the contrary, they are the result of gambling. For this argument, Dworkin's distinction between two kinds of luck is useful (Dworkin 2000, pp. 73ff.). If a person is made worse off because gambles he has made turned out badly, that is, because he has had poor *option luck*, then egalitarian concerns are not triggered. If on the contrary, he fares worse than others because of matters outside his control, then he is a victim of poor *brute luck*, and egalitarian concerns come to the fore.

All in all, the third argument in favor of holding individuals responsible for the consequences of their behavior makes individual choice central. In cases of health gambling the so arisen healthcare needs are no longer generic, archetypical, and common to all, but result from personal preferences or desires. So in that case, they are "volitional" or "adventitious" needs, resulting from poor option luck (Frankfurt 1988; Braybrooke 1987; Denier 2007). Basic health care needs and special health care needs that are due to brute luck are morally arbitrary. Volitional healthcare needs are not, because they result from individual reckless behavior. So when we do not allow morally arbitrary differences to determine how social burdens and benefits ought to be allocated, personal responsibility becomes relevant.

1.3.1.3 Mitigating Moral Hazard

The fourth argument is practical. Suppose society explicitly chooses to punish risk-taking behavior (whether by excluding individuals from some healthcare entitlements or by demanding higher insurance premiums), and suppose that this would scare a considerable number of people away from smoking, drinking, unsafe sexual activities, and other forms of hazardous behavior. Suppose furthermore that this would help raise additional financing for health care services caused by voluntary bad behavior? Wouldn't this be a very efficient way to prevent unnecessary and avoidable healthcare costs? If doing so would help to maximize cost effectiveness in healthcare, why would we be against it (Rakowski 1991)?

1.3.1.4 Merit

In the final argument the criterion of personal merit is made central. Meritarian conceptions are above all grading ones. They refer to all kinds of qualities or performances with respect to which individuals may be graded. Advantages are allocated in accordance with amounts of energy spent (efforts) or kinds of results achieved (achievements). What is judged is particular conduct that distinguishes persons from one another, and not the fact that all parties are human beings. Merits are "acquired," that is to say, they represent what its possessor has made of her natural endowments and environmental opportunities.

What should be stressed is the importance of meritarian criteria in our general thinking about justice (Miller 2001). Dworkin's argument of the responsibility cut has roots in common experience and perception. People generally see a difference between nonmeritarian health crises and nonpure cases in which merit considerations do not seem wholly irrelevant. People do tend to feel and think differently about the drunk driver who has caused a car accident and the teenage cyclist who was hit in the accident and now suffers brain damage; about the smoker having a heart attack who is seriously overweight and the 60-year-old man with a healthy lifestyle who is suddenly stricken by leukemia. Furthermore, cases like that of the leukemia patient who has always taken excellent care of himself raise reactions such as "this is so undeserved!" People generally sense that benefits and burdens should be distributed in a way that is proportional (or at least related) to effort. Common sense strongly supports the idea that merit considerations are not wholly irrelevant to the allocation of health care resources. If this were not the case, the issue of responsibility in healthcare would not be a topic of discussion.

1.3.2 Counterconsiderations

Several arguments, however, maintain that even if we agree that the notion of merit plays a very important role, the idea of justice is not exhaustively characterized by it (Dworkin 1981a; Denier 2005, 2007; Prah Ruger 2010). According to this line of reasoning, the notion of merit is especially ill-suited to play a primary role in the determination of policies that should govern a system of healthcare. Why is it so ill suited?

To begin with, the practical applicability of the admission of merit considerations in the instance of healthcare delivery appears limited. A policy of withholding societal funds cannot be justified unless several conditions are met. First, it must be possible to identify and differentiate various *causal factors* in morbidity, such as natural causes, social environment, and personal activities, and it must be confirmed that a pertinent disease or illness actually results from *personal activities*, rather than from some other cause. Additionally it must be shown that the personal activities in question were *autonomously undertaken* in the sense that the actors were aware of the risks and voluntarily accepted them. Furthermore, locating the autonomous risk takers would require a rigid and complex framework of research policy. To make such a policy legitimate, considerable moral objections, for instance privacy considerations, would have to be overcome. Moreover, all this would have to be cost-effective indeed. Finally we show that luck egalitarianism clashes with a consistent understanding of the principle of fair equality of opportunity.

1.3.2.1 Unambiguous Causality?

Regarding the first condition, although it is possible to define general risks from identifiable types of conduct, it is virtually impossible to draw an unambiguous link between an example of that conduct and a particular health consequence. Medical needs often result from many influences of very different kinds varying from genetic predispositions, personal actions and habits, and environmental and social conditions (Sen 2002; Wikler 2004a, b). It is often impossible to establish the respective roles of different factors on the basis of scientific evidence. Whereas it is mostly possible to determine responsibility for an injury in mountain climbing or skiing, it is not possible to determine with certainty whether a particular individual's lung cancer resulted from smoking, environmental pollution, occupational conditions, heredity, or some combination of these. Although we know that smoking increases the risk of lung cancer, we also know that many nonsmokers die of lung cancer each year and many smokers live to old age. All in all, while we can identify conduct that increases the risk of illness or injury, it remains very difficult to conclude that a particular health crisis was actually caused by a particular lifestyle choice. In these cases, social policy may rest more on ignorance of causal factors than on knowledge.

1.3.2.2 Autonomous Choice?

Second, the argument in favor of holding risk takers responsible shows great confidence in the free, voluntary, and independent character of individual choice making. However, if we want to make choice central, we have to be sure that the participation in risky behavior is *truly* voluntary. Nicotine is now widely recognized as a potently addictive drug, and alcoholism and eating disorders are diseases in their own right. But if many people in a cultural group or class behave similarly, this behavior might acquire the quality of a social or cultural norm, in which case we might wonder just how voluntary the behavior is (Wikler 2004a, b; Marmot et al. 1997; Marmot 2004; Wilkinson and Pickett 2009). A denial of a person's right to healthcare would be unfair if the person could not have acted otherwise or could have acted otherwise but only with great difficulty. At the very least, the proposition that individuals voluntarily bring many of their illnesses upon themselves must be challenged and tested in each situation in which it is invoked. This is far from easy to achieve.

1.3.2.3 Rigid Policy?

In addition to the previous issue, problems of rigidity in policing the system become relevant. To locate voluntary risk takers, officials would have to investigate the causes of accidents and diseases. In the worst-case scenario, these officials would be authorized to invade privacy, break confidentiality, and keep records in order to document health abuses that could result in restriction of the right to healthcare. In such cases the natural jungle, in which morally arbitrary differences (as in race, gender, or health) determine the results, makes room for a social jungle, in which people could be punished by society as a result of an infinite series of responsibility questions about their health behavior. This immediately raises doubts about the ethical viability of such measures. Too much insistence on the luck egalitarian claim to discredit responsible behavior might lead to harsh and counterintuitive results.

1.3.2.4 Freedom

Furthermore, we know that in real life people routinely trade health risks for other benefits. They do so when commuting longer distances for a better job, practicing certain sports, or taking a skiing holiday. So if patients needing treatment for smoking-related diseases can be fairly penalized because they smoke, we should apply the same stricture to those who drink too much alcohol, eat too much fat, drive too fast, work too hard, go out too late, go on skiing holidays, or indulge themselves in sports like mountain climbing or boxing. Within such a policy only few of us might qualify for the treatment we require in our hour of need. Although there is some plausibility to the claim that rational people should refrain from trading their health for other goods, refusing *ex ante* to allow *any* trade-offs of health for other goods may seem unjustifiably paternalistic.

1.3.2.5 Cost Effective?

Moreover, one might wonder whether health enforcement would indeed be cost-effective. One of the major reasons for the debate on responsibility in healthcare is the problem of increasing costs. The argument is based on the idea that those who choose to run health risks cost the rest of us money, and it is fair that they should pay it back, either by paying larger insurance premiums or by forgoing healthcare for their self-induced conditions.

However, there is reason to believe that this strategy would lead to counterintuitive outcomes. In addition to the fact that the organization of health enforcement would carry high financial costs besides its morally unattractive features, it ironically proves that some risk taking requires less rather than more medical care, because it results in earlier and quicker deaths. Cost-effectiveness research to compare healthcare costs has shown that low-risk, nonsmoking men with low blood pressure generate far higher healthcare costs per year of life than high-risk men who smoke and have high blood pressure (Manning et al. 1989). Ironically, it seems that people with unhealthy life styles actually might save society more in overall expenditures for both healthcare and social security than they cost (Leichter 1981; Russell 1989; Schwartz 1995). Would this be embarrassing for a luck egalitarian health system? If risk-takers do not, in fact, cost the rest of us money through reckless conduct, then there is no need to penalize them (Segall 2010a).

1.3.2.6 Forward-Looking Conceptions of Responsibility?

In addition to practical problems, the concept of fair equality of opportunity remains an important element in this discussion. A human right to healthcare is of fundamental importance in order to be able to enjoy fair equality of opportunity for good positions in society and for various life styles in one's personal life (Daniels 1985, 2008). This helps us to bear in mind two things.

Firstly, moral objections against a system of full private pocket payment of healthcare fundamentally come down to the fact that it results in a *policy of exclusion* (only the healthy and wealthy will be able to purchase insurance and medical care) from a domain that is *much too important* to allow exclusion, that is, the domain of guaranteeing fair equality of opportunity for all. A *policy of inclusion* is one of the basic reasons for a moral right to healthcare. In this same line of reasoning, Shlomi Segall (2010a) has addressed the "harshness objection" to the strict luck egalitarian reading of justice, which holds that society has no obligations of egalitarian distributive justice toward those who suffer bad option luck. Such a strict reading would imply "abandonment of the imprudent" (Anderson 1999). Segall's luck egalitarian proposal implies a guaranteed minimum for all, a "sufficientarian" distribution of resources justified on grounds of the moral requirement to meet basic needs (Segall 2010a). As such, even his luck egalitarian framework conceives of health care as a *normatively non-excludable* good, a social protection that no person could forfeit.

Additionally, fair equality of opportunity is a *forward-looking* concept. It provides the moral basis for a fallback framework that contributes to all persons' receiving a fair chance in life. Because of this, it would be unfair to cut off fair equality of opportunity in the future because of past behavior. Although it sounds paradoxical, holding people responsible for their ends means that in assuming the presence of fair institutions, we are acting as if they can exercise their underlying moral power to *form* but also to *revise* their conceptions of the good and valuable.

Does this mean that society is a trough of means and services, freely available to everyone after all? Is the debate on the role of personal responsibility with regard to the right to healthcare irrelevant? Of course not.

Most theorists on the subject agree about three elements in this regard. (1) Responsibility is an important value. People's behavior has an effect on their health, and society should not hesitate to underscore the importance of a sensible choice for a healthy lifestyle by making people conscious of the influence they have on their health needs. (2) However, society should continue to be forward-looking, both in providing incentives to avoid hazardous behavior and in offering medical help. Regarding incentives, consciousness raising health campaigns show respect for individual autonomy while appealing to people's rationality to take care of their health. The same goes for cost sharing. It is fair to require individuals who engage in risky actions that result in costly medical needs to pay higher premiums or taxes. Risk takers may be required to contribute more to particular pools such as insurance schemes or to pay a tax on their risky conduct, such as an increased tax on alcohol and tobacco. These requirements may fairly redistribute the burdens of the costs of healthcare, and they may deter risky conduct without disrespecting autonomy. The return individuals may expect from taxation of unhealthy behavior is healthcare protection for themselves. (3) It would be unjust to refuse care to people in need, even if it is clear that they were responsible for their condition. Contributing to fair equality of opportunity should continue to be one of the fundamental moral goals of healthcare. This should not change because of past behavior.

1.4 Justice and the Goal of Medicine and Health Care

What do we learn from the discussion about the relationship between justice, luck and responsibility in health care? There is a relatively broad consensus about the idea that just health care should be implemented in a multi-tiered system which involves

(1) a guaranteed minimum of decent-quality care for all, organized on a basis of solidarity (universal and mandatory insurance, risk-sharing, sometimes even with a progressive, income-based contribution system), (2) allowing that additional levels or higher levels of health care be voluntarily purchased by whoever has the possibility, income and desire to do this. (Dworkin 1993, pp. 215–216; Segall 2010a; Beauchamp and Childress 2008). The additional tier is then a matter of individual choice and responsibility, organized on the basis of various conditions determined by the insurance contract. In such a system, age and lifestyle would co-determine the height of the insurance premium.

The moral acceptability of such a system depends, of course, on the level, content and quality of the first tier. What exactly is included in the guaranteed minimum of decent-quality care for all? And how can we specify this? Here, three aspects play an important role in the discussion (Callahan 1987, 1990, 1993, 1998, 2008, 2009, 2011), *viz.* (1) the fact of infinite medical possibilities, (2) the scope and content of solidarity, and (3) our public understanding of the good human life.

1.4.1 Unlimited Medical Possibilities

First of all, we have to point at the simple contradiction between endless clinical possibilities of diagnosis and therapy on the one hand and economic affordability on the other hand, which underlies the increasing gap between supply and demand in health care (Denier 2008). This contradiction is inherently linked to scientific and technological progress. The history of medicine shows an exponential increase of diagnostic capabilities and of related therapeutic possibilities (for instance in AIDS and cancer research) (Porter 1999). Furthermore, it happens that every advance in medicine creates new needs that did not exist until the means of meeting them came into existence, or at least into the realm of the possible (like the various possibilities in assisted reproduction). As such, the history of medicine and health care disclose their infinite capacity to provide patients with ever more and ever more expensive treatments (Porter 1999; Butler 1999). The nature of health care is such that supply often generates its own demand; and to spend more on the provision of health care is often no more than to stoke the fires of further demand. As John Butler puts it:

> Since to conquer one peak is merely to reveal yet others to climb, we cannot assume that a doubling or even a trebling of the volume of resources allocated to [health care] would close the gap between supply and demand (Butler 1999, p. 7).

As such, the question of responsibility in health care re-enters the stage in a different form, *viz.* by asking what we can and may reasonably expect from the health care system. Can we reasonably continue to expect physicians to honor their Hippocratic duty of doing as much as possible for any patient? And is it reasonable to expect society to support this duty (Callahan 1987, 1990, 1998, 2008, 2009)?

According to Ronald Dworkin, we should reconsider a powerful ideal of justice in health care, which is *the ideal of insulation* (Dworkin 1993, 1994). This ideal has three features. The first involves the idea that life and health are the *Summum Bonum*, or as René Descartes put it in his *Discourse on the Method*, chief among all goods, which need to be protected and promoted by all means. Everything else is of minor importance besides them (Descartes 1994, p. 87). The second component is *equality*. The ideal supposes that even in a society that is otherwise very inegalitarian, medical care should be distributed in an egalitarian way so that no one is denied the care he needs simply because of inability to pay. The third component, which in fact flows from the other two, is the old *rescue principle*. It holds that it is unacceptable when people die, though their lives could have been saved, because the necessary resources were withheld on economic grounds.

This ideal of insulation has exerted great power throughout history. It has served medical practice for millennia and although critical voices crop up from time to time (Foucault 1963; Illich 1975; Hanson 2002; Callahan 2008, 2009), it is still instinctively accepted by most people and widely supported in political rhetoric. The power of the insulation ideal is so great that people think that it might easily be thought to provide the right standard for answering two fundamental questions of justice in health care: “How much should we spend on health care?” and “What exactly should we spend it on?” (Dworkin 1993, 1994).

However, so Dworkin urges, this is a serious mistake, for it would give the advice of spending *all* the society can on health care until it has reached the level at which no more gain in health or life expectancy is to be expected. With the increasing supply of medical technology during the last decennia, meaning that we have so much more to buy, it is unreasonable that society should treat health as lexicographically prior to all other values and treat longer life as a good that must be protected at all costs. And what should we spend it on? The egalitarian impulse of the ideal seems to recommend that medical care should be distributed according to some principle of need. However, the concept of medical need is multiply ambiguous and cannot solve the matter. Its very definition is highly contested. Who should be helped first? The person who is in urgent need of the one who can profit most from the treatment? Maybe the former will die quite soon anyway and maybe the latter still has the promise of a long and fruitful life. And how should we balance needs? Does someone need an operation if it might save his life but is highly unlikely to do so? Is someone’s need for life-saving treatment affected by the quality his life would have after successful treatment? Does someone need less treatment at 70 than at 40? Furthermore, we know that, with the increasing possibilities of contemporary medicine, the fulfillment of medical needs can still be a drain on social resources (Daniels 1981, 2001). So the old ideal of insulation fails to answer our second question, as well as our first (Dworkin 1993, 1994).

1.4.2 The Content and Scope of Solidarity

Dworkin’s alternative approach to justice in health care is based, not on the insulation of health care as a separate sphere of justice or activity, but on the contrary, on the *integration* of health care in a competition with other goods. The central idea is:

> We should aim to make collective, social decisions about the quantity and distribution of health care so as to match, as closely as possible, the decisions that people in the community would make for themselves, one by one, in the appropriate circumstances, if they were

looking from youth down the course of their lives and trying to decide what risks were worth running in return for not running other kinds of risks (Dworkin 1993, pp. 208–209).

Dworkin's *prudent insurance ideal* argues that we should allocate resources between health and other social needs, and among different patients who need treatment, by trying to imagine what health care would be like if it were left to a free and unsubsidized market that would be corrected in three ways (1993, pp. 209–210, 1994, pp. 310–312).

The first correction is that the economic structure, including the distribution of income and wealth, should be as fair as possible. In Dworkin's view, this means that the economic structure treats all members of the community with equal concern when it divides resources equally, and then leaves each member free to spend those resources designing a life that each believes valuable. Secondly, the public at large should have reliable information about the value, cost and effectiveness of different medical treatments. In other words, everybody knows what very good doctors know. Thirdly, adverse selection should not be possible for insurance companies. This means, they should dispose of no individualized knowledge about the health risks of any particular person. Information about genetic predispositions, cultural or social determinants of individual persons should not be available. No one would be in a position to say that a particular person has a higher than average probability to contract sickle-cell anemia, diabetes, or some other disease.

In this imaginary situation, each individual is free to purchase health care insurance as much or as little as he wishes to do. The question that Dworkin invites us to ponder is: which treatments would we prudently choose to be insured for, and which would we regard as not worth the cost of the insurance? What kind of health care arrangements would develop in such a community? How much of its aggregate resources would we want to be devoted to health care? And how would medical treatment be distributed?

Carrying the model through, he discusses its implications for our own society.

Of course, what is prudent for someone depends on that person's own individual needs, tastes, personality, and preferences, but we can nevertheless make some judgments with confidence that they would fit the needs and preferences of most [individuals in industrialized societies] (1994, p. 313).

It is important to consider what arrangements the hypothetical society would generally make, Dworkin argues, because these decisions can serve as a *guide* to what we should do to improve justice in our own real, imperfect and often unjust circumstances. The prudent insurance strategy presumably allows one to determine what justice would require in the way of a *decent minimum.* Dworkin speculates that private insurance would develop into large collective insurance arrangements, which might result in something close to a comprehensive public health insurance scheme for a *basic level* of provision, with supplemental private insurance possibilities. As such, Dworkin's position combines an argument for a moral right to health care with a limitation on that right, both based on the idea of the prudential insurer.

1.4.2.1 Probably Not Including…

Consequently, he identifies a number of disparities between the choices that people would probably make in this hypothetical world and the decisions of health care providers in the real world. Let's consider some of his proposals.

Dworkin suggests, for example, that few people would insure for life-sustaining treatment in case they fell into a persistent vegetative state; yet thousands of people are kept alive in such a condition at any time (Butler 1999). The substantial sum spent year after year in insurance premiums to provide that coverage would be at the expense of education, or job training, or culture, or investment, or travel experience, and other things that would enhance someone's actual, conscious life. The opportunity cost of such insurance would be irrationally high.

Furthermore, it is reasonable to think that almost no one would purchase insurance providing for expensive medical intervention, even of a life-saving character, after he will have entered the late stages of irreversible dementia. Almost everyone would rather prefer to make life before dementia more worthwhile. Although most prudent people would want to buy insurance to provide decent-quality custodial care, in conditions of dignity and adequate comfort, if they became demented, no one would insure for expensive, life-saving intervention in this situation. The same goes for relatively old age. The prudent insurer might not be inclined to insure for expensive technology whose main results benefit people in relatively *old age*, like life-saving treatment over the age of 85 (Dworkin 1993, p. 214, 1994, p. 315). According to Dworkin, most people would prefer to enjoy life before that age.

A further suggestion is that very few people would choose to insure for very expensive medical treatment in the last months of a terminal illness; treatment which would lengthen their lives for a few additional months. Yet some 40% of medical expenditure during the last year is on people in the last 4 months of their lives (Lubitz and Riley 1993).

This is not to say, Dworkin emphasizes, that most people would not *want* those additional months. For indeed, many people want to live as long as possible, provided they remain conscious and alert, provided they do not suffer too much pain, and provided the quality of their life stays reasonably good. The point is rather that they would not want those additional months *at too great a cost* of sacrifices in their earlier, vigorous life; a cost that would be necessary if they had to make that choice. On the other hand, they would certainly want insurance to provide the much less expensive care that would keep them as comfortable and as free of pain as possible.[1]

[1] Note, however, that the abstract ideas of age-based rationing and limiting expensive treatment in the terminal stages of life are contested. Critics contend that age-based rationing of life-extending technologies would not save substantially on resources, in part because the provision of care, including long-tem care and support services, is expensive and cannot always be sharply differentiated from the care that prolongs life. Experts argue that saving the costs of the last few weeks of life would not produce large reductions of costs overall, and they note great difficulties in predicting the final weeks of life for many patients. See: Zweifel et al. (1999), Jahnigen and Binstock (1991), O'Connell (1996).

How much further can we go down this road? How much more insurance can we be reasonably confident people would not buy in the circumstances we are imagining? Dworkin raises one further issue that is of major importance and will become increasingly more critical in the next decades. That is, how far would people in the imagined community go in making provision for access to the ultra-expensive high-tech medical equipment now in use or being developed, like the various forms of research in molecular biology (Dworkin 2000, pp. 427–452)? Undoubtedly these technologies will save *some* lives, but just as undoubtedly at a cost that would seem very high when we consider how a community might use the funds in other ways (like for instance enhancing economy and providing more jobs and a higher standard of living conditions for more people, which are, lest it be forgotten, important social determinants of health). In this line of reasoning, people might not spend to insure for highly expensive speculative technology even though it could save some lives, like for instance separating a Siamese twin when there is only a minute chance of their survival.

1.4.2.2 But Prudently Providing…

Inversely, we might use our speculations about what people in the imaginary community would consider prudent to provide for themselves, as a guide to help us define what justice demands everyone should have. As such, 'willingness to pay' becomes a strong determinant of solidarity in health care (Schokkaert 2009; ter Meulen and Jotterand 2008; ter Meulen and Maarse 2008). What should be included in the basic package of health care coverage that should be available to everyone, at a reasonable cost, and be supplied without charge to those who cannot carry that reasonable cost themselves?

Informed and reflective people in the imagined society, ultimately deciding for themselves how to allocate their resources, might make the following decisions. They might pay to provide for life-saving techniques for diseases that tend to occur relatively *early in life*, particularly when these techniques have a high probability of success. As such, most people would consider it prudent to insure for immediate and expert treatment for handicapping conditions in childhood, including treatments which are traditionally in short supply such as those for children with speech or learning difficulties (Butler 1999, p. 22).

The point of the prudent insurance principle is that if *most prudent* people would buy a certain level of medical coverage in a free market if they had average means – that is, if nearly everyone would buy insurance covering primary medical care, hospitalization when necessary, standard prenatal and pediatric care, routine examinations, inoculations and other preventative medicine, and finally, respectful, decent, and attentive long-term care – then the *fairness* or unfairness of our real time society can be measured according to the number of people that do not have such coverage now. The above quoted elements of medical coverage would constitute the basic package that any responsible health care system would establish.

If, at the contrary, very *few prudent* people would want to buy insurance covering a much higher level of coverage – like some heroic medical technologies – it would be unjust to force everyone to have such insurance through a mandatory scheme. There are of course exceptions to the prudent insurance principle: some people have special preferences and would make decisions different from those of most others. It seems fair however, to construct a mandatory coverage scheme on the basis of assumptions about what all but a small number of people would consider appropriate, allowing those few who want to spend more on special care to do so, if they can afford it, through supplementary insurance (Dworkin 1993, pp. 219–212, 1994, p. 315).

1.4.3 What Is a Good Human Life?

The discussion about how to deal with scarcity in health care and what forms of care are appropriate towards the end of our life ultimately points to deep philosophical questions: What is a good life, and maybe even more important: What is our public understanding of a good human life (Callahan 1990)?

1.4.3.1 A Healthy Life?

For a long time the primary focus of public policy has been on realizing equal access to health care for equal need. The reason for this has been that health was considered to be essentially a matter of natural or genetic factors of which we did not really have much control. Recently one has become aware of the fact that health depends only to a minor degree on the quality and quantity of health care, and much more on various social determinants that can be influenced by public policy (Marmot 2004; Wilkinson and Pickett 2009). Hence the focus has shifted to equality in health (Segall 2007b, 2010a, b; Daniels 2008). Significant inequalities in health between people trigger us to continuously reflect on the influence of social structures on people's health status. In this regard, incentives for health promotion can be considered as an important part of a just society. A very strong argument for this is the fact that health has an important instrumental value: it determines to a significant extent the possibility of forming and realizing our life projects. Nearly everything we want to do or be in life depends on our good health. Health is surely not our only concern in life, but definitely, health is special and it deserves special protection within a just health care system.

1.4.3.2 A Free Life?

Does this mean that it is the just society's assignment to get everyone as healthy as possible? After all, attempts to change unhealthy behavior through education, exhortation, penalties, taxes, restrictions, or prohibitions do involve or border on coercion and therefore must continue to be the subject of moral reflection. The fact that good health may be valued by every person does not by itself justify these interventions, since for some people health risks seem to be less important than the benefits derived from risk-taking behavior.

Freedom is an important aspect of the good human life, and each encroachment on individual autonomy is commonly regarded as standing in need of justification (Wikler 2004b). Three kinds of justification generally come into play: (1) paternalist concerns for the person's good; (2) protection of others from burdens involuntarily imposed by the risk-taking behavior, and (3) the public's stake in the nation's health. As such, interventions aimed at altering lifestyle choices have to be evaluated along the lines of (1) the harm for the person and the question whether or not it is a truly free choice with which the person identifies (e.g. the happy smoker) or an addiction, a handicapping taste (the unhappy addict); (2) the harm to others (e.g. AIDS-prevention); and (3) the health of the nation (e.g. compulsory vaccination against infectious diseases).

Within these lines of reasoning, continuous attention must be given to the precarious balance between health and liberty, thereby being careful not to overemphasize the goal of health at the expense of other important goals. The moral perspective from which lifestyle interventions are urged, has been criticized as *healthism*, a view whereby health is being elevated from a self-interested goal to a virtue, thereby entering into the conviction that healthy people (or at least those who choose health) are better people (Skrabanek 1994). Or, as Dan Wikler has put it:

> the behavior in question may be difficult to change without considerable meddling in the individual's culture and milieu, whether these champion "wine, women, and song", or risk taking or violence, or quiet (and unathletic) contemplation. The life of the fitness-loving moderate is not for everyone, even if it is most conducive to long life and good health (Wikler 2004b).

1.4.3.3 A Long Life?

Is a good human life a long life? Is living longer living better? And how long then, should it be? Should it be a certain minimum amount of life years, based on the society's average life expectancy, a certain form of normal life span (Daniels 1988, 2008), or an aggregation of quantities of well-being (Broome 2004)?

Or put another way: Is a short life less good? Although we might spontaneously be inclined to think it is, this is probably not always the case. Yes, we want to live long and grow old, but only and at least under favorable conditions of good health. Hence, it is not so much a matter of loose additional life years, but of Qualitative Life Years (QALY's), Disability Adjusted Life Years (DALY's), or Healthy Life Expectancy (Segall 2010a). As such, we generally believe that living well is favorable over merely living longer (Temkin 2011). But how then, should we interpret living well? Probably this is related to our desire to lead a meaningful life. And this has to do with living a life that is more or less 'to the point', i.e. appropriate to the various challenges each individual is confronted with.

1.4.3.4 A Meaningful Life?

In general, people strongly believe that death at a certain age, when having lived a full life to a good end, is easier to cope with than the death of a young person, who still had hopes to fulfill many important projects in life. As such, a good life indeed implies a certain number of life years, up to a point where it can be said that one's life has been complete and that everything has been fulfilled or accomplished.

In this regard, medicine and health care have achieved enormous results in expanding the life expectancy of people. We are able to let people grow much older than in previous centuries. The flipside of this, however, is the fact that medicine and health care cannot offer a perspective of a meaningful life. Medicine and health care are able to prolong the lives of people, but they cannot offer a meaningful life. As such, new problems crop up. How should we deal with people who are convinced that their lives have been lived to the fullest extent and are now ready to die (Hardwig 1997)? What should we do with people who say that they do not want to endure physical and/or mental deterioration, simply because such a situation would be contrary to their conception of a meaningful life? And what should we do, on the other hand, with people who wish to live their lives to the fullest extent? Can we expect society to support long-term care at a very old age? And how can we make a distinction between intensive treatment and intensive care for people at high age? What would be a meaningful thing to do for physicians in such cases (Callahan 1987, 1993, 2008, 2011)?

1.5 Outline of the Book

In the succeeding chapters of the book, all the above-raised questions are being dealt with in a particular way. All together, they provide a thorough reflection on the theme of justice, luck and responsibility in health care.

In the first part of the book the contributors tackle this theme from a more fundamental philosophical and ethical perspective. Daniel Hausman sketches how inequalities in health and health care may contribute to injustice, thereby providing a critical analysis of luck egalitarian considerations of health and health care. Shlomi Segall provides a defense of radical affirmative action in health. Yvonne Denier inquires into the question of prospective parents' moral responsibility in reproduction matters. Finally, Jeroen Luyten takes the matter onto the level of our mutual moral obligations in the prevention of infectious diseases.

In the second part of the book, we focus on the implications of these philosophical and ethical debates for an ethics of end-of-life care. It opens with a contribution of John Hardwig, who as advocates the idea that at a certain moment in life we might come to the point where we are confronted with something like a moral duty to die. In the following chapter, Martin Gunderson provides an analysis of our duty to care based on the theory of democratic equality and stresses the importance of people's freedom to choose. In his contribution, Chris Gastmans analyses the theme of advance euthanasia directives and defends the idea of dignity-enhancing care for people who suffer from dementia. In his answer to Chris Gastmans, Govert den Hartogh provides a thorough analysis pro advance euthanasia directives in the case of dementia. In the final contribution to the second part of the book, Thomas Nys discusses the question whether the principle of respect for autonomy can still be relevant in guiding our conduct for people who suffer from severe dementia, and offers an thorough analysis of what exactly frightens us when we talk about old age and dementia.

1.6 About Crickets and Ants...

When taking a general look – like the Owl of Minerva – at the issue at hand, we cannot but consider the past, present and future of the discussion. In this regard, we have to bear in mind that the story of the cricket and the ant has already been present in peoples' minds for centuries. Considering the fact that the fable's most early versions were present in the Aesopica (620–560 BC), that there are versions of it in ancient Indian philosophy (Sendabar, 100 BC), in Greek philosophy (Babrius, third century AC) and Latin literature (Avianus, fifth century), in the Hebrew Bible, in the late renaissance period with Faerno (1564) and L'Estrange (1692), and with Jean de La Fontaine in the seventeenth century, until its twentieth century adaptations by William Somerset Maugham (1924), James Joyce (1939) and John Updike (1987), it is clear that the question regarding the relationship between personal responsibility and justice offers thoroughly fundamental and dateless food for thought.

New evolutions and altered expectations in the field of medicine and health care ("a new life", "a new death") have made us ask the question again: Why should the ant provide support to the cricket? Answers to this question are not univocal; and they probably they never will. What is important, however, is the presence of a continuing debate on these matters, motivated by the urge to find the most humane and dignified solution for the problem at hand.

References

Anderson, E. 1999. What is the point of equality? *Ethics* 99: 287–337.

Arneson, R. 1989. Equality and equal opportunity for welfare. *Philosophical Studies* 54: 79–95.

Arneson, R. 1997. Egalitarianism and the undeserving poor. *Journal of Political Philosophy* 5: 327–350.

Arneson, R. 1999. Egalitarianism and responsibility. *Journal of Ethics* 3: 225–247.

Arneson, R. 2007. Desert and equality. In *Egalitarianism: New essays on the nature and value of equality*, ed. K. Lippert-Rasmussen and N. Holtug, 262–293. Oxford: Oxford University Press.

Arneson, R. 2011. Luck egalitarianism – A primer. In *Responsibility and distributive justice*, ed. C. Knight and Z. Stemplowska, 24–50. Oxford: Oxford University Press.
Beauchamp, T.L., and J.F. Childress. 2008. *Principles of biomedical ethics*. Oxford: Oxford University Press.
Berlin, I. 1955–56. Equality as an ideal. *Proceedings of the Aristotelian Society* 56: 301–326.
Braybrooke, D. 1987. *Meeting needs*. Princeton: Princeton University Press.
Brock, D. 1993. *Life and death: Philosophical essays in biomedical ethics*. Cambridge: Cambridge University Press.
Brock, D. 1998. Justice health care and the elderly. *Philosophy and Public Affairs* 18(3): 297–312.
Brock, D. 2002. Priority to the worst off in health care resource prioritization. In *Medicine and social justice*, ed. M. Battin, R. Rhodes, and A. Silvers, 362–372. New York: Oxford University Press.
Brock, D. 2004. Ethical issues in the use of cost effectiveness analysis for the prioritization of health care resources. In *Public health, ethics, and equity*, ed. S. Anand, F. Peter, and A. Sen. Oxford: Oxford University Press.
Broome, J. 2004. The value of living longer. In *Public health, ethics, and equity*, ed. S. Anand, F. Peter, and A. Sen, 243–260. Oxford: Oxford University Press.
Buchanan, A. 1985. *Ethics, efficiency and the market*. Oxford: Oxford University Press.
Buchanan, A. 2009. *Justice and health care: Selected essays*. Oxford: Oxford University Press.
Buchanan, A., D. Brock, N. Daniels, and D. Wikler. 2001. *From chance to choice: Genetics and justice*. Cambridge: Cambridge University Press.
Butler, J. 1999. *The ethics of health care rationing. Principles and practices*. London: Cassell.
Callahan, D. 1987. *Setting limits: Medical goals in an aging society*. Washington, DC: Georgetown University Press.
Callahan, D. 1990. *What kind of life. The limits of medical progress*. Washington, DC: Georgetown University Press.
Callahan, D. 1993. *The troubled dream of life: In search of a peaceful death*. New York: Simon & Schuster.
Callahan, D. 1998. *False hopes. Overcoming the obstacles to a sustainable, affordable medicine*. New York: Simon & Schuster.
Callahan, D. 2008. Finite lives and unlimited medical aspirations. In *The contingent nature of life. Bioethics and the limits of human existence*, ed. M. Düwell, C. Rehman-Sutter, and D. Mieth, 159–167. Dordrecht: Springer.
Callahan, D. 2009. *Taming the beloved beast: Why medical technology costs are destroying our health care system*. Princeton: Princeton University Press.
Callahan, D. 2011. End-of-life care: A philosophical or management problem? *The Journal of Law, Medicine & Ethics* 39(2): 114–120.
Cohen, G. 1989. On the currency of egalitarian justice. *Ethics* 99: 906–944.
Cohen, G. 2000. *If you're an Egalitarian, how come you're so rich?* Cambridge: Harvard University Press.
Daniels, N. 1981. Health-care needs and distributive justice. *Philosophy and Public Affairs* 10(2): 146–179.
Daniels, N. 1985. *Just health care*. Cambridge: Cambridge University Press.
Daniels, N. 1988. *Am I my parent's keeper? An essay on justice between the young and the old*. Oxford: Oxford University Press.
Daniels, N. 2001. Justice, health, and healthcare. *The American Journal of Bioethics* 1(2): 2–16.
Daniels, N. 2008. *Just health: Meeting health needs fairly*. Cambridge: Cambridge University Press.
Daniels, N. 2011. Individual and social responsibility for health. In *Responsibility and distributive justice*, ed. C. Knight and Z. Stemplowska, 266–286. Oxford: Oxford University Press.
Denier, Y. 2005. On personal responsibility and the human right to healthcare. *Cambridge Quarterly of Healthcare Ethics* 14(2): 224–234.
Denier, Y. 2007. *Efficiency, justice and care. Philosophical reflections on scarcity in health care*. Dordrecht: Springer.

Denier, Y. 2008. Mind the gap! three approaches to scarcity in health care. *Medicine Healthcare and Philosophy* 11(1): 73–87.

Denier, Y. 2010. From brute luck to option luck? On genetics, justice and moral responsibility in reproduction. *The Journal of Medicine and Philosophy* 2(35): 101–129.

Descartes, R. 1994. *Discourse on the method*, ed. and trans. Heffernan, G. Notre Dame: University of Notre Dame Press.

Dworkin, G. 1981a. Taking risks, assessing responsibility. *The Hastings Center Report* 11(5): 26–31.

Dworkin, R. 1981b. What is equality? Part 1: Equality of welfare. *Philosophy and Public Affairs* 10(3): 185–246.

Dworkin, R. 1981c. What is equality? Part 2: Equality of resources. *Philosophy and Public Affairs* 10(4): 283–345.

Dworkin, R. 1993. Justice in the distribution of health care. *McGill Law Journal* 38: 883–898. Reprinted in *The ideal of equality*, eds. M. Clayton, and A. Williams, 203–222. Basingstoke: Palgrave Macmillan.

Dworkin, R. 1994. Justice and the high cost of health, first appeared as will Clinton's plan be fair? *New York Review of Books* 41(1–2): 20–25. Reprinted in Dworkin, R. 2000. *Sovereign virtue. The theory and practice of equality*, 307–319. Cambridge: Harvard University Press.

Dworkin, R. 2000. *Sovereign virtue. The theory and practice of equality*. Cambridge: Harvard University Press.

Foucault, M. 1963. *Naissance de la Clinique*. Paris: Presses Universitaires de France.

Frankfurt, H.G. 1988. Necessity and desire. In Id., *The importance of what we care about*, 104–116. Cambridge: Cambridge University Press.

Hanson, R. 2002. Why health is not special: Errors in evolved bioethics institutions. *Social Philosophy and Policy* 19(2): 153–179.

Hardwig, J. 1997. Is there a duty to die? *The Hastings Center Report* 27(2): 34–42.

Hersch Nicholas, L., K.M. Langa, T.J. Iwashyna, and D.R. Weir. 2011. Regional variation in the association between advance directives and end-of-life Medicare expenditures. *Journal of the American Medical Association* 306(13): 1447–1453.

Hurley, S. 2001. Luck and equality. *Proceedings of the Aristotelian Society* 75(supp vol): 51–72.

Hurley, S. 2007. The 'what' and the 'how' of distributive justice and health. In *Egalitarianism: New essays on the nature and value of equality*, ed. K. Lippert-Rasmussen and N. Holtug, 308–334. Oxford: Oxford University Press.

Illich, I. 1975. *Medical nemesis – The expropriation of health*. London: Calder & Boyars.

Jahnigen, D.W., and R.H. Binstock. 1991. Economic and clinical realities: Health care for elderly people. In *Too old for health care? Controversies in medicine, law, economics, and ethics*, ed. R.H. Binstock, S.G. Post, and L.S. Mills, 13–43. Baltimore: Johns Hopkins University Press.

Leichter, H. 1981. Public policy and the British experience. *Hastings Center Report* 11: 32–39. Reprinted in Leichter, H. 1991. *Free to be foolish: Politics and health promotion in the United States and Great Britain*. Princeton: Princeton University Press.

Lubitz, J., and G. Riley. 1993. Trends in Medicare payments in the last year of life. *The New England Journal of Medicine* 328: 1092–1096.

Manning, W., E. Keeler, J. Newhouse, E. Sloss, and J. Wasserman. 1989. The taxes of Sin. Do smokers and drinkers pay their way? *Journal of the American Medical Association* 261(11): 1604–1609.

Marmot, M. 2004. Social causes of social inequalities in health. In *Public health, ethics and equity*, ed. S. Anand, F. Peter, and A. Sen. Oxford: Oxford University Press.

Marmot, M., C.D. Ryff, L.L. Bumpass, M. Shipley, and N. Marks. 1997. Social inequalities in health: Next questions and converging evidence. *Social Science and Medicine* 44(6): 901–910.

Miller, D. 2001. *Principles of social justice*. Cambridge: Harvard University Press.

Nozick, R. 1974. *Anarchy, state and utopia*. New York: Basic Books.

Nussbaum, M. 2000. *Women and human development*. Cambridge: Cambridge University Press.

Nussbaum, M. 2003. Capabilities as fundamental entitlements: Sen and social justice. *Feminist Economics* 9(2–3): 33–59.

O'Connell, J.M. 1996. The relationship between health expenditures and the age structure of the population in OECD countries. *Health Economics* 5: 573–578.

Pogge, T. 2004. Relational conceptions of justice: Responsibilities for health outcomes. In *Public health, ethics and equity*, ed. S. Anand, F. Peter, and A. Sen, 135–162. Oxford: Oxford University Press.

Porter, R. 1999. *The greatest benefit to mankind: A medical history of humanity*. New York: Norton.

Prah Ruger, J. 2010. *Health and social justice*. Oxford: Oxford University Press.

Rakowski, E. 1991. *Equal justice*. Oxford: Clarendon.

Rawls, J. 1971. *A theory of justice*. Cambridge: Harvard University Press.

Rawls, J. 1999. *A theory of justice*, revth ed. Cambridge: The Belknap Press of Harvard University Press.

Roemer, J. 1985. Equality of talent. *Economics and Philosophy* 1: 151–188.

Roemer, J. 1996. *Theories of distributive justice*. Cambridge: Harvard University Press.

Roemer, J. 1998. *Equality of opportunity*. Cambridge: Harvard University Press.

Russell, L.B. 1989. Some of the tough decisions required by a national health plan. *Science* 246: 892–896.

Schokkaert, E. 2009. Willingness to pay and solidarity. In *In sickness and in health. The future of medicine: Added value & global access*, ed. M. Wynants. Brussels: VUB Press.

Schwartz, R.L. 1995. Life style, health status, and distributive justice. In *Justice and health care: Comparative perspectives*, ed. A. Grubb and M.J. Mehlman, 244–248. New York: Wiley.

Segall, S. 2007a. In solidarity with the imprudent: A defense of luck egalitarianism. *Social Theory and Practice* 33(2): 177–198.

Segall, S. 2007b. Is health care (still) special? *Journal of Political Philosophy* 15(3): 342–361.

Segall, S. 2010a. *Health, luck and justice*. Princeton: Princeton University Press.

Segall, S. 2010b. Is health (really) special? Health policy between Rawlsian and luck egalitarian justice. *Journal of Applied Philosophy* 27(4): 344–358.

Segall, S. 2012. Why egalitarians should not care about equality. *Ethical Theory and Moral Practice* 15(4): 507–519. doi:10.1007/s10677-011-9306-7 (Online First™).

Sen, A. 1980. Equality of what? In *Tanner lectures on human values*, ed. S.M. McMurrin, 195–220. Salt Lake City: University of Utah Press.

Sen, A. 1985. *Commodities and capabilities*. Amsterdam: North-Holland.

Sen, A. 2002. Why health equity? *Health Economics* 11: 659–666.

Skrabanek, P. 1994. *The death of humane medicine and the rise of coercive healthism*. London: Social Affairs Unit.

Temkin, L. 2011. Is living longer living better? In *Enhancing human capacities*, ed. J. Savulescu, R. ter Meulen, and G. Kahane, 350–367. West Sussex: Wiley-Blackwell.

ter Meulen, R., and F. Jotterand. 2008. Individual responsibility and solidarity in European health care. *The Journal of Medicine and Philosophy* 33(3): 191–197.

ter Meulen, R., and H. Maarse. 2008. Increasing individual responsibility in Dutch health care: Is solidarity losing ground? *The Journal of Medicine and Philosophy* 33(3): 262–279.

ter Meulen, R., W. Arts, and R. Muffels (eds.). 2001. *Solidarity and health care in Europe*. Dordrecht: Kluwer Academic Publishers.

Veatch, R.M. 1980. Voluntary risks to health. *Journal of the American Medical Association* 243(1): 50–55.

Wikler, D. 1988. Ought the young make health care decisions for their aged selves? *The Journal of Medicine and Philosophy* 13(1): 57–71.

Wikler, D. 2004a. Personal and social responsibility for health. In *Public health, ethics and equity*, eds. S. Anand, F. Peter, and A. Sen, 109–134. Oxford: Oxford University Press. A shorter version of this essay is available. *Ethics and International Affairs* 16(2002): 47–55.

Wikler, D. 2004b. Lifestyles and public health. In *Encyclopedia of bioethics*, ed. S.G. Post, 1406–1409. New York: Macmillan.

Wilkinson, R.G., and K. Pickett. 2009. *The spirit level: Why more equal societies almost always do better*. New York: Bloomsbury Press.

Zweifel, P., S. Felder, and M. Meiers. 1999. Ageing of population and health expenditure: A red herring. *Health Economics* 8: 485–496.

Part I
Philosophy of Health and Health Care

Chapter 2
Injustice and Inequality in Health and Health Care

Daniel M. Hausman

2.1 Introduction

I chose the title of this essay in part because of the balanced alliteration between "injustice" and "inequality" on the one hand and "health" and "health care" on the other. But the parallelisms of sound in this case mirror analogies in the relations. In each pair, the first member is the more important and more general. Injustice is of obvious moral importance. Inequality is one source of injustice, though inequalities are not always unjust, and inequalities may have other ethically significant consequences. Similarly, health is much more important than health care, though health care obviously contributes to health and may have other morally significant effects on well-being and social solidarity.

In this essay, I shall sketch the ways in which inequalities – and especially inequalities in both health and health care – may constitute or contribute to injustice. More specifically, I shall address the following questions. In Sect. 2.2 I shall ask when inequalities are of moral concern. One answer is the luck egalitarian's: inequalities for which people are not responsible are unjust. Section 2.2 sketches and criticizes this view. Section 2.3 considers whether health and health care are special and whether the luck egalitarian can justify a demand for equality in health and health care. Section 2.3.1 considers what implications the other main version of egalitarianism – which I call "relational egalitarianism" – may have for the distribution of health and health care. Section 2.3.2 asks whether there is any other case for condemning inequalities in health and health care.

This essay draws on other work of mine, especially Hausman (2007, 2011, 2012). I am grateful to Paul Kelleher for comments on an earlier draft of this paper and to discussion of the talk based on this paper at the conference in Leuven on *Justice, Luck and Responsibility in Health Care* in May of 2011.

D.M. Hausman (✉)
Department of Philosophy, University of Wisconsin-Madison,
600 N. Park Street, Madison, WI 53706, USA
e-mail: dhausman@wisc.edu

Y. Denier et al. (eds.), *Justice, Luck & Responsibility in Health Care*,
Library of Ethics and Applied Philosophy 30, DOI 10.1007/978-94-007-5335-8_2,

2.2 Why Are Inequalities Unjust: The Luck Egalitarian Answer

What motivates egalitarians are the huge disparities in life prospects between those who grow up in affluent circumstances and secure and loving homes and those who grow up in extreme poverty or in abusive, chaotic circumstances. It is unconscionable that life expectancy in Angola should be half that in Japan. Similarly, most people feel that it is unjust that one person dies of a simple staph infection, because she could not get a simple antibiotic, while for others such infections are a minor irritation. Though not everyone shares the intuitions, most people feel that inequalities like these are seriously unjust. One explanation for these intuitions is that morality includes a fundamental egalitarian principle (EP) to the effect that

EP1: other things being equal, inequalities are unjust.

The "other things being equal" clause is crucial, because equality is not the only relevant consideration. All things considered, greater inequalities accompanied by greater welfare may be better.

A little reflection shows that EP1 is nevertheless absurd. No sane egalitarian wants to eliminate all differences between people. Egalitarians must specify which differences are of moral concern. The examples suggest that significant inequalities in life prospects or overall well-being are of moral concern, while small inequalities in prospects or well-being or other more specific inequalities in height, hair length, or numbers of handkerchiefs are not of moral concern. So perhaps what explains egalitarian intuitions is a principle to the effect that

EP2: other things being equal, significant inequalities in overall well-being are unjust.

For the moment, I shall speak of the object of distributive concern as overall well-being, because most luck egalitarians have taken well-being to be the "stuff" whose distribution they are concerned about, but as I will discuss later, other egalitarians are concerned about other goods.

Reformulating the purported egalitarian principle as EP2 does not answer all objections. Suppose that the individual mentioned above who dies of a simple staph infection was unable to get access to an antibiotic, because she lived in the twelfth century. Is it unjust that she died while individuals with the same infection today live? Is this inequality in any way morally wrong? Of course the early death of this woman in the twelfth century is sad and unfortunate, but is the inequality of any moral concern? Is there anything wrong about the inequality between health and comfort of people in affluent societies today and the situation of the medieval European aristocracy, whose lives were much less healthy and comfortable? People's intuitions differ on this point. Larry Temkin believes that such inequalities are morally bad, though he would grant that no one can be blamed for them (Temkin 2003). Kok-Chor Tan (2008), in contrast, takes the egalitarian to be concerned exclusively with the ways in which institutions influence inequalities and, like me, would find nothing morally objectionable about these inequalities. Egalitarians who share our intuition will want to modify the egalitarian principle further:

EP3: other things being equal, significant inequalities in overall well being that could have been addressed by human[1] action or social institutions are unjust.

Most contemporary egalitarians would have a further objection to make to EP3. Most would maintain that there is nothing unjust about inequalities, such as those that obtain between innocent citizens and convicted and imprisoned murderers.[2] It is open to an egalitarian to maintain that, other things being equal, the inequalities between a convicted murderer's well being and the well-being of others are morally objectionable, but to point out that other things are in this case obviously not equal and that the claims of equality are outweighed by considerations of retribution, protection, and so forth. But most egalitarians have instead felt that there may be nothing unjust at all inequalities in overall well-being among people, which are their own responsibility. So one arrives at a vague "luck egalitarian" sufficient condition for injustice:

EP4: other things being equal, significant inequalities in overall well being for which individuals are not responsible that could have been addressed by human action or social institutions are unjust.

Tan states what he takes to be the core of luck egalitarianism as "[P]ersons should not be disadvantaged or advantaged simply on account of bad or good luck" (2008, p. 665). If one stipulates that "opportunity for welfare" is equal if and only if overall well-being for which individuals are not responsible is equal, then one can restate EP4 as

EP4': other things being equal, significant inequalities in opportunities for welfare that could have been addressed by human action or social institutions are unjust.

EP4 and EP4' provide only a vague sufficient condition (other things being equal) for injustice. EP4 does not say that, other things being equal, inequalities for which individuals are responsible are just. It thus falls far short of defining how inequalities matter to justice. One way to proceed, is treat the condition in EP4 as both necessary and sufficient and thus to defend the following a vague version of luck egalitarianism:

EP5: other things being equal, significant inequalities in overall well being that could have been addressed by human action or social institutions are unjust if and only if individuals are not responsible for them.

There appear, however, to be serious objections to the necessary condition stated in EP5. I shall mention three. First, there is the problem of "the abandonment of the imprudent." For example, suppose that through imprudent choices in his early 20s, for which Albert is fully responsible, Albert finds himself at age 30 with few skills, a criminal record, physical and mental disabilities, and no friends or family

[1] This formulation assumes that humans are the only morally responsible agents.

[2] Indeed some egalitarians, such as Larry Temkin (1993, 2003), would argue that it would be unjust if murderers were living well. But this view seems to reflect considerations of desert, which are orthogonal to egalitarian concerns.

to care for him. His society offers no social services for people like Albert. The attitude his society takes, "He made their own beds; so let him lie in it." Though there may be non-luck-egalitarian moral objections to Albert's harsh society, there is no luck-egalitarian objection. Elizabeth Anderson (1999) argues that such a society fails to implement the most fundamental egalitarian concern for equal respect.

Second, consider the case of Amy, who is badly off because she has contracted a contagious disease in the course of heroically tending to others. Her society, like Albert's, does nothing for her, because she is responsible for her own bad health. EP5 says that an egalitarian has no grounds upon which to criticize abandoning the self-sacrificing. This strikes many egalitarians as implausible.

In the face of these counterexamples, the luck egalitarian has two choices. One alternative is to accept the verdict that there are no luck-egalitarian objections to Albert's or Amy's societies and emphasize the other, non-egalitarian grounds upon which to criticize them. The luck egalitarian might argue that such societies are cruel, destructive, mean-spirited, and ungrateful but they are not unjustly inegalitarian. Most luck egalitarians, including Tan (2008) and Shlomi Segall (2010), instead retreat and deny that inequalities for which individuals are not responsible are necessary for an egalitarian complaint of injustice. They maintain instead that inequalities may be unjust, even when people are responsible for them and that there are other egalitarian considerations, such a requirement that everyone's basic needs be met, which are not satisfied by societies such as Albert's or Amy's.

A third objection to EP5 is that it favors leveling-down. Here is one version: It is possible to destroy enough of the productive resources of societies across the earth so as to lower everybody's well-being to the level achieved by members of some isolated destitute indigenous tribe, who know nothing of the rest of the world. Assume that this destruction of productive resources has no benefits at all either now or in the future for members of the indigenous tribe or for anybody else. Since EP5 has an 'other-things-being-equal' clause, those who endorse EP5 can agree that, all things considered, the drastic immiseration of almost the whole of the earth's population would be unjust. But if, as EP5 maintains, the only grounds for an egalitarian objection are inequalities for which individuals are not responsible, then with respect to specifically egalitarian concerns, egalitarians should prefer the distribution that results from this immiseration. Those who make this objection regard this as an absurd implication. How could there be *anything* good about causing so much harm without benefit to anyone. Surely any reasonable version of egalitarianism must object to this immiseration.

I do not find this objection compelling. I think it confuses the moral assessment of the distribution of well-being before and after productive resources are destroyed with the moral assessment of destroying those productive resources. Luck egalitarians should condemn the latter because this destruction fails to show equal respect to individuals whose well-being is sacrificed. But that does not imply that the resulting distribution cannot be better from an egalitarian perspective. So I do not think that the leveling down objection has much to it. Those impressed with the objection have been drawn to luck prioritarianism,[3] which weights the interests of individuals in proportion to how badly off they would be if they were not responsible for their well-being. Luck prioritarianism avoids the leveling down objection, but it is subject to versions of the problems of the abandonment of the imprudent and of the self-sacrificing.

So let us retreat to EP4 and concede that it only captures a portion of what the egalitarian demands:

EP4: other things being equal, significant inequalities in overall well being for which individuals are not responsible and that could have been addressed by human action or social institutions are unjust.

The responsibility here is moral responsibility of some sort. According to Richard Arneson people are responsible for "the foreseeable consequences of their voluntary choices," (1989, p. 88). Causal responsibility and hence, as G.A. Cohen (1989) insists, free will are necessary for the relevant sort of moral responsibility, but not sufficient. Until it became known that smoking causes lung cancer, smokers could not be held responsible for contracting lung cancer. By linking responsibility to free will, Cohen and Arneson make it questionable whether people are ever responsible, and they have a hard time accommodating intuitive distinctions between just and unjust inequalities. Ronald Dworkin, in contrast, does not require free will. In his view, what distinguishes those actions for which individuals should be held responsible from those that one should regard as matters of luck is whether the actions stem from "those beliefs and attitudes that define what a successful life would be like, which the ideal assigns to the person, and those features of body or mind or personality that provide means or impediments to that success, which the ideal assigns to the person's circumstances" (1981, p. 303). But this is vague, and it is questionable whether, as Dworkin's view implies, people are not responsible for the consequences of psychological impediments to the pursuit of their objectives, such as compulsions or whims. Segall holds that an individual is not responsible for an outcome if it would have been unreasonable for society to expect the individual to avoid it. Segall's account is attractive as a sufficient condition on responsibility. For example, since it is reasonable to expect an individual to avoid driving while intoxicated, the individual is responsible for doing so. But it is not necessary for responsibility for some action and its consequences that it is reasonable to expect someone to avoid the action. For example, it would be unreasonable for society to expect a Jehovah's witness to accept a blood transfusion, but Jehovah's witnesses are in the relevant sense responsible for refusing to accept a transfusion and for the consequences that follow. A luck egalitarian should not object to the worse outcomes experienced by Jehovah's witnesses. As this cursory discussion shows, it is not easy to provide an adequate account of responsibility.

[3] For the classic discussion of prioritarianism, see Parfit (1991). Segall discusses luck prioritarianism in Segall (2010, pp. 111–12, 118–20).

Moreover, even if luck egalitarians possessed an adequate account of responsibility, they would face the problem that responsibility appears to be typically shared: outcomes are almost always due both to individual choice and to contingent circumstances. Those who smoke increase their risk of lung cancer, but they are still unlikely to get cancer, and if they do, there may be no way to tell whether their smoking caused it. If we assume that smokers are responsible for their smoking, how much responsibility should they bear for the inequalities due to bad outcomes that smoking makes somewhat more probable?

This section began with the intuition that the gross inequalities we observe in the world today constitute serious moral wrongs. One way to explain this intuition is to invoke an egalitarian principle to the effect that inequalities in the distribution of benefits and harms are morally objectionable. Other intuitions concerning responsibility pushed us toward a version of luck egalitarianism. But luck egalitarianism faces counterexamples, falls short of a comprehensive account of egalitarianism, and conflicts with some central egalitarian intuitions.

The luck egalitarian offers one explanation for the central intuition that the gross inequalities we observe in the world today constitute serious moral wrongs, but there are others. One possibility is that what is wrong with these inequalities is not the inequality, but the suffering and misery of those who are doing badly.[4] The importance specifically of the inequality lies in its demonstration that the suffering and misery of those doing badly is avoidable and hence a moral wrong. On this view, there is nothing intrinsically unjust or morally wrong about inequalities themselves; though the actual inequalities we observe, which involve great suffering and deprivation, constitute serious wrongs.

Another possibility, which I defend elsewhere (Hausman and Waldren 2011), is that egalitarianism is a family of related positions with different egalitarians focusing on the distribution of different goods and with different reasons explaining why they take the distribution of these goods to be of moral importance.[5] So some egalitarians are concerned about the distribution of benefits and burdens by societies and especially by the state as the agent of society. A commitment to fairness and a particular construal of impartiality explains why egalitarians of this sort are so concerned with the distribution of benefits and burdens. Other egalitarians are concerned with the distribution of status, power, and respect, because they think that morality rests upon equality of respect and moral standing and that relations among human beings should be governed by reciprocity. Still other egalitarians are motivated by a concern with solidarity and fraternity and for that reason condemn large inequalities in wealth, status, and power. What

[4] "[…] what makes us care about various inequalities is […] the hunger of the hungry, the need of the needy, the suffering of the ill, and so on. The fact that they are worse-off in the relevant respect than their neighbors is relevant. But it is relevant not as an independent evil of inequality. Its relevance is in showing that their hunger is greater, their need more pressing, their suffering more hurtful, and therefore our concern for the hungry, the needy, the suffering, and not our concern for equality makes us give them the priority" (Raz 1984, p. 240).

[5] For a related view, see O'Neill (2008).

makes those concerned with solidarity, like those concerned with reciprocity, equality of respect, or impartiality all egalitarians is the fact that certain kinds of distributional equalities constitute, not merely cause, the realization or frustration of these ideals.

From this perspective, luck egalitarianism appears to be *superficial* as well as problematic. Luck egalitarianism stipulates a concern with significant inequalities in welfare without providing any philosophical foundations for this concern. It never explains why distributive inequality matters. For example, Tan argues that what distinguishes luck egalitarianism is that it is a "grounding principle" that answers the question, "Why does distributive inequality matter?" (2008, p. 667) – that is, that it answers the question that I am accusing it of failing to answer. What then, in his view, is the answer? According to Tan, the luck egalitarian holds that "persons should not be disadvantaged simply because of bad luck" because "individuals can only be held responsible for outcomes that are due to their own choices" (2008, p. 667). But the uncontroversial premise concerning responsibility says nothing at all about how advantages or disadvantages for which individuals should not be held responsible should be distributed. Tan never tells us how the luck egalitarian answers the question, "Why does distributive inequality matter." Both to justify luck egalitarianism and to explain how it should cope with the difficulties canvassed above, more needs to be said about its moral foundations

The author who has taken this challenge most seriously is Larry Temkin, who grounds his version of luck egalitarianism in considerations of desert.[6] His view condemns both undeserved inequalities and undeserved equalities. What explains why undeserved equalities in well-being are wrong cannot, of course, be some fundamental concerning about inequality in the distribution of well-being, since, by hypothesis, there is none. What drives the theory is the view that rewards should match deserts. The emphasis on desert nicely explains the intuition that the imprudent should not be fully compensated, nor abandoned altogether, while those who have been disadvantaged as a result of their own choices in course of doing something admirable should be compensated. The principle that people should get what they deserve is not itself an egalitarian principle. But, with the additional assumption that there is a baseline equality of desert or that equality is the default when desert is not defined, Temkin's position is arguably egalitarian – though only marginally so.[7]

---

[6] I am indebted to Matt Waldren for this reading of Temkin (which Temkin accepts). Segall explicitly rejects such a justification (2010, pp. 16–17), and argues that his concerns are completely independent of questions of desert. But he provides no alternative philosophical rationale for his qualified luck egalitarianism. The only consideration in its favor is its questionable ability to match our intuitions.

[7] See Kagan (1999). Serena Olsaretti (2002) disputes Kagan's view that notions of desert completely displace egalitarian concerns. She argues that valuing equality makes a difference when considering starting points, where no one yet deserves anything, or when considering different patterns of desert.

2.3 Equality of Health and Health Care

Luck egalitarians want to eliminate differences in opportunities for welfare. Health strongly influences opportunity for welfare, and so the distribution of health will be of concern to luck egalitarians. The provision of health care influences health and thereby influences well-being. It may also affect well-being by providing financial security in the face of illness. As a significant influence on well-being, the distribution of health-care will also be of interest to luck egalitarians. But is there any reason why luck egalitarians should want specifically to equalize health outcomes for which individuals are not responsible or why luck egalitarians should want to equalize access to health care?

To address this question, something must be said about what is meant by equality in health. (One could also ask for some clarification concerning what constitutes equality of access to health care, but I shall assume here that the idea is clear enough.) One might maintain that the health of two individuals is unequal if there is any time period during which they are in different health states. But to attempt to redress all temporary inequalities in health for which individuals are not responsible would not be sensible. Among other things, it would shift the emphasis in medical care toward addressing temporary ailments. Most people think that two individuals can be equally healthy if one has the flu a few weeks before the other. At the other extreme, one might say that individuals are equally healthy if they have the same lifetime quantity or value of health. This presupposes some way to measure or value overall health at a time and to aggregate it over a lifetime. Luck egalitarians would not, of course, insist on equality of realized health, because individuals are responsible for a good deal of their health and because many health differences cannot be eliminated by human action. Equality of lifetime health *expectations* comes closer to what the luck egalitarian aims for. But equality in lifetime health expectations is consistent with compensating inequalities in health in different life stages, and an egalitarian might be unwilling to accept inequalities within life stages.

Having at least laid out some alternative conceptions of equality in health, I can return to the question of what reason luck egalitarians might have to seek equality in health. Consider two people, Abby and Alan. Abby is better off than Alan, but she is sick, while he is in full health. Neither is responsible for the inequalities. If one rules out leveling down, the only way to equalize health is to cure Abby. But curing Abby will amplify rather than mitigate the inequality in *overall* well-being. In these circumstances, a luck egalitarian should oppose equalizing health. To mitigate the inequality, Alan needs other, non-health related resources. Suppose instead that Abby is both better off and healthier than Alan. In that case, it may be possible to equalize well-being either via separately equalizing health and other determinants of well-being or via compensating inequalities in health and other resources. As far as I can see, nothing in luck egalitarianism favors equalizing health. Luck egalitarianism offers no general justification for equalizing health.

There is, however, one special case where luck egalitarianism does favor equalizing health. To describe that case, some distinctions are needed. Some health deficiencies are preventable or curable – call these "remediable" – while others are not. Some health deficiencies are compensable – individuals can be made just as well off by providing them with more of other resources – while others are incompensable. For example, a diabetic coma is incompensable, but remediable. Congenital blindness is irremediable but compensable. Tay Sachs disease is neither remediable nor compensable. Mild myopia is both remediable and compensable. Only serious health conditions will be incompensable.[8]

Consider then a case in which Abby is better off than Alan because he has a remediable and incompensable health deficiency that Abby does not have. If Alan is not responsible for his health problem, then the luck egalitarian finds this state of affairs unjust. Since Alan's health problem is incompensable, the unjust inequality in well-being can only be addressed by eliminating the inequality in health. When health problems are remediable and incompensable and individuals are not responsible for them, then equalizing opportunity for welfare will often require equalizing health. But this is a special case. In general, luck egalitarianism provides no justification for equalizing health.

Neither is there a luck egalitarian case for equalizing access to health care. There are many ways to equalize opportunity for welfare or to eliminate inequalities in welfare for which individuals are not responsible. Some of these may involve equalizing access to health care. Many will not. Nothing in luck egalitarianism tells us to favor those that involve equalizing access to health care. If one seeks a justification for equalizing health or health care, he or she needs to look beyond luck egalitarianism.

2.3.1 Relational Egalitarian A pproaches

As I mentioned, though all too briefly, near the end of Sect. 2.2, I maintain that egalitarianism is a family of positions motivated by several distinct moral commitments, which are egalitarian in their spirit, rationale, and implications. The most-discussed alternative to luck egalitarianism sees equality as a matter of how individuals relate to one another and consequently focuses on equality of standing, respect, and political power. This "relational egalitarianism," versions of which one finds in the work of Rawls (1971), Daniels (1985, 2007), Anderson (1999), Scheffler (2003, 2005), and Freeman (2007) is grounded in a moral commitment to equal respect and a political commitment to reciprocity and liberty (in the sense of non-domination). It is not mainly concerned with the distribution of benefits and burdens

[8] I first drew these distinctions in Hausman (2007). There is more to be said about them. It might be possible to mitigate the inequalities between Abby and Alan that are due to Alan's irremediable bad health by providing Alan with additional non-health resources or by making Abby otherwise worse off. I count only the former as "compensation." The fact that one might be able to make Alan and Abby equally well off by making Abby sufficiently miserable does not make Alan's ill-health compensable.

by state or society or with holdings of goods, except insofar as these impinge on the relations among individuals and threaten to subordinate some to others or to diminish the liberties of some relative to the liberties of others.

A relational egalitarian has an easier time defending policies that mitigate health inequalities than does a luck egalitarian. Though it would be hard for a relational egalitarian to make the case for strict equality, large inequalities in health undermine reciprocity and equal liberty. They render individuals vulnerable to domination by others and diminish their political voice. The case for mitigating inequalities in access to health care is more tenuous, but it is arguable that failing to take steps (or to make it easy for individuals to take their own steps) toward protecting the health of some individuals fails to show them equal respect. The case for equalizing health then rests on the claim that significant inequalities in health, unlike inequalities in goods in general, are crucial to maintaining equality among citizens. Although the effects of ill-health on well-being are often compensable, the effects on the political and social relations among individuals are not readily compensable, and there is consequently an egalitarian case to be made for mitigating health inequalities, even in circumstances in which there are inequalities in well-being that might be aggravated by the lessening of health inequalities.

Norman Daniels' influential and well-known argument for equality of access to health care (1985, 2007) and for equalizing health (2007) is a hybrid that inherits the problems that arise when luck egalitarians try to argue for equality with respect to health and health care, and it ultimately lacks any clear egalitarian rationale. Daniels rejects luck egalitarianism and draws on Rawl's relationally egalitarian *Theory of Justice*. Daniels takes the distribution of health and health care to be governed by generalizations of Rawls' two principles of justice, and in particular by a generalization of a portion of Rawls' second principle, which Rawls calls "Fair Equality of Opportunity." In Rawls' work (which abstracts from all health disparities), fair equality of opportunity obtains when people's social circumstances do not affect their career prospects. This principle diverges from luck egalitarianism, because it is not concerned with the distribution of overall well-being and because it permits career prospects (as well as well-being) to be influenced by an individual's talents and skills, even though individuals are typically not responsible for them.

Daniels points out that if one relaxes Rawls' simplification and allows for the possibility of ill health, then one must recognize that society can influence opportunity not through social resources such as education and personal contacts, but also via health care. Since it would be bizarre to measure the importance of health entirely by its impact on careers, Daniels broadens the notion of opportunity. If individuals *P* and *Q* have the same talents, then *P* has greater opportunities than *Q* if and only if *P* can access a larger portion of the range of life plans accessible in that society to individuals with these talents than *Q* can. Rather than opportunity for welfare, which is what the luck egalitarian is concerned with, or opportunity for careers, which is what Rawls is concerned with, Daniels is concerned with opportunities for carrying out life plans.

Daniels's reinterpretation of the fair equality of opportunity principle requires that those whose talents are the same should have available to them the same range of life plans. This diverges from luck egalitarianism, since it calls for no compensation for differences in talents, even though individuals are typically not responsible for those differences. But it faces the same difficulties in justifying equalizing health or access to health care that the luck egalitarian faces. Suppose that despite being sick, Annabelle has access to a larger portion of the range of life plans open to someone with her talents than does Alphonse, who has the same talents, comes from a poor family, and is healthy. In such circumstances fair equality of opportunity does not imply that society should attempt to improve Annabelle's health or provide her with better access to health care. One can equalize opportunities by compensating inequalities in health and social advantages or by separately equalizing each; and nothing in Daniels' theory favors the latter (Sreenivasan 2007).

Moreover, in revising Rawls' fair equality of opportunity principle, Daniels undermines its egalitarian rationale. As Daniels emphasizes, his version of the fair equality of opportunity principle requires prevention and treatment of disease or disability, not enhancement of non-pathological traits, even when these traits lead to overall functioning that significantly diminishes opportunity. Non-pathological traits – abilities and skills – define what someone's fair share of the normal opportunity range is, while pathological traits prevent individuals from enjoying their fair share. So fair opportunity, as Daniels interprets it, requires that someone whose short stature is due to a (pathological) growth-hormone deficiency be treated with growth hormone while someone of equal stature who lacks the pathology but who is equally sensitive to growth hormone, need not be treated.

Daniels' position on treatment versus enhancement is obviously inconsistent with luck egalitarianism, and one might wonder how a relational egalitarian could defend it. Crucial to its defense is Daniels' view that fair equality of opportunity requires mitigation of pathologies but tolerates inequalities due to differences in talents. This way of distinguishing the cases thus places a great deal of weight on the distinction between "low talent" and pathology,[9] which, according to the account of health that Daniels relies on, is in fact largely arbitrary.[10] But what reason could a relational egalitarian have to favor remediation or compensation for conditions depending on whether they are due to pathologies or to talent deficiencies? What is relevant appears to be how a condition affects people and the possibilities and costs of remedy or compensation, not whether it is a disease.

[9] Lesley Jacobs makes a similar point, "Daniels could respond that from the perspective of equality of opportunity, the effects of some natural differences—those originating from differences in talents—are fair, but the effects of other natural differences—those originating from illness and disease—are unfair. The cogency of this response depends on the basis for this distinction" (1996, p. 337).

[10] Daniels adopts Christopher Boorse's view (1977, 1997), according to which health is the absence of disease or pathology. According to Boorse, there is a pathology in some part of an organism when the level of functioning or capacity to function is in the lower tail of the distribution of efficiency of part function. Exactly where to draw the line between low normal and pathological functioning is in Boorse's view arbitrary. There is nothing in theoretical medicine or biology that tells one whether the bottom 5% or 1% or .001% of liver function among some reference class divides the pathological from the non-pathological. For a critique of this view, see Schwartz (2007).

The fact that Daniels' version of fair equality of opportunity principle justifies the disparate treatment of conditions depending on whether they result from pathology or from low talent casts doubt on the principle. In Rawls' hands, the principle had a clear rationale from a relational egalitarian perspective. Allowing social factors such as one's family's wealth and status to influence opportunities for careers and positions fails to show equal respect and facilitates domination of some people by others, while allowing talents and motivation to influence opportunities for careers and positions does not. But why should a relational egalitarian believe that permitting health deficiencies to influence what life plans are accessible fails to show equal respect and facilitates subjugation, while maintaining that permitting talents to have such influence is unobjectionable? From a relational egalitarian perspective, there is no reason to be more concerned about inequalities due to poor health than there are to be concerned about inequalities due to differences in talents. Daniels' version of fair equality of opportunity has no relational egalitarian rationale.

If Daniels were instead to regard inequalities in opportunities to achieve life plans due to talents as just as unacceptable as inequalities due to poor health, then his view would become a form of luck egalitarianism where the object of distributional concern consists in the range of accessible life plans rather than well-being. The resulting view would have much the same rationale as more standard variants of luck egalitarianism; and it would be no better able to justify equalizing health or access to health care.

2.3.2 *Justifying Equality of Health and Health Care*

Most luck egalitarians have been concerning about inequalities in overall well-being for which individuals are not responsible. Relational egalitarians have been concerned about differences in moral standing, political influence, and extent to which some individuals can dominate others. Other versions of egalitarianism have, I have suggested, been concerned about impartiality or solidarity. If health inequalities or inequalities in access to health care are of egalitarian concern, it must be because of their bearing on inequalities in well-being for which individuals are not responsible, their implications for the relations among citizens, whether they conflict with the impartiality and fairness required of the state, or what they imply about solidarity. Since equalizing health or equalizing access to health care is not a necessary condition for achieving the goals of the luck egalitarian and indeed sometimes impedes those goals, luck egalitarians cannot justify the claim that health inequalities and inequalities in access to health care are *prima facie* unjust. Relational egalitarians, in contrast, can make a case, but not in the way that Norman Daniels hopes.

Are there then no other grounds upon which to condemn health inequalities and inequalities in health care? In addition to a variety of not altogether convincing practical political considerations, I think that two arguments can be made. The strongest egalitarian criticisms of inequalities in health and health care rest, I think, on the values of solidarity and reciprocity, which, as I argued above, I take to be egalitarian values. Very few of us are never sick and in need of aid, and collectively we are able (to varying extents) to protect, cure, or comfort those who are stricken. By guaranteeing that we will be there to assist one another in times of need, we recognize our common vulnerability and affirm our common humanity. Though some health care differs little from the personal services one might purchase at a private spa, the protection of life and basic functioning and the alleviation of physical and mental suffering have a special significance, since everything of value in human life depends on them. To permit some to suffer, to die, or to be disabled needlessly is to fail to embrace them as partners in the human enterprise. This is, in rough outline, what I believe to be the central egalitarian basis for condemning inequalities in health and access to health care.

A second reason to object to inequalities in health and access to health care rests on benevolence rather than equality: As a matter of fact, inequalities greatly lessen total well-being and involve enormous suffering. Relatively small transfers of resources to the impoverished to improve nutrition and sanitation and to provide treatments for common diseases would diminish inequalities in health and at the same time limit suffering and increase total well-being both directly and through improvements in the labor force.[11] Though one can easily imagine circumstances in which those who are worse off are not badly off and in which inequalities in health and health care would increase rather than decrease total well-being, those circumstances are not ours. This argument for the egalitarian conclusion that we should lessen inequalities in the distribution of health and health care does not rest on any egalitarian premises, but it is none the worse for that. Indeed, given how contentious egalitarianism is, the possibility of making non-egalitarian arguments for diminishing inequalities in health and health care should be welcomed.

References

Anderson, E. 1999. What is the point of equality? *Ethics* 99: 287–337.

Arneson, R. 1989. Equality and equal opportunity for welfare. *Philosophical Studies* 56: 77–93.

Boorse, C. 1977. Health as a theoretical concept. *Philosophy of Science* 44: 542–573.

Boorse, C. 1997. A rebuttal on health. In *What is disease?* ed. J. Humber and R. Almeder, 1–134. Totowa: Humana Press.

Cohen, G.A. 1989. On the currency of egalitarian justice. *Ethics* 89: 906–944.

Daniels, N. 1985. *Just health care*. Cambridge: Cambridge University Press.

Daniels, N. 2007. *Just health*. Cambridge: Cambridge University Press.

Dworkin, R. 1981. What is equality? Part 2: Equality of resources. *Philosophy and Public Affairs* 10: 283–345.

Freeman, S. 2007. Rawls and luck egalitarianism. In *Justice and the social contract*, ed. S. Freeman, 111–142. New York: Oxford University Press.

[11] One might question this claim on the grounds that improving the health of those who are worst off would lead to a population explosion which in the future would diminish total well-being. The tragic scenario suggested by this objection might come to pass. But the future is too uncertain to justify a certain present loss of well-being.

Hausman, D. 2007. Are health inequalities unjust? *Journal of Political Philosophy* 15: 46–66.
Hausman, D. 2011. A Lockean argument for universal access to health care. *Social Philosophy and Policy* 28: 166–191.
Hausman, D. 2012. Egalitarian critiques of health inequalities. In *Measurement and ethical evaluation of health inequalities*, ed. O. Frithjof Norheim, S. Hurst, N. Eyal, and D. Wikler. Oxford: Oxford University Press.
Hausman, D., and M.S. Waldren. 2011. Egalitarianism reconsidered. *Journal of Moral Philosophy* 8(4): 1–20.
Jacobs, L. 1996. Can an egalitarian justify universal access to health care? *Social Theory and Practice* 22: 315–348.
Kagan, S. 1999. Equality and desert. In *What do we deserve: A reader on justice and desert*, ed. L. Pojman and O. McLeod. Oxford: Oxford University Press.
Olsaretti, S. 2002. Unmasking equality? Kagan on equality and desert. *Utilitas* 14: 387–400.
O'Neill, M. 2008. What should egalitarians believe? *Philosophy and Public Affairs* 36: 119–156.
Parfit, D. 1991. *Equality or priority? (Lindley lecture)*, 1–22. Lawrence: University of Kansas.
Rawls, J. 1971. *A theory of justice*. Cambridge: Harvard University Press.
Raz, J. 1984. *The morality of freedom*. Oxford: Oxford University Press.
Scheffler, S. 2003. What is egalitarianism? *Philosophy and Public Affairs* 31: 5–39.
Scheffler, S. 2005. Choice, circumstances, and the value of equality. *Politics, Philosophy and Economics* 4: 5–28.
Schwartz, P. 2007. Defining dysfunction: Natural selection, design, and drawing a line. *Philosophy of Science* 74: 364–385.
Segall, S. 2010. *Health, luck, and justice*. Princeton: Princeton University Press.
Sreenivasan, G. 2007. Health care and equality of opportunity. *The Hastings Center Report* 37(2): 21–31.
Tan, K.-C. 2008. A defense of luck egalitarianism. *Journal of Philosophy* 11: 665–690.
Temkin, L. 1993. *Inequality*. Oxford: Oxford University Press.
Temkin, L. 2003. Egalitarianism defended. *Ethics* 113: 764–782.

Chapter 3
Affirmative Action in Health

Shlomi Segall

3.1 Introduction

The ideal of equality of opportunity has long been considered central to health equity. Rawlsians, such as Norman Daniels, speak of health care as a means to (fair) equality of opportunity (Daniels 1985), whereas luck egalitarians have suggested the (diametrically opposed) ideal of equality of opportunity for health (LeGrande 1987, 1991, ch 7; Roemer 1998, ch 8; Segall 2010, ch 7). What unites both egalitarian camps, however, is the view that to achieve substantive (rather than merely formal) equality of opportunity we must often practice affirmative action. And yet, health equity and affirmative action have not (to my knowledge) been linked. My purpose in this paper, then, is to try and elucidate what 'affirmative action in health' might mean. I want to do so, in particular, by constructing and evaluating Rawlsian and luck egalitarian accounts of affirmative action. The former I glean from Daniels's most recent work. He says there that we have a good reason to prioritize the medical needs of those whose ill health is the product of unjust social circumstances. The alternative account of affirmative action in health, with which I want to contrast Daniels's, speaks of prioritizing the needs of members of groups who ex-ante face worse health prospects (African-Americans, say, and, somewhat more controversially, men).

The discussion to follow is premised on a number of assumptions for which I cannot argue here. It assumes, of course, that health (and not just health care) is a subject of justice (Segall 2010, ch 6), and that health inequalities could be unjust

I am grateful to the participants of the *Priority-Setting in Health Care* workshop at the Karolinska Institute, Stockholm in January 2011, and the conference on *Justice, Luck and Responsibility in Health-Care* at the Center for Economics & Ethics, KU Leuven, in May 2011, for their comments and suggestions. I am particularly grateful to Gustaf Arrhenius and Niklas Juth for their feedback.

S. Segall (✉)
Department of Political Science, Hebrew University of Jerusalem,
Jerusalem 91905, Israel
e-mail: ssegall@mscc.huji.ac.il

Y. Denier et al. (eds.), *Justice, Luck & Responsibility in Health Care*,
Library of Ethics and Applied Philosophy 30, DOI 10.1007/978-94-007-5335-8_3,

(Segall 2010, ch 6). In addition, the discussion also assumes that we may discuss health inequalities in isolation from other inequalities. Let me quickly qualify this last premise. It hardly needs stating that a discussion of health inequalities does not presume that these are the only morally significant inequalities, or that health inequalities are more unjust than other inequalities (e.g. in income). [Although I do think the latter statement is not far off the mark, as health does seem to underwrite much of human welfare. So for welfarist egalitarians, at least, health inequalities should be tremendously important (Sen 2002)]. Rather, the point is to try and isolate the discussion of health inequalities for analytical, rather than practical purposes.

Daniels's position amounts to what is often called the (left) liberal approach to affirmative action. Assessing that liberal approach as it applies to health entails examining the grounds underlying affirmative action. These normally divide between backward-looking and forward-looking considerations. Section 3.2 presents Daniels's position, and then assesses whether backward-looking considerations may ground a liberal approach to affirmative action in health. Concluding that they cannot, I turn, in Sect. 3.3, to examine and rebut forward-looking justifications. Section 3.4 then presents and defends an alternative to liberal affirmative action in health, one derived from the luck egalitarian account of radical equality of opportunity.

3.2 Liberal Affirmative Action in Health

Let us, then, examine the liberal account of affirmative action in health. According to Daniels, all health inequalities are bad from a moral perspective, and we have an obligation to meet all health needs. However, health inequalities that result from an unjust distribution of the socially controllable factors affecting health are not merely bad but also unjust. So, we have a duty to reduce *all* health inequalities, but we have an 'extra reason', Daniels says, to reduce health inequalities when they are *inequities*, that is, when they are owed to an unjust distribution of the social determinants of health.[1] This principle yields concrete policy implications. Suppose we are faced with two equally needy patients, where one's neediness is the result of natural factors whereas the other's illness is due to racism or (unjust) poverty. It follows from Daniels's account that we must assign priority to the latter patient. He acknowledges, admittedly, that this reason might be outweighed by other considerations.[2] Daniels in fact goes as far as saying that some people may plausibly think that we ought to not give *any* priority to the patient who is a victim of racism. He thus

[1] 'There is considerable force to the claim that we should increase the priority we grant to those whose health is worse if this is a result of racist or sexist policy or individual acts of racism or sexism' (Daniels 2008, p. 304).

[2] 'Although we may give additional priority to meeting a group's health needs if they are the result of unjust social practices, we cannot give their needs complete priority' (Daniels 2008, p. 305).

concludes that whether or not the victim of racism ought to be given priority over the patient whose illness is no one's fault is something over which there might be reasonable disagreement,[3] and that, consequently, this ought to be subject to a deliberative decision mechanism.

Contra Daniels, I want to claim that there is *no* reasonable disagreement over the case in question, and that it would be wrong (because unjust) to give priority to the patient who is the victim of racism (call her Clare) over the patient who is the victim of ordinary bad luck (call her Doris). One way of teasing this out is to try and imagine how things would look from Doris's perspective once we have automatically[4] passed-over her in favour of Clare (on account of the particular social circumstances that have led to Clare's illness). To examine the case in its pure form, we must assume, of course, that Doris was not herself complicit in the racist or otherwise unjust social practice that has lead to Clare's disadvantaged health status. And we must also assume, note, that Doris did not benefit in any way from Clare's disadvantage.[5] Under those circumstances, Doris may plausibly say that it is *not her fault* that Clare was a victim of racism. Moreover, now that she lost out the priority in medical treatment to Clare, Doris wishes that she herself had been the victim of racism. (That is, she would prefer it to simply being the victim of bad luck in the natural lottery of genes). Giving priority to Clare over Doris thus seems arbitrary and unjust. We might even say [to use Daniels's terminology regarding deliberation (see Daniels and Sabin 1997)] that there is nothing reasonable we could say to Doris to convince her that she was not discriminated against.

Now, one thing that could be said in support of Daniels's position, and in favour of giving priority to Clare (the victim of social injustice), is to invoke affirmative action. We often do assign priority to those who were the victims of social injustice, so the claim goes, and crucially, over and above equally suitable individuals who did not suffer such injustices. Just think of standard cases of affirmative action where among equally qualified candidates we give priority to the one who belongs to a group that has suffered some historical injustice. Recall, for example, the landmark Bakke case in which a medical school practiced quotas for African-Americans, in the name of affirmative action. The court, admittedly, ruled in favour of Bakke, but nevertheless established that, in principle, majority candidates have no legitimate complaint against the policy of affirmative action even when they are equally qualified to the candidate eventually chosen (Dworkin 1985, ch 14). The practice of affirmative action is of course not beyond dispute but it is certainly not prima facie implausible. And that, crucially, is all that Daniels needs to show here. (Since, as we

[3] 'Reasonable people will continue to disagree about how much additional priority to grant. Some of this disagreement may be the result of the original disagreement about how to make the trade-offs in the morally neutral distributive problems. But some of it may be the result of disagreement about how much weight to give to the underlying fact of injustice, be it race or gender based' (Daniels 2008, pp. 305–6).

[4] I should stress that Daniels allows that prioritizing Clare over Doris is not automatic. Since he talks about 'non-absolute priority' it follows that we may adopt here something like a weighted lottery.

[5] Daniels, it is worth noting, adopts the same assumption (Daniels 2008, p. 304).

saw, his claim is that the priority of those suffering a social disadvantage over those suffering a natural one is something that ought to be subject to deliberation, because reasonable people may disagree over its proper extent). If we think it is right (as the US Supreme Court evidently did) to allow for priority to be given to the minority candidate who was no more qualified than Bakke, then at the very least, one might say, it is not implausible to give priority to Clare (the victim of racism) over Doris. If we ask, then, what affirmative action in health could possibly mean, the (reconstructed) Rawlsian answer would be: of two equally needy patients assign priority to the one who suffered some social injustice.

I disagree, however, that we ought to give priority to Clare, and I further doubt that we may derive such priority from any parallel one might draw from affirmative action in employment and higher education. To see this it would be useful to recall the various potential rationales for affirmative action (say, in higher education). These conventionally divide between backward-looking and forward-looking considerations. A typical backward-looking argument for affirmative action says that it compensates the minority candidate for past injustices (whether committed against him personally or against the group to which he belongs).[6] (This rationale for affirmative action is not beyond controversy, of course, but we are setting such reservations aside for the sake of argument). On this rationale, the minority candidate would have been even more qualified than the (currently) equally qualified majority candidate, had it not been for the past racism. Among other things, this rationale clearly shows why affirmative action does not, in fact, discriminate against the white (majority) candidate. This rationale, however, does not apply easily to the case before us. It is *not* the case that Clare would have been more deserving of the treatment (or of priority for the treatment) than Doris had it not been for the social injustice. If anything, it is quite the opposite. If it wasn't for the racial injustice, Clare would have been healthier, and as such, would have deserved *lower* priority for the treatment. There seems, then, to be an asymmetry between merit (an arguably determining factor in higher education) and need (a determining factor in the allocation of health care). Merit and need, in other words, simply pull in opposite directions.

It could be objected, though, that I haven't analyzed the case before us correctly. One might say, instead, that what is at stake here is not the entitlement to the medical *care* but the entitlement to the health *status* in question. If it wasn't for the social injustice, Clare would indeed have had better health, but that is precisely why she has a stronger claim to that level of health. She ought, therefore, to be given priority in the competition for the scarce medical care. It is therefore not a question of need but one of merit, owing to the imperative of restoring one to the position one would have occupied in the absence of social injustice. This revised claim also shows a

[6] Notice that backward looking justifications do not necessarily rely on there being a past injustice. They may, for example, strive to correct the outcome of a just lottery. Suppose that at time T an indivisible good A had to be distributed between groups X and Y, and X won the (fair) lottery. This gives us a reason, at time T+1 to award group Y with some good B. This can be seen as a measure of affirmative action, based on backward-looking considerations, and one which does not correct for an injustice. I am grateful to Dan Hausman for pointing this out to me.

nice parallel with affirmative action in employment and higher education. On this interpretation, affirmative action does not, in fact, undermine meritocracy (i.e. the appointment of the best qualified) because it rewards those who *would have been* the most qualified if it was not for the systematic past discrimination against them. Similarly, we might say that affirmative action in health restores individuals' life expectancy to what it would have been if it wasn't for the social injustice. Affirmative action thus operates here as a restorative device.

Notice, then, that what affirmative action accomplishes here is the removal of (arbitrary) social obstacles to individuals' ability to enjoy the fruits of their innate good health. This is, again, in parallel with meritocracy in employment and education. Meritocrats (including left-liberals such as Rawls) strive to level the playing field between equally talented individuals in the pursuit of jobs and university-places for which their talents qualify them. The point of affirmative action is then to correct the distortion brought on by social injustice. Equally, then, someone like Daniels might say, the point of affirmative action in health is to level the playing field, as it were, between individuals who possess equal genetic makeup, in the pursuit of long and healthy life. But drawing such a parallel has problematic implications. While meritocracy in employment is certainly not implausible, neither is it beyond doubt, especially for egalitarians. One might say that the talented deserve the better jobs for which they are qualified (Miller 1999, chs 7, 8). And alternatively, one might say (Rawls 1971, p. 84) that, while not itself a requirement of justice, it would *not be unjust* to assign good jobs to the talented. Yet, however persuasive these claims are (cf. Segall 2012), both lose force when applied to health. It is one thing (for critics of EOP in health) to claim that justice *does not require* equalizing health between the genetically lucky and unlucky. But it is quite another matter to hold that the genetically-endowed *deserve* better health, compared to the genetically worse off. It is moreover hard to see a reason why there should be such a requirement of justice. To put this differently, one may claim (falsely in my opinion, but leave that aside) that it is permissible to allow the genetically-endowed to enjoy their better health. But it is a different matter altogether to claim that health policy should be structured in such a way as to ensure that the genetically-endowed can enjoy their better innate health. It is not obvious why the winner of the natural lottery (in genes) deserve this institutional privilege.

One reason invoked by Rawls in defence of his 'careers open to talent' which might be relevant here is that levelling the playing field between equally talented individuals benefits society as a whole. (Notice that with this reply we are moving to the realm of forward-looking considerations). It is socially useful to allocate competitive positions of employment and higher education to the best talented. But the case is far less obvious when applied to health. There might be a utilitarian case for allocating scarce medical care to those who are genetically superior, since it may produce more overall life-years. But this is not the case in our example: ex hypothesi, Doris and Clare will derive equal benefit from the treatment. There does not, therefore, seem to be any social value in prioritising the naturally-gifted in this case.

3.3 Forward-Looking Considerations

Let us, then, turn to consider forward-looking considerations for affirmative action in health. Affirmative action in higher education and employment is sometimes said to be motivated by the social value entailed in boosting the representation of some historically excluded groups.[7] We commonly think that there are substantial benefits to having academic faculty, say, proportionally drawn from both genders and from the various ethnic and racial groups that make up society. (This is the case, notice, whether or not any of these groups were themselves subject to past injustices). Consider how this rationale applies to health. There is certainly social disvalue in the fact that different ethnic groups enjoy unequal levels of healthy life expectancy.[8] And quite apart from the egalitarian imperative of narrowing down these inequalities there does, admittedly, seem to be value in achieving greater racial equality in life expectancy. But this, notice, does not yet mean that there is social benefit to having the group of 'treated patients' (or even 'cured patients') made up of all strands of society. One potential benefit of having the group of 'treated patients' mirror the make-up of society as a whole is that it allows medical staff the opportunity to interact with diverse patients, each representing different culture and customs, thus adding to the overall training of doctors and nurses. But note that this instrumental rationale does not give us a reason to draw patients *proportionately* from society, but only to have significant numbers of them so as to allow contact with medical staff. One need not deny this instrumental value, but it might be the case here that the potential harm in trying to achieve this goal may well outweigh the expected gain.

A related forward-looking consideration for affirmative action often invoked in the literature is the 'role-model' effect (Dworkin 1985, p. 299). Having more women and members of ethnic minority as academic faculty, medical doctors, and CEO's sends an important message to young members of these groups that they, as well, may strive for these positions. But again this does not seem true in the case of health. In considering backward-looking considerations for affirmative action we saw that merit and need pull in opposite directions. Here, with regard to forward-looking considerations, a different disanalogy seems to be at work. Namely, while higher education and jobs carry some prestige, health does not. In other words, individuals do not normally gain social status merely by being healthy. That is why forward-looking considerations for affirmative action do not seem to apply to health, and that is also why, conversely, liberal affirmative action, whether or not appropriate in higher education and employment, is not appropriate to health.

To see the point more fully, consider cases where we have reasons to think that affirmative action (and anti-discrimination legislation more generally) may

[7] There is a good discussion of this in Anderson (2010, ch 7).

[8] For example in Belgium, Walloon males have a life expectancy that is 2 years lower than Flemish males: Life expectancy at 15 was 73.9 for Flemish males, as opposed to 71.6 for Walloon males (Van Oyen et al. 1996).

effectively narrow one type of inequality but at the same time exacerbate another. It is often noted, for example, that affirmative action benefits women and minorities at the cost of widening socio-economic gaps. The reason behind this is that it is often those who are already privileged and well-connected who are in a position to take advantage of the opportunities offered by affirmative action. Recognizing that affirmative action may well widen socio-economic gaps we often still think it is overall desirable to pursue it. And one reason that may explain why we feel that way is that we think of the long-term benefits of breaking the glass ceiling that may be restricting the employment of women and members of ethnic minorities. We also often think that hiring more women and people of colour will not only reduce gender- and racial- inequality here and now, but would also have a trickle down effect and, in the long term, increase opportunities for women and blacks (say) of *all* socio-economic classes. Crucially however, this rationale does not seem to obtain in the case of health. Health carries no prestige (Margalit 1996, pp. 241–2), and having more of it is therefore unlikely to have any role-model effect on those lacking it. Having more faculty members that are black is different, in that sense, from extending African American life expectancy from 65 to 67. Affirmative action in health cannot therefore be motivated by a consideration for breaking down some glass ceiling in the health gains of disadvantaged groups. To put this differently, we find it repugnant that life expectancy in some neighbourhoods of Glasgow is 12 years or so shorter than in the more affluent neighbourhoods of that city. And we do think that narrowing down that gap is valuable in itself (even while recognizing that this value does not trump other values such as the value of aggregate health, thus potentially resisting levelling down). But crucially we do not normally think that narrowing that gap will serve the end of smashing some imagined glass ceiling in some group's life expectancy.

In considering backward-looking considerations we witnessed the disanalogy between merit and need. In reviewing forward-looking considerations, we now see the disanalogy between the expressive value in affirmative action in employment (and higher education), compared with the absence of such value in health. This disanalogy has some concrete implications, some of which may prove controversial. Suppose we are forced to choose between policy X which would benefit middle class black men and policy Y which would benefit poor white men. Measure X is likely, then, to decrease racial inequality in health, but increase class inequality, whereas measure Y will do precisely the opposite. Which should we prefer? If we were discussing employment, we would probably opt for policy X (the one narrowing racial inequalities) because it has the more pronounced expressive effect, and because it is more likely, in the long term, to reduce overall inequalities (that is, both racial and class-based), precisely through breaking some glass ceiling. In the case of health things are made easier, in a way, by the absence of such expressive value. In the absence of glass ceilings to break, we should simply look at which measure benefits those who are worse off (which, in this example, may well be policy Y).

It might be said, finally, that contrary to the assertion just made, health does carry some prestige. This is manifested, for example, in the case of bad teeth, which often carries a social stigma. But notice that whatever stigma bad teeth may have hinge on the particular medical condition and not on the *level* of health that it may manifest. This is further evidenced in the fact that some medical conditions carry a positive message of prestige, such as broken legs around Christmas break. It is the particular condition, not the level of health that tracks prestige. The case is different in goods such as income or employment, where (at least some of) the prestige resides in the quantity of the good the person controls. (Prestige varies with how much money we have and how highly ranked is the university which we attended). So while certain medical conditions (bad teeth, mental illness) do obviously carry negative stigma, low level of health, in and of itself, typically does not.

3.4 Radical Affirmative Action in Health

The liberal ideal of affirmative action does not seem very suitable to health. Consider, then, the alternative account, the luck egalitarian ideal of radical equality of opportunity. Very briefly, what distinguishes radical from substantive EOP is that the former 'treats the inequality that arises out of native difference as a further source of injustice' (Cohen 2009, p. 17). Applied to health, radical affirmative action would strive to assign priority to those whose need is caused by an ex-ante worse-off health prospect, whether generated by social or natural factors. We know, for example, that being poor, black, male, and so forth entails worse health prospects. (Radical) affirmative action in health directs us, then, to improve the health prospects of members of these groups. I should quickly qualify this. This ideal of affirmative action is meant to inform health policy rather than medical care narrowly understood. The suggestion here is not to practice affirmative action at the point of delivery. For rather obvious reasons, it might not be such a good idea for doctors and nurses to prioritize patients on the basis of anything but their medical condition, let alone on the basis of race, sex, and socio-economic status. My suggestion, I hope, escapes this undesirable effect by focusing on the way in which health policy is set up rather than the way in which health care is delivered. (In any case, in this respect Daniels's account and mine rise and fall together).

Notice also that the contrast between Daniels's account and mine applies not only domestically but also globally. Whichever account we adopt is something that has potential implications for aid policy in developing countries. Luck egalitarians commonly think that individuals ought to have equal opportunities, including opportunities for health, no matter in which country they happen to be born (Caney 2001). This has potential implications for priority-setting in global health policy. Suppose health-aid institutions (say, the WHO) are forced to decide between two countries, Colonia and Independensia. The former's low health status is a legacy of its colonial past, its resources having been ransacked and its civil society undermined by the colonial power. Independensia, in contrast, had no colonial past, but rather has suffered a series of droughts (none of them owed to human agency), which has left its population malnourished and stunted. Assuming life expectancy is equally low in both countries, Daniels's principle would give priority to Colonia. But we may similarly anticipate the legitimate reaction on the part of the citizens of Independensia to such hypothetical WHO decision, possibly expressing regret over never having a colonial power rule over them. If all this is plausible, then contra Daniels, it seems that countries whose disadvantaged life expectancy is owed to natural factors deserve the exact same priority as countries whose low health is owed to unjust international practices.[9] Looked at from the perspectives of such developing nations, I suggest, it does not matter whether one's short life expectancy is owed to a ruinous colonial past or to some unfortunate act of nature.

Now, it might be suggested that some of the general objections to liberal affirmative action are true also of radical affirmative action in health. A common objection to affirmative action says that its direct beneficiaries have often not themselves suffered any disadvantage. Critics, thus, often point out that it is mostly middle-class blacks, for example, who benefit from affirmative action in higher education. And it is, furthermore, doubtful that these individuals are more deserving than some other poor white candidates. The ideal of radical affirmative action in health that I defended can be said to suffer from the same objection: a health policy that prioritizes blacks as a rule may end up benefiting some such patients who happen to be healthier than some more deserving white patients. This might motivate an objection, say, to public sponsorship of BiDil (a drug for heart condition that is said to be particularly effective for African-Americans). Similarly, shifting research funds from breast cancer into prostate cancer (due to the ex-ante worse health prospects of men compared to women) may end up being beneficial primarily to well-to-do male patients who are overall healthier than many female patients.

Of course, one thing to note is that this objection afflicts also the other account of affirmative action in health. Recall that Daniels's account prioritizes medical needs that are the product of unjust social practices, which he proposes to do by targeting socially disadvantaged groups. It is implausible, and Daniels indeed does not recommend doing so, to identify *individuals* who have suffered some social injustice. So that proposal, as indeed any account of affirmative action, is likely to be vulnerable to the objection that it would sometimes benefit well-off members of worse-off groups. My first reply, then, is that the objection is common to any account of affirmative action in health, and is not particular to the one I advance here. But let me add a further response. While affirmative action targets groups (or individuals qua members of groups), it is, to be sure, individuals as such that it is ultimately concerned with. That is the case with affirmative action in employment and higher education, and is moreover so the case with regard to health (moreover so because of the absence of the abovementioned expressive value in breaking glass-ceilings). The reason behind health policy targeting groups rather than individuals is a practical rather than a principled one. The currency of health inequalities is life expectancy. And so long as (technically speaking) life expectancy is an attribute of groups rather

[9] Both would count as 'circumstance' or 'bad brute luck' and as such equally deserve to be neutralized. For a luck-egalitarian-informed approach to international aid which emphasizes circumstance vs. effort see Llavador and Roemer (2001). The same model is applied to health aid in Roemer (1989).

than individuals, affirmative action in health could target individuals qua members of groups rather than target individuals as such. Notice, though, that with the continuing advent of medical research we are likely to be able to have an increasingly refined account of life expectancy. This fact, we can see, casts a more favourable light on my account than it does on Daniels's, because mine is not restricted to salient groups who have suffered some social injustice. An account whose concern is social *as well as* natural sources of ill health may therefore appeal to an account of groups that is as refined and specific as can be. Returning to the example of Bidil, we may identify not only African-Americans but 'African-Americans with an income below 40k$ a year' as the worse off, health-wise, group in society. And if, crucially, we can devise health measures that would target such a specific group, the radical account of affirmative action in health would endorse it.

It might be said, finally, that since my account of affirmative action in health makes only an instrumental rather than a principled allusion to groups it cannot then properly qualify as affirmative action. Affirmative action is by definition concerned with individuals qua members of groups. If it weren't, then it would just be an account of simple equality of opportunity. I don't have much to say by way of reply apart from pointing out that I do not think my overall account is undermined by this ('what's in a name') objection. I am happy to concede that equality of opportunity is what this account of justice in health is fundamentally concerned with.

3.5 Conclusion

I have contrasted, in this paper, two accounts of affirmative action in health. The first, Norman Daniels's liberal affirmative action, sought to prioritize patients whose medical condition is the result of social injustice. The second account, radical affirmative action, sought to prioritize the needs of all patients who ex-ante face worse off health prospects, whether owed to social *or* natural factors. I hope to have shown that radical affirmative action in health is the more defensible and attractive of the two ideals.

References

Anderson, E. 2010. *The imperative of integration*. Princeton: Princeton University Press.
Caney, S. 2001. Cosmopolitan justice and equalizing opportunities. *Metaphilosophy* 32: 113–134.
Cohen, G.A. 2009. *Why not socialism?* Princeton: Princeton University Press.
Daniels, N. 1985. *Just health care*. Cambridge: Cambridge University Press.
Daniels, N. 2008. *Just health: Meeting health needs fairly*. Cambridge: Cambridge University Press.
Daniels, N., and J. Sabin. 1997. Limits to health care: Fair procedures, democratic deliberation, and the legitimacy problem for insurers. *Philosophy and Public Affairs* 26: 303–350.
Dworkin, R. 1985. *A matter of principle*. Cambridge: Harvard University Press.
LeGrande, J. 1987. Equity, health, and health care. *Social Justice Research* 1: 257–274.

LeGrande, J. 1991. *Equity and choice: An essay in economics and applied philosophy*. London: Harper Collins.
Llavador, H.G., and J.E. Roemer. 2001. An equal-opportunity approach to the allocation of international aid. *Journal of Development Economics* 64: 147–171.
Margalit, A. 1996. *The decent society*. Cambridge: Harvard University Press.
Miller, D. 1999. *Principles of social justice*. Cambridge: Harvard University Press.
Rawls, J. 1971. *A theory of justice*. Oxford: Clarendon.
Roemer, J.E. 1989. *Distributing health: The allocation of resources by and international agency*. Washington, DC: World Institute for Development Economics Research of the United Nations University.
Roemer, J.E. 1998. *Equality of opportunity*. Cambridge: Harvard University Press.
Segall, S. 2010. *Health, luck, and justice*. Princeton: Princeton University Press.
Segall, S. 2012. Should the best qualified be appointed? *The Journal of Moral Philosophy* 9(1): 31–54.
Sen, A. 2002. Why health equity? *Health Economics* 11: 659–666.
Van Oyen, T., J. Tafforeau, and M. Roelands. 1996. Regional inequities in health expectancy in Belgium. *Social Science and Medicine* 43: 1673–1678.

Chapter 4
On Justice, Luck and Moral Responsibility Concerning Prenatal Genetic Diagnosis

Yvonne Denier

As the possibilities for significant and large-scale genetic interventions on human beings come closer *to being actualized, we may be forced to expand radically our conception of the domain of justice by including* natural *as well as social assets among the goods whose distribution just institutions are supposed to regulate, to abandon the simple picture of justice being about distributing goods among individuals whose identities are* given *independently of the process of distribution, and to* revise *certain basic assumptions about the relationships between justice, human nature, and moral progress.*

– Allen Buchanan, Dan Brock, Norman Daniels & Dan Wikler, *From Chance to Choice* –

4.1 Introduction

Though many ethical reflections on genetics are of a speculative and futuristic kind, concentrating on techniques that "come *closer* to being actualized," it is reasonable to say that in contemporary Western societies, at least one type of genetic intervention has *already* become widely actualised and well-established,

This essay is a slightly revised and updated version of earlier work (Denier 2010). As such, it is the result of several discussions on many occasions. I am thankful to John Alexander, Bart Capéau, Bart Engelen, Chris Gastmans, Jimmy Geutjens, Sylvie Loriaux, Stijn Neuteleers, Thomas Nys, Erik Schokkaert, Joris Van Damme, Antoon Vandevelde, Carine Vande Voorde, and all the participants to the May 2011 Conference on 'Justice, Luck and Responsibility in Health Care' in Leuven.

Y. Denier (✉)
Centre for Biomedical Ethics and Law, Catholic University of Leuven,
Kapucijnenvoer 35, box 7001, 3000 Leuven, Belgium
e-mail: Yvonne.Denier@med.kuleuven.be

Y. Denier et al. (eds.), *Justice, Luck & Responsibility in Health Care*,
Library of Ethics and Applied Philosophy 30, DOI 10.1007/978-94-007-5335-8_4,

viz. the framework of techniques of prenatal genetic diagnosis (PGD). Put shortly, these techniques make it possible to know in advance about the genetic condition and health status of the unborn child, thus making it possible either to prepare for the birth of a disabled child or to avoid this by aborting the foetus with congenital disorder.

By becoming common practice, these techniques indeed challenge the traditional conception of justice according to which *natural* inequalities among human beings are taken to be morally arbitrary, to be simply *given* facts that do not belong to the domain of justice (Rawls 1971, p. 102, 1999, p. 87). Put another way, they challenge the established idea that justice has to do with *agency*, with *directing* capacity, with things we can *control*, with a state of affairs that has either *resulted* from the actions of societies or individuals, or is at least capable of being *changed* by such actions. This conception of justice is convincingly expressed by David Miller's example of rain:

> … though we generally regard rain as burdensome and sunshine as beneficial, a state of affairs in which half of [the country] is drenched by rain while the other half is bathed in sunshine cannot be discussed (except metaphorically) in terms of justice – unless we happen to believe that Divine intervention has caused this state of affairs, or that meteorologists could alter it. As long as a state of affairs is regarded simply as a product of natural causes, questions about its justice or injustice do not arise (Miller 1976, p. 18).

The challenge that techniques of PGD pose on this characterisation of justice resides in the fact that "the natural" no longer seems to be something that is simply "beyond our control." They urge us to reconsider or at least refine the above definition of justice, since their existence makes it possible to say that "it is *unfair* to be born with lesser natural assets," or "that it is an *injustice* to give birth to a handicapped child when you could have *prevented* it by genetic testing." Arguments of this sort generally underlie claims of "wrongful birth" and "wrongful life." In "wrongful birth," the parents of a disabled child initiate a lawsuit, typically against a physician who is accused of not performing proper genetic screening or not adequately counselling prospective parents. The essence of wrongful birth is that the defendant's negligence resulted in the birth of a disabled child whom the parents would have aborted had they received adequate medical information. In "wrongful life," the disabled child – or those acting on the child's behalf – sues for being alive. In the latter case, the parents may become defendants. In essence, the child claims that being born damaged him and that he should be compensated for his suffering and for extra financial costs, such as special education and medical care.

Claims of wrongful life and wrongful birth usually create general uneasiness in society, which results in much public debate, often of a heated and highly emotional kind. In this paper, I will sketch the philosophical background of this uneasiness in a threefold way. I will start with a short overview of some recent examples of wrongful birth and wrongful life (Sect. 4.2), followed by an analysis of the luck egalitarian approach to PGD (Sect. 4.3). Luck egalitarian theories of justice are very influential in contemporary political philosophy. They are essentially – though with internally differing interpretations – based on the distinction between choice and luck, in the sense that natural and social inequalities that are *involuntary* should be compensated for; inequalities that are the result of *choice*, however, should not. Using PGD as a case, I will show that this distinction between choice and luck leads both to conceptual difficulties (in Sect. 4.4) and to moral problems (in Sect. 4.5). I argue that it is precisely these difficulties and problems that form the basis of the general indignation over claims of wrongful life and wrongful birth, when they come up in society. The case of PGD shows that the luck egalitarian approach fails to express equal respect for the individual choices of people, however diverse these choices may be.

4.2 About Nicola, Keeden, Chelsea and the Others...

Let me start with a quick look at some recent examples of wrongful birth and wrongful life cases. The most prominent cases are the French case of Nicolas Perruche, the Australian cases of Keeden Waller, Chelsea Edwards, and Alexia Harriton, the Dutch case of Kelly Molenaar, and the Belgian case of Rukiyé.

In November 2000, France's Supreme Court awarded damages to Nicolas Perruche, a 17-year old boy born with severe mental and physical disabilities, on the basis of wrongful life. His mother contracted rubella during the pregnancy and she argued that if doctors had correctly diagnosed the illness, she would have had an abortion. In 1992, the parents were already awarded damages on the basis of wrongful birth. The legal ruling of 2000, which established the "right not to be born" outraged the country and caused strong protests by disability communities, parents of people with disabilities, doctors, ethicists, theologians, and politicians. As a result, the French parliament has voted to overturn the legal ruling by stating that nobody can claim to have been harmed simply by being born. The law, which has come into effect on March 4, 2002, has thus brought an end to a year-long moral and legal controversy. Wrongful birth claims are still possible, but only on the grounds of a blatant error by doctors.

On June 13, 2002, a Supreme Court in Australia rejected the wrongful life cases of three disabled people. The first, IVF-baby Keeden Waller, 17 months at that time, inherited a blood-clotting disorder that screening could have detected. The second, Chelsea Edwards, 2, was born with a chromosome disorder after a failed vasectomy. The eldest, Alexia Harriton, 20 at that time, is blind, deaf, spastic and mentally retarded after her mother's rubella was not diagnosed during pregnancy. The central arguments of the judge were fourfold. (1) To recognise a duty to prevent the conception of these people, or to advise prospective parent's not to give birth to such children would be contrary to public policy. (2) Acceptance of such claims would pass over the precious nature of human life itself and the erosive effect that it would have upon the value to be accorded to human life. (3) Recognition of this class of claim would have a pervasive impact on the self-esteem of those born with disabilities and upon their perceived worthiness by other members of society. (4) In order to calculate the damages, it would be necessary to compare existence with non-existence, which is an impossible exercise.

Kelly Molenaar, 11 in 2005, was born with multiple mental and physical disabilities. She cannot walk, talk, or recognise her parents. She has deformed feet;

is believed to be in constant pain; and has had several heart operations. Like the cases of Nicolas Perruche and of the Australian girls, the parents of Kelly said that they would have had her aborted if they had known she would be disabled. On March 18, 2005, the Dutch Supreme Court awarded damages to Kelly Molenaar for having been born. Earlier, in 2000, the mother had been awarded damages on the basis of wrongful birth. Like in France, the legal ruling caused strong protests by disability communities, parents of people with disabilities, doctors, ethicists, theologians, and politicians, who are all urging the ministries of health and justice to take up the French example by voting a law to prohibit wrongful life claims. However, there is, as yet, no evidence of a parliamentary backlash such as arose in France.

In December 2010, the Court of Appeal ordered a Belgian hospital to pay €400,000 damages to the parents of Rukiyé. The girl had been born after a prenatal test, which was meant to show whether or not the foetus suffered from the hereditary metabolic disorder Sanfilippo. This disease leads to irreparable damage in tissue and organs and very limited life expectancy (Rukiyé became 10 years old). The parents of the girl had already had a child with Sanfilippo, which had died at the age of 12. As such, they knew they were carrier of the disease and had a significant chance for another child with Sanfilippo. They wanted PGD and an abortion in case of positive result, because they wanted to avoid a repetition of the experiences with their first child. The ultimate result of the test, however, was false-negative. The Hospital wants to lodge an appeal against the verdict by referring to technical flaws in the products that are being used in the tests (thereby referring to the responsibility of the firm that produces and delivers the tests). The verdict caused a public discussion, which was predominantly determined by the fear of over-legalisation of medicine, whereby a specific legal industry explicitly looks for medical flaws with a view to financial compensation. Another element in the discussion was the fact that PGD never provides 100% certainty. As such, the discussion was predominantly of a legal and scientific rather than ethical kind.

4.3 A Luck Egalitarian Viewpoint on Prenatal Genetic Diagnosis

According to the luck egalitarian view, which is a family of positions associated principally with the works of Ronald Dworkin, Gerald Cohen, Richard Arneson John Roemer and more recently Shlomi Segall, a person should not be worse off than anyone else in respect of some given metric of goods, as a result of *brute bad luck*, i.e. as a result of factors over which agents have *no control*. The fundamental impulse behind luck egalitarianism is the urge to correct, to compensate for, or to neutralise, *involuntary* inequalities between individuals. Accordingly, when inequalities are not involuntary – i.e., when they can be attributed to factors over which agents have control – they do not trigger egalitarian concerns (Dworkin 1981a, 2000a;

Cohen 1989; Arneson 1989, 2011; Roemer 1993, 1995, 1996, 1998; Segall 2007a, b, 2010a, b, forthcoming).

A fundamental issue in the luck egalitarian doctrine is Ronald Dworkin's famous distinction between brute luck and option luck (Dworkin 1981a, pp. 293–298, 2000a, pp. 73–77). *Option luck* is the sort of luck we might have in gambling, whereby we willingly take a risk in the full knowledge of its possible consequences. *Brute luck* is a matter of how things turn out without being a deliberate gamble. It refers to a result one could not anticipate or did not choose to run. It happens to someone without being the result of choice. Dworkin argues that while option luck is consistent with egalitarian theory – after all, it is reasonable to hold people responsible for the consequences of their willingly undertaken actions – he does not think that brute luck is consistent with equality, simply because it is not a matter of deliberate choice. Accordingly, egalitarian theory requires inequalities that result from brute luck to be redressed, but it does not require redress in the case of option luck, provided that the individuals had the opportunity to insure themselves against losses.

According to Dworkin's view, the welfare state functions as a large insurance company, which insures its citizens against all forms of brute bad luck (Dworkin 1981a, pp. 283–302, 2000a, pp. 65–82). Taxes for redistributive purposes are the equivalents of insurance premiums and welfare payments compensate people against losses traceable to brute bad luck, just like insurance policies do. The state provides social insurance when private insurance is not available to all on equal and affordable terms. Where private insurance is available, brute luck is automatically converted into option luck, for society can hold individuals responsible for purchasing insurance on their own behalf. In its pure form, luck egalitarian theory would insist that if individuals imprudently fail to do so, no demand of justice requires society to bail them out. However, Dworkin makes room for paternalist additions to justify a mandatory insurance scheme, in order to avoid imprudent insurance choices as much as possible.

An important part of the appeal of the luck egalitarian approach comes from its apparently humanitarian impulse that no one should suffer from *undeserved* disadvantages and that those undeservingly disadvantaged by nature – i.e. for their genetic endowments – or by social circumstances – i.e. for who their parents are or where they were born – should be compensated for this. To many people it seems unfair that some have fewer opportunities as a result of factors over which they have no control, and because of circumstances that did not result from their choices.

Furthermore, much of its appeal comes from the fact that the luck egalitarian approach has been most responsive to criticisms of equality, entailing the idea that just inequalities between people exist, namely those that are due to individual differences in effort and responsibility. The luck-egalitarian approach is able to respond to the ancient question why, in the name of equality, the ant who chose to work hard should subsidise the grasshopper who chose to sing and laze away the day (de La Fontaine 1693). Because the luck egalitarian distinction between choice and luck incorporates the idea of individual effort and responsibility into our egalitarian concerns, it finds much support not only among many contemporary egalitarians, but also among people's spontaneous intuitions about distributive justice (World Values Survey 2005–2008).[1]

A third aspect of its appeal comes from its being responsive to a fundamental characteristic of our contemporary knowledge-societies, in which many previous uncertainties have been transformed into risks, that can be taken or not (Beck 1986, 1992; Giddens 1990, 1999). Today, we know much more than we used to know. On closer look, however, this is a dubious appeal. On the one hand, our increased knowledge is generally considered as a welcome gift. For instance, it improves the quality and effectiveness of social policy, since we know much more about the causal relations between various phenomena. On the other hand, however, there is reason to believe that this may turn into a poisoned gift, especially when we consider the various ways in which the transition from brute luck to option luck appears in many domains in which welfare payments are at stake, such as for instance in issues of unemployment (Rosanvallon 1995), or in discussions of life style and responsibility for one's own health condition (Dworkin 1981b; Schwartz 1995; Denier 2005, 2007) and also in discussions of responsibility for the health condition of one's children, as it happens in claims of wrongful life and wrongful birth.

The luck egalitarian background of the latter discussion is the following. Whereas the genetic constitution of our children has long been a matter of brute luck, i.e. the result of the natural lottery over which we did not have any control, widespread techniques of prenatal genetic diagnosis have given the impression that this has become less and less the case. More specifically, they have given questions about the morality of reproduction – What sorts of children should we be attempting to create? What sort of children is it permissible to create? (Savulescu 2001) – an urgency that they may have previously lacked. It is an urgency of the following kind: when people choose to have a child, and can easily find out what birth defects are possible, and how often they occur, one may say that they choose to gamble. Accordingly, giving birth to a child that will have a certain type of condition has become less, it seems, a matter of *chance* than of *choice*. Put in Dworkin's terms, it has become less, it seems, a matter of *brute luck* than of *option luck*. Or put another way, though being born with a congenital handicap or disease, may remain a matter of brute luck for the child, it has become a matter of option luck for the parents: they knew, or should have known the gamble they were taking in choosing to have children. This gives rise to a complex series of questions regarding preventability, responsibility, attributability, source and kind of compensation, et cetera.

We may wonder whether this is a good evolution. Below, I will argue that even though the luck egalitarian distinction between choice (controlled) and luck (beyond

[1] In the fifth wave of the World Values Survey (2005–2008), carried out in 57 countries all over the world, 76.9% of the respondents (n=71,421) found the following situation fair: "Imagine two secretaries, of the same age, doing practically the same job. One finds out that the other earns considerably more than she does. The better paid secretary, however, is quicker, more efficient and more reliable at her job. In your opinion, is it fair or not fair that one secretary is paid more than the other?" World Values Survey is accessible online: www.worldvaluessurvey.org. I am grateful to Erik Schokkaert for pointing my attention to this.

control) is most appealing, it cannot overlap respectively with the distinction between fairness and fortune. Although we might spontaneously think that both distinctions coincide, the case of PGD shows otherwise. Even more, it shows that too great an emphasis on the aspect of choice and control in matters of justice, leads to results that go *against* the essence of justice.

4.4 Conceptual Difficulties

First of all, there are several conceptual difficulties underlying the luck egalitarian approach. They become clear when we apply the approach to the case of PGD. Below, I will address three such difficulties. The first refers to the content of the concepts of "nature" and "the natural", the second arises from the distinct varieties of luck that come into play, and the third difficulty comes with the question which concept of responsibility we have to use.

4.4.1 Nature and the Natural

The first difficulty resides in the fact that the content of the concepts of "nature" and "natural inequalities," understood as "being beyond human control", evolves alongside technological and medical evolution. At first sight, this is nothing new. It is merely a statement saying that technological and medical progress equals increasing control over nature. The boundary between what we can control and what we cannot is not static (Bayertz 2003). What is particularly interesting, however, is that this causes a peculiar shift in our understanding of the relationship between nature and justice; a shift that has been designated by Buchanan et al. as "The colonization of the natural by the just" (Buchanan et al. 2000, pp. 82–84).

On the one hand, "nature," or "the natural" is often thought to be not only that which is *given* but also that, which must be accepted as something that is beyond human control, as something that is a matter of brute luck. It concerns our natural endowments, as Dworkin would say. To say that something is "natural" is to subsume it under the category of fortune and misfortune, rather than of justice and injustice. It is not surprising that traditional thinking about justice has associated natural disadvantages with misfortune, rather than injustice, since there was little or nothing that could be *done* to *prevent* them. What could be done, on the other hand, was to *compensate* for natural inequalities in the distribution of *social* goods, by providing additional welfare payments, special education, subsidies for extra medical or social support services, et cetera.

However, if it becomes within our powers to achieve greater natural equality by controlling the distribution of *natural* goods, by intervening in the natural lottery by which genetic endowments have previously been distributed, it follows that natural inequalities are no longer fully *given* facts that are morally arbitrary.

Instead, they might become goods whose distribution just institutions are supposed to regulate. Or as Buchanan et al. put it, we bring "within the sphere of social control, and thereby within the domain of justice, what was previously regarded as the natural, and as merely a matter of good or ill fortune," i.e. of good or bad luck (2000, p. 83). Paradoxically, we may say that nature brought within human control is no longer "nature."

It is this shift that underlies claims of wrongful birth or wrongful life. For if it becomes within human power to *prevent* what we would regard as the misfortune of a congenital disorder or the tragedy of a genetically based degenerative disease, then we may no longer be able to regard it as a misfortune. Instead, we may come to view the person who suffers from these disabilities (in the case of wrongful life), or the parents who care for them (in the case of wrongful birth) as *victims of injustice*. As techniques of PGD make it possible to avoid a genetically based disadvantage by avoiding the birth of the individual who would have it, they may make it possible to say "that it is unfair to have been born with a congenital handicap" or "that it is an *injustice* to give birth to a handicapped child when you could have prevented it by genetic testing and selective abortion in the case of congenital disorder." This line of reasoning underlies the concept of genetically responsible parenthood.

Two points can be made in response to this colonisation of the natural by the just. First, we encounter the problem of breakdown of the distinction between the subjects and objects of distributive justice, i.e. between persons and goods (Buchanan et al. 2000, p. 85). The basic problem of distributive justice, as it has always been conceived, is how goods ought to be distributed among persons when their *identities*, at least for purposes of justice, are *given*, independently of the distribution of goods. We think of justice as justice to given persons, whose natural endowments are beyond human control so that any resulting inequalities must be *compensated* for, rather than attacked directly by avoiding the birth of particular persons. But if it becomes possible to distribute the genetic bases of "natural" characteristics, including those that are constitutive of the identity of persons, then this fundamental assumption – of subjects receiving objects through an allocative mechanism – will no longer be applicable. Instead of asking what kinds of compensation we are indebted to people with lesser endowments, the main question becomes: what kinds of people are we allowed or even obliged to create? (Savulescu 2001) The special oddity of this problem of breakdown of the distinction between the subjects and objects of distributive justice becomes clear in the case of wrongful life claims and the related non-identity problem, to which I will come back below in Sect. 4.4.2.3.

The second point has to do with the relationship between justice and control. If a theory of justice is to be more than a mere utopian ideal, control, understood as directing capacity and capability to change the situation, is indeed a *necessary* condition for justice. Conversely, however, it is essential to bear in mind that not *everything* we can control is a matter of justice or injustice. As such, control is a *necessary* but not a *sufficient* condition for justice. We need further refinement of our conception of control as related to distributive justice and to the primary goal of just institutions. Since there are many things we can control that do not belong to the domain of justice, the mere distinction between control and luck is not enough to determine the demands of justice. In this regard, it is necessary to determine *which* goods we can control are so important that they belong to the realm of justice. I will come back to this in Sect. 4.5.4. For now, it is sufficient to say that with this line of reasoning, we are moving away from taking the traditional distinction between fortune and justice, natural and social goods, luck and control, chance and choice, as a sufficient basis for determining society's distributive duties.

4.4.2 Varieties of Luck

The second conceptual difficulty follows from the first. The continuous alteration of the content of the concept of the *natural* implies that the related concept of *luck* also needs to be refined. After all, techniques of genetic testing and engineering, such as PGD, undermine the assumption that the results of the natural lottery depend on *mere* luck, and therefore escape our moral responsibility.

At first sight, this does not seem to pose much problems for the luck egalitarian approach since it has already introduced a fundamental refinement of the concept of luck in the discussion by its distinction between *brute luck* and *option luck*, i.e. between the kinds of luck that are involved in situations that are beyond our choice and control and the kinds of luck that are involved in gambling whereby we willingly take a risk in the full knowledge of its various possible consequences.

On closer look, however, it turns out that this distinction does not bring much clarity in the discussion about justice and the morality of reproduction. As Susan Hurley puts it, luck is a treacherous and curious concept, which ramifies into a *wide variety* of conceptions of luck, which very often may cut *across* moral responsibility (Hurley 2001, pp. 79–80, 2003, pp. 106–107). The case of PGD provides a very good example of this. This becomes most clear when we ask what *kinds* of luck are involved in cases of PGD, and *whose* luck we are talking about.

Let us take up the last question first: whose luck is involved in cases of PGD? This question derives its relevance from the fact that we normally only speak of something being a matter of luck, good or bad, if it is relevant to someone's interests in some way. As such, luck is identity-dependent (Hurley 2001, pp. 86–88, 2003, pp. 118–120). It is always luck *for someone*. Even more, there must be someone whose identity is *constant* between the various alternatives that would count as good or bad luck, in order for these alternatives to count as good or bad luck *for that someone*. Related to this, luck can be good or bad, involving benefit or harm. Consequently, we can speak of identity-dependent benefit or harm when it is benefit or harm *to someone*. Important, in a second instance, is that this constant identity, this *someone* in question, need not actually be a human person. It could also be an animal for instance, or a society, or a company, or a group of people. Nevertheless, it must be an entity treated as having a *constant identity* across the alternative ways in which luck may befall.

Applied to the case of PGD, it is relevant to distinguish three kinds of interests, which should be taken into account in questions about the morality of reproduction. Firstly, there are the direct personal interests, which are the interests of the child that will – or presumably, will not – be born. Secondly, there are the indirect personal interests, which are the interests of the child's parents and family affected by his existence – or non-existence. And thirdly, there are the general, impersonal interests of the society in which the child will – or will not – be born. By taking a closer look at the various ways in which these interests – i.e., *whose* luck we are talking about – can take form, the various *kinds* of luck come in the forefront more clearly.

4.4.2.1 Society

Let us start with the interests of society. Although we are initially inclined to think that a society's interests in questions about the morality of reproduction are very indirect and impersonal, maybe even non-existing, they are nevertheless highly influential because social institutions and the way in which they are organised shape the general framework and social climate in which people generally tend to think and feel about responsible parenthood. As such, they may influence people's reproductive decisions. For instance, if a society would give dominant priority to *economic and productive interests*, the profit motive may provide the basis for a climate in which avoiding the birth of severely disabled people is generally considered to be preferable because their existence could be seen as a drain on social resources. From such a one-sided economic viewpoint, the society may have an interest in interpreting the birth of a congenitally handicapped child no longer as a matter of *brute luck*, which requires social compensation, but rather as a matter of *option luck* for the parents. By stressing the point that once people try to get pregnant, they deliberately choose to gamble. If consequently, they refuse PGD and abortion in the case of handicap, their life with a handicapped is the result of their conscious and deliberate choice, for which they have to bear the consequences themselves. This kind of reasoning would relieve society of bearing the extra costs of congenitally handicapped life (like compensation in the form of welfare payments, subsidies for special care, special education, supporting material like wheelchairs, etc.).

This leads us into a dynamics in which PGD becomes an instrument intended for the sole end of either avoiding the extra costs that come with congenitally disabled life completely, or shifting the responsibility for the extra costs of care for the disabled child fully to the prospective parents. Within such a climate, the social pressure on the prospective parents to undergo PGD and avoid giving birth to a congenitally disabled child may be very high. On the other hand, however, the just society has important *moral interests* as well, including issues of humanity, of moral sensitivity, and of providing the social bases of equal respect. It is reasonable to say that the degree of moral refinement and justice of a particular society is reflected in the way in which it shows equal respect to everyone, i.e. *also* to the congenitally handicapped. The basic expression of this equal respect is to show, on a public level of society, that they are just as welcome in the world, and deserve to be treated with the same respect as everyone else, by providing the care and support that is needed for them to live their lives with dignity.

4.4.2.2 Parents

A second category of interests is that of the indirect personal interests of the parents. This category contains important *emotional interests*, which may come into conflict in the case of PGD. On the one hand, there is the prospective parents' wish to have children. On the other hand, there is the parents' fundamental concern for the quality of their child's life, which may be very low in certain cases of severe handicap. Additionally, there are interests concerning the *family's strength and capacity* (emotionally and mentally, as well as practically and financially) to care for the disabled child in a sufficient and respectful way. Furthermore, there are important *moral interests* involved. Within the context of PGD, the prospective parents may come to face a choice, i.e. whether or not to terminate the pregnancy of a handicapped child. By providing this choice, it is reasonable to say that techniques of prenatal genetic diagnosis have converted the former brute luck-situation of giving birth to a congenitally handicapped child into an option luck-situation involving choice.[2] However, the nature of choice varies according to the moral beliefs of the prospective parents. For some people, the decision to terminate the pregnancy may be a logical consequence of PGD and the right thing to do, whereas for others it creates a huge moral dilemma in which the right choice is not clear at all. For yet a third category of prospective parents it cannot even be rightfully said to be a matter of option luck, since for them there *is* no option: abortion is out of the question in any case. Nevertheless, with PGD, choice returns in yet another form. For choosing not to choose is also a choice, and thus an option. For instance, if the prospective parents consciously decide *not* to undergo PGD, and therefore willingly *choose* to take part in the natural lottery that determines the child's constitution, the result may still be said to be a matter of *option luck* for the parents.

Be that as it may, however, in order to clarify the important differences in the nature of choice one needs to bring in these differences in moral beliefs. The *mere* distinction between chance and choice, or more specified, between brute luck and option luck is not sufficient. Paradoxically enough, it seems that an important feature

[2] Here, I am expressly assuming that the situation of giving birth to a congenitally handicapped child *before* techniques of PDG became common practice indeed *was* a brute luck situation in the following sense. In previous times, before the sexual revolution of the 1960s, people gave birth to children on the rhythm of nature. As for the amount of children, or their health status, there was little to nothing that could be done to control it (except for fully abstaining from sexual activity). It was, much more than today, a matter of nature's course. Today, however, we can decide on much in these matters: whether or not to have children, when we want to have them, and whether or not we want the fetus to be tested for congenital disorder, and whether or not to continue the pregnancy in case of a congenital disorder. All this has become, much more than before, a matter of choice (see also van Tongeren 1995).

of people's lives is not covered by the luck egalitarian distinction, and that is the fact of reasonable pluralism[3]: people differ in their opinions about the good life, in their moral convictions and in their interpretations of luck. What counts as option luck for one person may not be thought of in the same way by another person. The same goes for the interpretation of good or bad luck. What counts as good or bad luck for one person, is not necessarily so for the other.

4.4.2.3 Child

Finally, we need to take a third category of interests into account, that is, the direct personal interests of the child. Although techniques of PGD may be said to convert a brute luck-situation into a situation of option luck *for the parents*, this does not change anything *for the child*. For him, his constitution remains a matter of *brute luck*, i.e. of *constitutive luck* understood as *lack of control of the causes* of who and what he is, of the causes of his native endowments and capacities (Nagel 1979, p. 28; Hurley 2001, p. 82, 2003, pp. 111–112). For the child, his constitution is the result of the way the natural lottery turns out *for him*, something that is beyond his control. Nevertheless, in taking the child's interests into account, the primary concern is that of the child's quality of life. In limiting cases, this concern comes down to the question whether it is possible to say that someone has been (or will be) born with a life that is so miserable that it is not worth living; that it is of no benefit to him. The combination of the possibility of PGD with such quality judgements forms the basis of claims of wrongful life (from the perspective of the child) and wrongful birth (from the perspective of the parents).

Two points can be made in response to this. Firstly, claims of wrongful life meet the non-identity problem (Parfit 1984, pp. 351–379). This problem originates from the identity-dependence of luck, and more specifically of lottery luck. Lottery luck requires that there is an agent whose luck is in question and whose identity is *constant* across the different possible results of the lottery (Hurley 2003, pp. 118–123). This condition is not fulfilled in the case of wrongful life, since here, the alternative is that that the person in question would not have existed at all. This creates a rather peculiar conception of "worth" or "benefit" *for that person*. From the statement that life is of no benefit to someone, it does not automatically follow that non-existence

[3] With this, I refer to John Rawls's concept of *Reasonable Pluralism*, as an inherent feature of all modern democratic societies. It entails the recognition that citizens endorse different, often incompatible, comprehensive doctrines, that is, a pluralism of religious, philosophical, or moral worldviews, which include "conceptions of what is of value in human life, and ideals of personal character, as well as ideals of friendship and of familial and associational relationships, and much else that is to inform our conduct, and in the limit to our life as a whole." (Rawls 1996, p. 13). Many of these comprehensive and incompatible doctrines are endorsed by citizens who are "reasonable" in the sense that they recognize that there are limits to what can be justified to others and "will think it unreasonable to use political power, should they possess it, to repress comprehensive views that are not unreasonable, though different from their own." (Rawls 1996, p. 60).

would have been better *for him*, since there would *be* no *him*, whose interests would be better served. Susan Hurley denotes this problem as the "bare self illusion" (Hurley 2001, pp. 88–90, 2003, pp. 120–123). Claims of wrongful life presuppose a pre-entity, a proto self, or bare self, who might have existed as me, or who might have existed as someone else, whose good or bad luck it is to have one or another identity, to have one or another constitution. But this does not apply here. It is not a question of a person being either such or such. On the contrary, it comes down to Hamlet's question: "To be or not to be?"

Secondly, wrongful birth claims are based on the fact that parents would have terminated the pregnancy had they known in advance that their child would be disabled. Mostly, such a claim is directed against a physician who is being accused of not having given the parents the *option* to abort. Therefore, they claim that they should be compensated for the unwanted extra burdens (financial, material, emotional...) that come with having to take care for a disabled child, which is a child that would not have been born, had the parents have had the choice. This creates a situation in which a person is *explicitly* and *publicly* judged by the parents to have an inferior and burdensome constitution, something that is for the child itself a matter of constitutive luck, i.e. something he did not cause and cannot change. This is an astonishingly strange situation, presupposing a very peculiar expression of parental love. How can the interests of the child be served well if it is the parents' message that the child would never have been born, had they had the choice? Among the worst problems that disabled people must confront are the condescending attitudes of many other people (Anderson 1999; Feder Kittay 1999; Glover 2001; Nussbaum 2004). A society that supports claims of wrongful life and wrongful birth, risks to reinforce those attitudes and to equality of respect for all human beings. As explained in Sect. 4.2, this has been the basic reasoning of the Australian Supreme Court in rejecting the wrongful life cases of Waller, Edwards and Harrington.

4.4.3 Responsibility?

The distinction between brute luck and option luck implies that people are responsible for the results of bad option luck. Applied to the case of PGD, this may lead to the conclusion that the prospective parents or, in some cases, the negligent physicians, are responsible for the extra costs that come with the life of a congenitally disabled child. From this, the third conceptual difficulty underlying the luck egalitarian approach can be deduced. Which conception of responsibility is adequate here? Let us concentrate on two conceptions that are relevant in this case.[4]

[4] For this I am much indebted to Kurt Devooght. See his *Essays on Responsibility-Sensitive Egalitarianism and the Measurement of Income Inequality* (non-published Ph.D., KU Leuven, Faculty of Business and Economics), Leuven, 2003, esp. ch. 1, pp. 7–36 for an extensive and detailed analysis of various conceptions of responsibility.

4.4.3.1 Backward-Looking Responsibility: The Forfeiture View

The mainstream view on responsibility – with which the luck egalitarian approach agrees – holds that people are responsible for what they have chosen voluntarily. Responsibility as voluntariness assigns liability for the results of one's own choices made knowingly, consciously, and freely (i.e. what I *want* to do, taking into account internal convictions). Closely related to this view is the conception of responsibility as control (which refers to what I am *able* to do – taking into account external limitations). According to this conception, inequalities due to factors within a person's control are equitable. The basis of the mainstream view is the distinction between fortune or luck, on the one hand, and free will or control on the other hand. One can only be held responsible for what stems from free will or what one could control. As Thomas Scanlon puts it: "… a person to whom a certain outcome was available, but who knowingly passed it up, cannot complain about not having it" (Scanlon 1988, p. 193). If, on the other hand, fortune or luck determines the situation, people cannot be held responsible and should even be indemnified for the bad consequences; i.e. they are in a situation of brute bad luck.

Another important distinction that is relevant in this regard is the distinction between *actual* responsibility and *moral* responsibility, i.e. respectively between *being* responsible (in the causal chain of events) and *being held* responsible (which is possible even if a direct causal link is absent). If a theory assumes that these two variants of responsibility coincide with each other – as the luck egalitarian approach does – three problems crop up.

The first is the metaphysical problem of free will and control. If choice and control are the criteria for assessing responsibility and if the question of *moral* responsibility implies having to answer the question of *actual* responsibility, we have to be sure that people's choices are *truly* voluntary, that they are freely and consciously made, and that they truly are within their control, i.e. that they could have done otherwise, but that they freely and consciously decided not to. This assumption shows great confidence in the free, voluntary and independent character of individual choice making. However, in view of the physical, psychological, social and economic determinants of preference formation – as shown by Jon Elster's arguments of the contented slave and of the sour grapes (Elster 1982, 1989) – and therefore in view of the related metaphysical question of how free the free will *really* is and how much is *truly* within our control, the problem of distributive justice and responsibility no longer seems to be solved by the mere distinction between chance and choice, between luck and control.

Related to this is the problem of infinite regression. Responsibility as voluntariness and as control are both *regressive* conceptions of responsibility. In this regard, Susan Hurley has pointed at the problem that comes with Thomas Nagel's regressive control conception of responsibility, which implies that in order to be responsible for something, one must also be responsible for its causes. According to this conception, responsibility requires control all the way back the chain of causes. Indeed, this makes *actual* responsibility impossible because human actions, thoughts and decisions are always, in one way or another, related to a variety of events and factors beyond one's control (Nagel 1979, p. 35; Hurley 2001, pp. 80–84, 2003, pp. 109–114). Applied to the case of PGD, a regressive conception of responsibility may give rise to the following question: Who is responsible for the child's genetic constitution? Initially, one might say that it is caused by the genetic constitution of the parents. But it seems hardly right to speak of responsibility here, since there is an essential element of constitutive luck or brute luck in having genes for certain talents or for certain diseases, both for the parents themselves regarding their own genetic constitution, and for the child regarding his constitution. Nevertheless, claims of wrongful birth and wrongful life show that when a congenitally disabled child is born, the possibility of PGD may generate a chain of regress of the following buck passing kind: the child sues the parents (because they did not make use of the necessary genetic screening) or the physician (because he did not offer it to the parents, or wrongly interpreted the results) for being born; or the parents sue the physician, or the hospital, for negligence in prenatal care; the physician or hospital, in turn, might sue the producer of the genetic tests or the distributor of the medical equipment in case it was due to faultiness on their behalf, et cetera.

The idea of genetically responsible parenthood conceives of responsibility in this same regressive, backward-looking spirit. Furthermore, it is a conception of responsibility with a negative bias to it. In this regard, we may reasonably refer to Aristotle's conception of corrective justice (*Nicomachean Ethics*, V in Aristotle (2000)). Something went wrong and has to be corrected for. The situation has to be rectified by punishing the guilty party and by compensating the party that is the victim. The punished party has to pay a *forfeit* of a certain kind. However, the problem of the negative bias is less of a conceptual than of a moral kind and I will come back to this in Sect. 4.5 below. For now, suffice to say that by using the forfeiture view on responsibility in issues of distributive justice, we risk mistaking distributive justice for corrective justice. It is, however, important to bear in mind that these are quite distinct types of justice.

4.4.3.2 Forward-Looking Responsibility: Attributability

An alternative way of interpreting responsibility is, what I would like to call, the progressive, or forward-looking way. This perspective sheds a different light on the distinction between *actual* responsibility and *moral* responsibility. For next to the question of responsibility for the birth of a handicapped child, the question of responsible parenthood also refers to issues as meeting the child's needs in surroundings characterised by love, care, respect, et cetera. From this perspective, PGD receives a different significance. Instead of being merely an instrument for avoiding the birth of a handicapped child, it may also become an important instrument, which helps people to prepare (psychologically, emotionally, but also practically) for the birth of a child with a certain disorder and for the very specific forms of care that their child will need in order to lead a good life, however confined that life may seem to be.

A different conception of responsibility enters the stage here. It is a conception of a non-metaphysical and non-regressive kind, and is defended, among others, by Thomas Scanlon. Scanlon rejects, what he calls, the *forfeiture* view because it puts too much weight into the hands of choice:

> [The Forfeiture View] exaggerates the importance of the fact of choice relative to that of the [social] conditions under which the choice was made. The Forfeiture View suggests that these conditions are important only insofar as they bear on the voluntariness of the choice. This is a mistake. The fact that a choice was voluntary does not always establish that we 'did enough' for an agent by placing him or her in the position from which the choice was made. Nor does the fact that an agent did not voluntarily choose an outcome, or choose to take a certain risk, establish that what resulted was not his fault (Scanlon 1988, p. 196).

Scanlon's view is known as 'responsibility by delegation' or as 'responsibility as attributability.' According to this view neither control, nor voluntariness are the criteria for the assessment of responsibility. On the contrary, we are responsible because we are given the opportunity to choose by the society who has made sufficient efforts to provide the necessary conditions for us to make decisions, the outcomes of which we are ourselves responsible for. Whether we have made our choices voluntarily is unimportant. Whether we have control over our decisions is equally unimportant. The real issue is whether *society* provides the *necessary social conditions* for people to make responsible decisions. This means that responsibility is not to be traced back to metaphysical assumptions on how free the free will really is, but is simply assigned, or attributed, by society.

Why is this viewpoint forward-looking? Because instead of focusing on the regressive question of responsibility, searching for the guilty party (as happens in claims of wrongful birth or life), one now looks at society's role in providing the *framework* in which people – in our case, the prospective parents, possibly in deliberation with the physician – can make responsible choices with regard to their own future according to their own conception of the good life. Scanlon's conception of responsibility shows the importance of reflecting on the role of *society* in fulfilling the conditions for people to make free and responsible choices according to their own conception of the good. Applied to the case of PGD, this implies that *society* has a moral responsibility in providing for appropriate social support (such as providing for caring institutions, special education, financial and material support) of people with special needs (which are not only the cared-for, but also their family members and other care-takers). Only then, one can say that prospective parents can truly make a free and responsible choice in the context of PGD. Only then, the choice to whether or not give birth to a disabled child is not reduced to the question: "Can I afford this?"

In the following and final section, I will focus on the relation between social and personal responsibility in matters of PGD by examining the social conditions for technological progress to be moral progress as well. Or put another way, by examining the conditions that have to be fulfilled for issues of PGD to meet the requirements of social justice.

4.5 Technological Progress – Moral Progress?

Let us now focus on the moral problems, which found the public debate that comes with claims of wrongful life and wrongful birth. These moral problems are all aspects of one and the same movement, *viz.* of the transition from the natural jungle to the social jungle.

As I have mentioned before, the boundary between the natural and the social, and between the realm of fortune and of justice, is not static. Moreover, what we have long taken to be *moral progress* has often consisted in pushing back the frontiers of the natural; in bringing within the sphere of social control, and thereby within the domain of justice, what was previously regarded as 'the natural.' As such, compensation for arbitrary natural inequalities is a matter of human and moral progress. It is a way of countering the capriciousness and harshness of the natural jungle. And this is also, as we have seen, one of the main appeals of the luck egalitarian approach, which advocates that the fundamental aim of egalitarian theory is to compensate people for undeserved bad luck, such as being born with poor native endowments within a poor social environment, and suffering from brute accidents and illnesses.

The flipside of this idea is that people should bear the costs of chosen or preventable inequalities themselves. However, by making personal choice central, we run the risk of replacing the natural jungle by a *social jungle*, in which people could be stigmatised and even marginalised by society as a result of individual choice. The problem is that this social jungle might be just as harsh and merciless as the natural jungle. In her influential article 'What's the Point of Equality?', Elisabeth Anderson analyses the various ways in which the luck egalitarian approach runs this risk (Anderson 1999). By focusing on correcting a supposed cosmic injustice, Anderson argues, luck egalitarian theory has lost sight of the distinctively political aims of egalitarianism. The essence of the argument is that the luck egalitarian approach or equality of fortune, as she also calls it, fails "the most fundamental test every egalitarian theory must meet: that its principles express equal respect and concern for all citizens" (Anderson 1999, p. 289). Below, I will address four main arguments illustrating the above-mentioned stigmatisation and marginalisation by using the case of PGD.

4.5.1 Abandonment Objection

The first problem is that of exclusion of the imprudent, which comes down to the fact that hard-core luck egalitarianism may treat the victims of bad option luck most harshly for once people risk and lose due to bad option luck they have no claims on others to help them (Anderson 1999; Segall 2007a, b, 2010a). They become excluded from the realm of social compensation and support. Anderson calls this the problem of lack of a safety net, which is only there either for the victims of brute bad luck or for those who prudently decided to prevent such fates by purchasing private insurance, but not for the so-called “imprudent”. The essence of the problem is that an egalitarian approach that

> guarantees equality only *ex ante*, before adults start making choices for themselves, and makes no provision for people *after* that, will in fact generate substantial inequalities in people’s fates as they lead their lives to the point where the worst off might be extremely badly off (Anderson 1999, p. 300).

Applied to the case of PGD, and the possibility it creates of understanding parenthood of a congenitally disabled child as a question of bad option luck, the position of the parent as a willingly and consciously chosen dependent caretaker becomes very vulnerable. As John Roemer says, explaining Arneson’s and Cohen’s position:

> Society should not compensate for their choice of [a more altruistic, self-sacrificing] path because it owes people no compensation on account of their moral views (Roemer 1996, p. 270).

This assimilates the performance of moral obligations to care for the disabled child to the class of *voluntary expensive tastes* for which people are supposed to take full individual responsibility.

The same idea seems to be included in Dworkin’s view of the welfare state as a large insurance company (Dworkin 1981a, pp. 283–302, 2000a, pp. 65–82). Dworkin argues that basic insurance (for welfare, health care, and unemployment schemes) should be provided for everyone, and it must be financed out of income taxation or some other compulsory insurance at a fixed premium. The insurance coverage and the level of the premium can be computed, Dworkin argues, by modelling a *hypothetical* insurance market in which insurance is offered to everyone on the basis of community rating, that is, based on the question how much coverage the average member of the community would purchase. As such, the hypothetical insurance mechanism would function as a theoretical guide with which we can determine the real-time issues for which we are collectively, if not, then personally responsible. The point of the hypothetical insurance principle is that if *most* prudent people would buy a certain level of coverage in a free market if they had average means then the fairness or unfairness of our real time society can be measured according to the amount of people that do not have such coverage now. On the other hand, if very *few* people would want to buy insurance covering a much higher level of coverage it would be unjust to force everyone to have such insurance through a mandatory scheme. There are of course exceptions to the insurance principle: some people have special preferences and would make decisions different from those of most others. It seems fair however, Dworkin argues, to construct a mandatory coverage scheme on the basis of assumptions about what *all* but a small number of people would consider appropriate, allowing those few who would be willing to spend more on special insurance to do so, if they can afford it, through supplementary private insurance (Dworkin 2000a, p. 315, endnote 10, p. 492).

This is a very reasonable argumentation. However, against the background of our problem in hand, we must be cautious and raise the following question: what happens if the majority of the average community members would terminate the pregnancy in case of certain handicapping conditions of the foetus? This is a reasonable question, since surveys show that, in the case of children with Down’s syndrome, about 80% would want the pregnancy terminated when asked hypothetically, and over 90% in such cases chooses to terminate in reality (Glover 2001, pp. 429–444; Christiaens and Kloosterman 1997, pp. 52–61; Vamos et al. 1997, pp. 7–13). Given these facts, what does it imply with regard to the *hypothetical* insurance mechanism as it is meant to be a guide to determine the issues for which we are collectively, if not, then personally responsible? Two possibilities remain.

The first is that we interpret giving birth to a congenitally disabled child as a matter of option luck. Together with the fact that most people would terminate the pregnancy, it would be unjust then to force everyone through a mandatory scheme to share in the extra costs that come with caring for the congenitally disabled child. Accordingly, the parents of the child lose every form of *social* protection and support, and are left to purchase additional *private* insurance. It is doubtful, however, whether it would be possible to purchase private insurance in such cases. One may reasonably doubt whether such cases are insurable at all on the private market.[5]

If we want to avoid such forms of exclusion, we could move over to the other possibility, which contains that we "on average" consider purchasing insurance for protection and support in the case of giving birth to a congenitally disabled child as a prudent thing to do, thus making it part of our *collective* responsibility. In this case, however, the scope of solidarity is not determined by the mere distinction between choice and luck or between brute luck and option luck, but by other arguments to which I will come back in Sect. 4.5.4. The essence of these other arguments is that some things are basic entitlements for every human being, i.e., they are just *too important* for human functioning to allow exclusion. This point is also being stressed by Shlomi Segall (2007a, 2010a) who develops a luck egalitarian approach that wants to escape the abandonment objection and justify universal and unconditional health care.

4.5.2 Problem of Paternalism

The second problem follows on the first. I have mentioned before that the luck egalitarian approach makes room for the imprudent to be entitled to special paternalistic

[5] Insurance is a form of risk management, primarily used to hedge against the risk of a contingent loss. Insurance is defined as the equitable transfer of the risk of a loss, from one entity to another, in exchange for a premium, and can be thought of as a guaranteed small loss to prevent a large, possibly devastating loss. A crucial element in insurance is *uncertainty* about the *probability* of the loss. If the likelihood of the insured event is high, and the cost of the event is known to be large, the premium to be paid will be high as well. Furthermore, the event that constitutes the trigger of a claim should be *fortuitous*, or at least outside the control of the beneficiary of the insurance. The loss should be 'pure' in the sense that it results from factors we don't control. Otherwise, the events are generally not considered insurable. Congenital handicaps are problematic in these respects since techniques of PGD make it possible to *know* in advance about the genetic condition and health status of the unborn child and to *avoid* the birth of a handicapped child by aborting the handicapped foetus. Furthermore, the costs that come with the birth of a handicapped child – life-long support of special needs – may be so high that the premium to be paid becomes unaffordable or even useless, or insurance companies may simply deny coverage on grounds of the fact that the insurance does not involve an unpredictable risk, but a given fact.

protection by society against their poor choices (Arneson 1989, p. 239; Dworkin 1981a, pp. 293–295, 2000a, pp. 74–77). As Anderson puts it: paternalism is the only way to escape the problem of lack of safety net (Anderson 1999, p. 289). But whereas she gives the impression that paternalism is a problem *tout court*, I believe it is necessary to make a distinction between legitimate and illegitimate forms of paternalism. In this regard it is illuminating to recapitulate Nussbaum's threefold answer against an oversimplified critique of paternalism (Nussbaum 2000, pp. 51–60).

Firstly, Nussbaum argues that not *all* forms of paternalism are illegitimate. For if paternalism means telling people that they cannot behave in some way that they want to behave, then any system of law and any bill of rights is paternalistic with respect to certain inhuman practices that treat people with insufficient or unequal respect. It is clear that this is hardly a good argument against the rule of law, or, more generally, against opposing the attempts of some people to tyrannise over others. We dislike paternalism because we like each person's liberty of choice in fundamental matters. Therefore, it is fully consistent to reject some forms of paternalism while supporting those forms that are liberty-supporting.

Next, we should note that liberty has *material preconditions*. Liberty is not just a matter of having rights on paper, it requires being in a position to *exercise* those rights. And this requires material and institutional resources, including legal and social acceptance of claims. A state that is going to *guarantee* people rights *effectively*, is going to have to take a stand about more than the importance of these basic rights themselves. It will have to take a stand on the distribution of resources to guarantee citizens what John Rawls has called the "fair value" of the various liberties – for example by raising revenue through taxation in sufficient quantity to make education and health care available to all. Such redistributive measures are paternalistic, meaning interference with activities that some people choose. The question is, is this acceptable or not? It is when it is meant to create forms of *empowerment* that are crucial to making liberties *truly* available to people.

And finally, Nussbaum argues, there is the *principle of each person as end*. If we agree that citizens are worthy of equal respect, and grant that they live their own lives, we ought to conclude that politics should treat each of them as ends, as sources of agency and worth in their own right, with their own plans to make and their own lives to live, therefore as deserving of all necessary *support* for their equal opportunity to be such agents. To do this implies that we have to take a stand on some fundamental values that will be made central for political purposes, and *against* some ways of treating persons disrespectfully. However, taking a stand in this way should not raise the charge of illegitimate paternalism, since we do so in order to treat *each* person as an end and permit *all* citizens to search for the good in their own ways.

Against this threefold argument of liberty-supporting paternalism, the material preconditions of liberty, and respect for persons as ends in themselves, it is reasonable to ask whether the luck egalitarian protection of the imprudent against poor choices is a legitimate form of paternalism. In order to answer this question we must ask, in a luck egalitarian spirit: what is a prudent decision in the case of PGD? Or put inversely: who are the imprudent? What exactly is a poor choice? Within the spirit of the distinction between brute luck and option luck, it is reasonable to believe that it is the choice *not* to undergo PGD. Or as Dworkin puts it:

> Suppose it were possible to correct serious genetic defects of different kinds in embryos, for example, either through genetic engineering or through more conventional forms of therapy. Then the principle of special responsibility [i.e., every person is individually responsible for the success of his own life] would no longer justify allowing a pregnant woman to *refuse* tests to discover such a defect in an embryo she carries, and the first principle of ethical humanism – an objective concern that any life, once begun, be a successful one – would counsel *mandatory testing*. It is true that modern democracies share a visceral distaste for requiring anyone to submit to a medical procedure to which she objects, particularly when the objection is founded, as an objection to genetic testing and the treatment that follows might well be founded, on religious conviction. The flat principle of bodily integrity may, however, be one of those artefacts of conventional morality that seemed well justified *before* the possibilities suggested by modern genetic medicine were plausibly imagined, but *not after*. If we are to accept a more fundamental principle of concern for the lives of everyone, that principle of bodily integrity may one day have to be qualified (Dworkin 2000b, p. 450, my addition, my italics).

This quotation perfectly illustrates the way in which the possibility of achieving control over our children's genetic structure undermines our most basic assumptions about the boundary between what we are responsible for choosing and what lies beyond our control because it is fixed by nature. Our genetic identity – who we and our children are – has long been a paradigm of nature's responsibility and not ours, and a substantial shift of that determination to the sphere of our own responsibility destabilizes much of our conventional morality. What can we reasonably say about this?

I agree with Dworkin that we must take up the challenge of improving our understanding of what happens here rather than to turn back from it. However, I strongly believe that the only legitimate way to do this would be to take up this challenge but *without* putting social pressure on the prospective parents to undergo PGD, that is, to make testing mandatory. This is the risk we take if we subsume procreative decisions under the category of option luck. The same goes for the idea of genetically responsible parenthood and for cases of wrongful life. These can hardly be called cases of legitimate paternalism, since the latter is meant to *create* space for choice and liberty, to provide the material preconditions for making free choices, and all this with respect for *each* person as an end, permitting *all* citizens to search for the good *in their own ways*.[6]

[6] In this context, it is necessary to reflect on the distinction between two ways in which the previously mentioned idea of constitutive luck appears, that is in the *natural* and in the *social* way, and their respective implications in matters of social justice. Both natural endowments (having genes for certain talents) and the social conditions (the social environment) in which individuals were born are given facts, things that are bestowed on them. They did not cause them, nor can they change them, and both are integral or essential to people's constitution or self-identity. Why then, are corrections of social conditions (like eradicating poverty, compensating for racial or gender discrimination in the past) necessary measures to be taken by every just society, whereas correcting natural conditions (like avoiding congenital handicaps on a large-scale social level) is problematic? What's the difference? Two things can be said by way of reply. Firstly, it is important to point at the fact that measures like eradicating poverty or compensating for discrimination intend to *support* people by eradicating social obstructions to their possibilities to lead a good life. These obstructions are generally seen as bad social circumstances. This is not necessarily the case for

Again, we must bear in mind that the content of what is imprudent and what it is that makes a particular choice a poor choice is a matter in which everything depends on the *individual* case, and on the individual beliefs of who decides. There is a relevant pluralism of conceptions of the good that strangely enough, does not seem to be backed up by the luck egalitarian approach. Or as Anderson puts it:

> Equality of fortune, in attempting to ensure that people take responsibility for their choices, makes demeaning and intrusive judgements of people's capacities to exercise responsibility and effectively *dictates* to them the *appropriate* uses of their freedom (Anderson 1999, p. 289, my italics).

4.5.3 A Social Signal of Hierarchy

The third problem is related to the already mentioned problem of the condescending attitude towards handicapped life that is reflected in claims of wrongful life and wrongful birth (cf. supra, Sect. 4.4.2.3). These claims express the idea that their life is actually not worth living. Put sharply, such claims send the message that people are products that can be rejected if quality control failed. In such cases, and especially against the background of a regressive conception of responsibility, someone is to blame.

Consequently, another group of people also becomes stigmatised, that is, the prospective parents who choose imprudently. Either, they have to be protected by society against their poor choices, or they lose all form of social compensation and support. On the one hand, however, we have seen that, in the case of PGD, it is far from clear to judge objectively what a poor or prudent choice is without meeting the problem of illegitimate paternalism. On the other hand, they meet the problem of exclusion for the lack of an adequate safety net for victims of bad option luck deprives them of the claim for social support.

As such, we come to a society of two groups of people. On the one hand, we have the good and prudent, who act responsibly. They are 'the insiders,' so to say. On the other hand, there are the imprudent, who either have to be protected against their

measures like eradicating congenital handicaps. It is much less clear that mandatory testing can be said to support people in leading a good life, since many people do not see congenitally handicaps, such as Down syndrome, for instance, as bad circumstances, necessarily to be avoided by collective measures. Secondly, the flip side of this first argument is the following: a given natural or social fact can become a blessing or a burden by the way in which societies and social institutions deal with them. The basis of corrections of social conditions (like avoiding discrimination on the basis of social class, race, gender or sexual preference) has been the idea of equality of respect. The idea of correcting natural conditions (by preventing the birth of congenitally handicapped people) does not start from equality of respect. On the contrary, it implies discrimination on the basis of handicap. Instead of collectively preventing handicapped people to be born by making testing mandatory, a just and respectable social policy should compensate for it by providing the necessary social support for these people to lead a good life.

poor choices, or else are left outside the realm of social compensation and support, becoming marginalized, an inferior group.

Contrary to this, I believe that if the primary subject of social justice has to do with providing basic institutional arrangements that generate people's opportunities over time; and with providing the social conditions of freedom and *equal* respect; with assuring that *all* citizens have the means to develop and exercise their capacities as citizens; while guaranteeing them the freedom to pursue their own conception of the good life, provided that they comply with the principles of justice, Thomas Scanlon is right in saying that the luck egalitarian forfeiture view: "exaggerates the importance of the fact of *choice* relative to that of the *[social] conditions* under which the choice was made" (Scanlon 1988, p. 196, my italics). The just society should not make a social signal of hierarchy about its citizens. This has been illustrated by the many and heated social reactions against the legal ruling in France (cf. Sect. 4.2).

4.5.4 The Scope of Solidarity

If we decide to make choice central in determining the demands of justice, we risk creating a society in which solidarity only means solidarity with the good and prudent. As such, claims of justice generate endless questions of regressive responsibility, voluntary choice and blameworthiness in order to decide who are the good and prudent and who are not. With this, we have done nothing more but to replace the natural jungle by the social jungle.[7] Within such a climate, certain groups of people, like for instance dependent caregivers, become very vulnerable. For one could say

[7] One might consider whether replacing the natural jungle with the social jungle does not constitute progress, albeit incomplete progress toward a goal of increased justice. Two points are important to bear in mind in this regard. The first is based on the idea of moral arbitrariness and refers to what we consider as being relevant or irrelevant in matters of justice. In *A Theory of Justice* John Rawls writes: "The natural distribution is neither just nor unjust [...]. These are simply natural facts. What is just and unjust is the way that institutions deal with these facts" (Rawls 1971, p. 102, 1999, p. 87). Here, Rawls refers to the fact that natural differences (such as race, gender, sexual preference, ...) can be reinforced or mitigated by social policy. Bear in mind the fact that in previous times, being black or being a woman implied that one was less worthy, and that homosexuality was a disease, necessarily to be cured. This brings me to the second point. The answer to the question whether replacing the natural jungle with the social jungle does not constitute progress, is that it all depends on what is being reinforced or mitigated, to what extent, and in which respects. We condemn gender or race discrimination because the principle of equal respect demands that social barriers to equal treatment are being removed (*negative action*) rather then being reinforced. On the other hand, though, it is sometimes necessary that certain *positive actions* are being taken in order for people to be able to participate in social life on an equal basis (such as the provision of ramps in buildings or wheelchair access in busses, etc.). The essence of the argument is the following: in dealing with natural differences, social institutions have to promote and preserve equality of respect. Only then, one can speak of progress toward the goal of justice. When speaking of the natural jungle, I refer to the opposite, *viz.* to the fact of socially reinforcing inequality of respect.

that it has been their own choice to do this. By taking this path, we risk creating an atomistic society. Or as Anderson puts it:

> People who want to avoid the vulnerabilities that attend dependent caretaking must therefore decide to care only for themselves. This is egalitarianism for *egoists* alone. One wonders how children and the infirm are to be cared for, with a system that offers so little protection to their caretakers against poverty and domination (Anderson 1999, p. 300).

Contrary to this, it is reasonable to say that the scope of solidarity cannot be determined by choice, option, regressive responsibility and blameworthiness. Rather, it should be determined by our common humanity and the things that are necessary for every human being in order to lead a good life. This means that we have to concentrate on those things that are so *important* for every human being's opportunities in life that they become *entitlements* of citizens based upon justice (such as the right to life, education, health care, the right to vote, being part of the political community, etc.).[8] With this, we enter a domain that is just too important to allow exclusion. As Martha Nussbaum argues, when any one of these entitlements is abridged this is an especially grave failure of the socio-political system. The abridgement is then not just a huge cost to be borne, but also a cost of a special kind, involving a violation of basic justice (Nussbaum 2001, 2003). In the same line of reasoning, Thomas Scanlon loosens the connection between equality and responsibility by arguing that it depends on the *objective value* of the equalisandum whether inequalities are just or unjust. Preferences and tastes are excluded from the distribution problem, not because people can be held responsible for them, but because they are less *urgent*. That people can be held responsible for their preferences should only mean that they can do *without* them. They are not necessities and thus lose their urgency. Responsibility for preferences is in itself not a reason for rejecting claims; it is at most a sign of their not being very urgent. The degree of urgency depends on the *objective value* of the claim, not on the subjective stress one can lay on it (Scanlon 1975, 1986, 1988).

---

[8] With this, we touch upon the rights and freedoms, as laid down in the Universal Declaration of Human Rights, especially article 1, "All human beings are born free and equal in dignity and rights", article 3 "Everyone has the right to life, liberty and security of person", article 22 "Everyone, as a member of society, has the right to social security and is entitled to realization, through national effort and international co-operation and in accordance with the organization and resources of each State, of the economic, social and cultural rights indispensable for his dignity and the free development of his personality", article 25 "Everyone has the right to a standard of living adequate for the health and well-being of himself and of his family, including food, clothing, housing and medical care and necessary social services, and the right to security in the event of unemployment, sickness, disability, widowhood, old age or other lack of livelihood in circumstances beyond his control", article 26 "Everyone has the right to education. Education shall be free, at least in the elementary and fundamental stages. Elementary education shall be compulsory. Technical and professional education shall be made generally available and higher education shall be equally accessible to all on the basis of merit. Education shall be directed to the full development of the human personality and to the strengthening of respect for human rights and fundamental freedoms." We also touch upon the list of Central Human Capabilities, which are the central elements of truly human functioning, as formulated by Martha Nussbaum (2003). For an extensive discussion of the capabilities, and their function within just health care, see also Denier (2007).

Interestingly, Shlomi Segall has stressed in his luck egalitarian approach, that luck egalitarianism can only escape the abandonment objection if it is *complemented* with *other* moral considerations like those of meeting basic needs. This means that the solution cannot be found from *within* luck egalitarianism, but has to be found in a basic needs theory that provides a universal and unconditional, non-exclusive layer of sufficientarian concern for meeting everybody's basic needs regardless of their antecedent health-related conduct or choices (Segall 2007a, 2010a).

So, if we want to avoid a situation in which legal rulings such as wrongful life and wrongful birth are the *only* possibility for people to receive the funds that are necessary to cover the extra costs that come with caring for disabled life, the scope of solidarity cannot be determined by the mere distinction between choice and luck. On the contrary, justice and solidarity have to do with a *forward-looking* policy of inclusion. A policy of inclusion is based on the idea that justice does not permit the abandonment of *anyone*, not even the imprudent, in matters of *objective, intrinsic importance*. In this line of reasoning, Elisabeth Anderson rightly argues that consistent egalitarian theory should *identify* certain types of goods to which *all* citizens must have effective access over the course of their whole lives, because they are more important from an egalitarian point of view than others (Anderson 1999, pp. 316, 327). A policy is forward-looking when it has to do with providing a 'fallback framework' that contributes to *all* persons' receiving a fair chance in life, that is, a safety net below which *no one* would be allowed to fall. Because of this, it would be unfair to cut off fair equality of opportunity in the *future* because of *past* choices. Although it sounds paradoxical, holding people responsible for their ends means that in assuming the presence of fair and just arrangements and institutions, we are acting as if they can exercise their underlying moral power to *form*, *pursue*, and possibly to *revise* their own conceptions of the good and valuable. Or as Norman Daniels has put it: "I think Cohen misses the mark. It is not actual choice that matters but *the underlying capacity for forming and revising one's ends* that is at issue" (1996, p. 222).

Taking it all together, the argumentation with regard to the scope of solidarity is threefold.

4.5.4.1 Freedom of Choice Presupposes a Real Range of Options

People are indeed responsible for the consequences of their freely made choices. However, in order for a choice to be free, the range of actual alternatives has to be sufficiently broad. This means that certain choices have to be supported by society. Otherwise, these choices will be *de facto* impossible. Nowadays, for instance, people can choose to have children, they can choose to undergo PGD, and they can choose to terminate the pregnancy in the case of congenital disorder. Within a just society, it should also be possible to choose otherwise, i.e., not to undergo PGD, and to keep and raise a handicapped child. Equal respect for both alternative choices, presupposes that society provides sufficient support also for people who choose to keep the handicapped baby. Otherwise, this alternative is not a real option.

4.5.4.2 Not All Options Have to Be Supported by Society

The second point of the argument refers to the question why society has to support the life and care for people with a congenital handicap? Because the choices that people have to make in the case of PGD do not involve superficial things like having to choose between chocolate or vanilla ice cream. Neither does it involve an expensive champagne taste. On the contrary, the choice to have children, even when they have a handicap, is of a *fundamental* and *existential* nature. It determines the lives of the prospective parents in a fundamental and significant way. This requires respect and support by society. The necessity of support by society also goes for having healthy children, as the saying 'It takes a village to raise a child…' aptly expresses.

4.5.4.3 Not Infinitely

The third point of the argument refers to the question whether these options have to be funded *infinitely* by the public for a society to be just? Does it involve limitless support in all possible ways? No it does not. It involves the support that is necessary for people to have a fair chance in life. The just society guarantees fair equality of opportunity in life for all. This implies that some people – like the handicapped – need more support than others in order to actually have a fair chance in life (like special education, supportive material like a wheelchair for instance, or a special telephone for the deaf, etc.) and that society has to make a special effort to create a culture of respect for people with a handicap (by providing adapted entrances to public buildings, by stimulating job creation for people with a handicap, etc.), thus supporting their participation in public and social life. In essence, these forms of social support (in education, in supportive care, in job creation) are the same for everyone, for they refer to things that people need in order to have a fair chance in life. For people with a handicap, it involves just more of an effort to realize this. But all in all, it refers to the basic things (education, care, a job) that constitute a person's well-being and that people need in order to have a fair chance in life.

Within this general framework, I argue that the only legitimate value that can be attached to PGD is that it serves as an instrument that prospective parents may or may not use, in all freedom, in accordance with their own capacities and their own conceptions of the good life. No one, in this regard, should be forced to undergo prenatal genetic testing, or otherwise, be excluded from the realm of social support. Or put differently, if our solidarity becomes reduced to solidarity with the "prudent" only, then it seems that legal claims of wrongful birth and wrongful life are the only possibility left to get the necessary funds to cover the extra costs that come with caring for congenitally disabled life. Or one should be rich enough to cover the costs privately.

4.6 Conclusion

In this paper I have explicitly chosen not to concentrate on the prevailing and typical problems that are usually tackled in ethical reflections on issues of wrongful birth and wrongful life – such as harm, identity, degree of disability, playing God-arguments, eugenics, etc. On the other hand, it has been my aim to concentrate on the *principles of justice* that should guide our social dealings with issues of PGD, wrongful birth and wrongful life; and more specifically, to analyze the influential *luck egalitarian* view on such issues.

It is true that the crucial boundary between chance and choice is the spine of our ethics and morality, and that any serious shift is thoroughly dislocating. As was already suggested by the opening quotation, it asks us to rethink certain basic assumptions about the relationships between justice, human nature, and moral progress. Perhaps the most important conclusion of my analysis is that if we want technological progress in genetic medicine to be moral progress, then it is the responsibility of the just society to make sure that it is guided by principles of justice, which above all, serve the *equal freedom* of *all* its citizens. The case of PGD shows that the luck egalitarian approach cannot vouch for this.

References

Anderson, E.S. 1999. What is the point of equality? *Ethics* 109: 287–337.

Aristotle. 2000. *Nichomachean ethics*. Trans. and ed. R. Crisp. Cambridge: Cambridge University Press.

Arneson, R.J. 1989. Equality and equal opportunity for welfare. *Philosophical Studies* 56: 77–93.

Arneson, R. 2011. Luck egalitarianism – A primer. In *Responsibility and distributive justice*, ed. C. Knight and Z. Stemplowska, 24–50. Oxford: Oxford University Press.

Bayertz, K. 2003. Human nature: How normative might it be? *The Journal of Medicine and Philosophy* 28: 131–150.

Beck, U. 1986. *Risikogesellschaft. Auf dem Weg in eine andere Moderne*. Frankfurt: Suhrkamp.

Beck, U. 1992. *Risk society: Towards a new modernity*. New Delhi: Sage.

Buchanan, A., D.W. Brock, N. Daniels, and D. Wikler. 2000. *From chance to choice. Genetics and justice*. Cambridge: Cambridge University Press.

Christiaens, G.C.M.L., and M.D. Kloosterman. 1997. Ik heb helaas geen goed nieuws voor u. Over ongunstige uitslagen van invasieve prenatale diagnostiek en afbreken van zwangerschap. In *Prenatale diagnostiek*, ed. H. Brandenburg, 52–61. Houten: Bohn Stafleu Van Loghum.

Cohen, G.A. 1989. On the currency of egalitarian justice. *Ethics* 99: 906–944.

Daniels, N. 1996. *Justice and justification: Reflective equilibrium in theory and practice*. Cambridge: Cambridge University Press.

de La Fontaine, J. 1693. *The complete fables of Jean de La Fontaine*. Trans and ed. N. Shapiro. 2007. University of Illinois Press.

Denier, Y. 2005. On personal responsibility and the human right to health care. *Cambridge Quarterly of Healthcare Ethics* 14: 224–234.

Denier, Y. 2007. *Efficiency, justice and care. Philosophical reflections on scarcity in health care*. Dordrecht: Springer.

Denier, Y. 2010. From brute luck to option luck? On genetics, justice and moral responsibility in reproduction. *The Journal of Medicine and Philosophy* 2(35): 101–129.
Dworkin, R. 1981a. Equality of resources 'What is equality? Part 2: Equality of resources'. *Philosophy and Public Affairs* 10: 283–345.
Dworkin, G. 1981b. Taking risks, assessing responsibility. *The Hastings Center Report* 11: 26–31.
Dworkin, R. 2000a. *Sovereign virtue. The theory and practice of equality*. Cambridge: Harvard University Press.
Dworkin, R. 2000b. Playing god: Genes, clones, and luck. In Id, *Sovereign virtue,* 427–452. Cambridge: Harvard University Press.
Elster, J. 1982. Sour grapes – Utilitarianism and the genesis of wants. In *Utilitarianism and beyond*, ed. A. Sen and B. Williams, 219–238. Cambridge: Cambridge University Press.
Elster, J. 1989. *Solomonic judgements: Studies in the limitations of rationality*. Cambridge: Cambridge University Press.
Giddens, A. 1990. *Consequences of modernity*. Cambridge: Polity Press.
Giddens, A. 1999. Risk and responsibility. *Modern Law Review* 62: 1–10.
Glover, J. 2001. Future people, disability, and screening. In *Bioethics*, ed. J. Harris, 429–444. Oxford: Oxford University Press.
Hurley, S.L. 2001. Debate: Luck, responsibility, and the natural lottery. *The Journal of Political Philosophy* 10: 79–94.
Hurley, S.L. 2003. *Justice, luck, and knowledge*. Cambridge: Harvard University Press.
Kittay, E.F. 1999. *Love's labor. Essays on women, equality, and dependency*. New York: Routledge.
Miller, D. 1976. *Social justice*. Oxford: Clarendon.
Nagel, T. 1979. *Mortal questions*. Cambridge: Cambridge University Press.
Nussbaum, M.C. 2000. *Women and human development*. Cambridge: Cambridge University Press.
Nussbaum, M.C. 2001. The costs of tragedy: Some moral limits of cost-benefit analysis. In *Cost-benefit analysis: Legal, economic, and philosophical perspectives*, ed. M. Adler and E. Posner, 169–200. Chicago: Chicago University Press.
Nussbaum, M.C. 2003. Capabilities as fundamental entitlements. Sen and social justice. *Feminist Economics* 9(2–3): 33–59.
Nussbaum, M.C. 2004. *Hiding from humanity. Disgust, shame, and the law*. Princeton: Princeton University Press.
Parfit, D. 1984. *Reasons and persons*. Oxford: Clarendon.
Rawls, J. 1971. *A theory of justice*. Cambridge: Harvard University Press.
Rawls, J. 1996. *Political liberalism*. New York: Columbia University Press.
Rawls, J. 1999. *A theory of justice* (rev. ed.). Cambridge: The Belknap Press of Harvard University Press.
Roemer, J.E. 1993. A pragmatic theory of responsibility for the egalitarian planner. *Philosophy and Public Affairs* 22: 146–166.
Roemer, J.E. 1995. Equality and responsibility. *Boston Review* 20(2): 3/15–7/16.
Roemer, J.E. 1996. *Theories of distributive justice*. Cambridge: Harvard University Press.
Roemer, J.E. 1998. *Equality of opportunity*. Cambridge: Harvard University Press.
Rosanvallon, P. 1995. *La Nouvelle Question Sociale: Repenser l'Etat-Providence*. Paris: Seuil.
Savulescu, J. 2001. Procreative beneficence: Why we should select the best children. *Bioethics* 15: 413–426.
Scanlon, T.M. 1975. Preference and urgency. *The Journal of Philosophy* 72: 655–669.
Scanlon, T.M. 1986. Equality of resources and equality of welfare: A forced marriage? *Ethics* 97: 111–118.
Scanlon, T.M. 1988. The significance of choice. In *The tanner lectures on human values*, vol. 8, ed. S. McMurrin, 149–216. Salt Lake City: University of Utah Press.
Schwartz, R.L. 1995. Life style, health status, and distributive justice. In *Justice and health care: Comparative perspectives*, ed. A. Grubb and M.J. Mehlman, 244–248. New York: Wiley.
Segall, S. 2007a. In solidarity with the imprudent: A defense of luck egalitarianism. *Social Theory and Practice* 33(2): 177–198.

Segall, S. 2007b. Is health care (still) special? *Journal of Political Philosophy* 15(3): 342–361.
Segall, S. 2010a. *Health, luck and justice*. Princeton: Princeton University Press.
Segall, S. 2010b. Is health (really) special? Health policy between Rawlsian and luck egalitarian justice. *Journal of Applied Philosophy* 27(4): 344–358.
Segall, S. Forthcoming. Why egalitarians should not care about equality. *Ethical Theory and Moral Practice*. doi:10.1007/s10677-011-9306-7 (Online First™).
Vamos, E., K. Vandenberghe, and J.J. Cassiman. 1997. Prenatal diagnosis in Belgium. *European Journal of Human Genetics* 5(suppl. 1): 7–13.
van Tongeren, P. 1995. The paradox of our desire for children. *Ethical Perspectives* 2: 55–62.
World Values Survey (2005–2008). Available: www.worldvaluessurvey.org. Accessed 4 May 2011.

Chapter 5
Mutual Moral Obligations in the Prevention of Infectious Diseases

Jeroen Luyten

5.1 Introduction

Not so long ago health policy was about little more than the provision of medical care. The availability of treatment is important for those in need of cure, but by now it is a well-shown fact that health is generally determined to a much greater extent by other factors. Genetic constitution, lifestyle choices and socio-economic environment largely explain why some of us become ill or die earlier than others who remain healthy (Mackenbach 1996; McKeown 1976; Wilkinson and Marmot 2003). While some of these factors fall under the control of an individual, the majority does not. Research increasingly indicates how remarkably sensitive our health seems to be to what has become known as the 'social determinants of health'. These factors generally fall beyond the control of an individual, but can nonetheless be influenced on a population level. This causes a shift in the focus of health policy from the classic provision of health care to policies specifically designed to influence the causal factors of ill-health in different non-medical fields. The flipside of that evolution is a significant increase of the state's influence in the sphere of individual lives. A pertinent question remains the one that asks for the legitimate role of governments in modifying, discouraging or prohibiting behaviors that lead to ill-health. To what extent can and should we hold public policy responsible for us leading a healthy life? Most scholars will

I am grateful to Yvonne Denier, Chris Gastmans, Tom Grimonprez and Antoon Vandevelde for giving me the opportunity to contribute to this book and to the preceding conference in Leuven on *Justice, Luck and Responsibility in Health Care* in May 2011. I want to acknowledge the other speakers and the audience for their valuable remarks and insights that improved this text. Furthermore I want to thank Philippe Beutels for his thoughtful comments on an earlier version. Financial support came from the Fund for Scientific Research – Flanders (FWO n° G098911N).

J. Luyten (✉)
Centre for Health Economics Research and Modeling Infectious Diseases,
University of Antwerp, Universiteitsplein 1, 2610 Wilrijk, Belgium
e-mail: Jeroen.Luyten@ua.ac.be

Y. Denier et al. (eds.), *Justice, Luck & Responsibility in Health Care*,
Library of Ethics and Applied Philosophy 30, DOI 10.1007/978-94-007-5335-8_5,

argue that governments indeed have a role to play, but that the limits will be reached when public health measures would imply large sacrifices of individual liberty.

In those private spheres where government intervention is perhaps undesirable, ethical values, norms and customs that guide our voluntary behavior are an important public health variable. One of these domains is infectious disease prevention. Infectious diseases are a major cause of ill-health worldwide; they are often easily preventable and the dynamics of their transmission are mainly situated in the private sphere. Therefore, policy makers that aim to reduce the incidence of infectious diseases will largely depend on the voluntary efforts and customs of individual citizens. Many forms of prevention are at everyone's free disposal. Many of them are effective in breaking the transmission chain of pathogens and consequently in avoiding infections. Vaccination is possible for many diseases and is likely to ensure immunity, with often close to 100% effectiveness. Behavioral precautions like safe sex practices or personal hygiene can also prevent many infections in ourselves and in others. There is evidence that wearing mouth masks, gloves, gowns, head covers or regular hand washing (more than ten times a day) are effective measures to reduce the spread of respiratory viruses (Jefferson et al. 2008; Mitka 2007). Moreover more and more screening possibilities exist to test whether someone carries infectious diseases. However the voluntary use of these preventive measures depends on our perceived necessity to implement them. Few people exhaust all possibilities and most people would not consider this as morally wrong, even though the consequences of forgoing these measures can be serious for themselves and for others. In this chapter I want to explore from an ethical perspective what our mutual obligations are in the prevention of infectious diseases. In a first section I will discuss the epidemiological importance of infectious diseases and the ethical relevance of prevention. Then I will explore the role of the state in enabling and enforcing preventive measures. In the final section two basic ethical perspectives that often serve to guide moral reasoning will be translated to the context of infectious disease prevention. A first perspective is a deontological one in which the moral quality of an action or a choice depends upon its conformity with certain principles or rules. The second perspective is a consequentialist one and will judge actions and choices based on the consequences they will bring about.

5.2 The Importance of Infectious Disease Prevention

Historically, the share of infectious diseases in the total disease burden has been large. Since the early appearance of human beings, infectious diseases have made so many casualties that they reduce the impact of war to only a footnote in history. The Black Death, i.e. 'the plague', raged for centuries in Asia before it finally came to Europe in the fourteenth century where it killed – in 2 years time – about one third of the European population (Williamson et al. 2008). After burning down city after city, religious processions were organized all over the continent to break the spell, but were likely instrumental into the further spread of the virus (Beran 2008). The smallpox, probably the most dreadful disease for humans, killed an estimated

400,000 Europeans each year by the late eighteenth century (Henderson et al. 2008) and approximately 300–540 million people in the twentieth century alone (Selgelid 2004). In 1918 a mutation in the influenza virus strain, resulted in the Spanish influenza epidemic with a number of deaths – predominantly among young and healthy persons – between 20 and 100 million people (Johnson and Mueller 2002).

However, about half a century ago, infectious disease was thought by some in the medical community to be on the verge of being vanquished through progress in sanitation, antibiotics and the development of safe and effective vaccines. In 1972 the Nobel Laureate Macfarlane Burnet concluded that "the most likely forecast about the future of infectious disease is that it will be very dull" (Selgelid 2005). That appeared to be an overly optimistic, perhaps hubristic prediction. Today infectious diseases are still worldwide the number one cause of death in children (Bryce et al. 2005), the biggest cause of overall mortality in low-income countries and the second biggest cause of mortality worldwide (WHO 2011). More than 90% of all human illnesses may somehow be caused by virus infections (Norkin 2010). In 2009, 33.3 million individuals were HIV seropositive while 1.8 million died from their infection (WHO 2009b). Tuberculosis killed an estimated 1.7 million people in 2009 (WHO 2009c). Epidemics of seasonal influenza result every year in about three to five million cases of severe illness, and about 250,000–500,000 deaths worldwide (WHO 2009a).

Infectious diseases are likely to remain an important concern to our health. Global warming will affect the introduction and dissemination of many serious infectious diseases (Patz et al. 2005). From 1940 to 2004 several hundred new infectious diseases have emerged as we have witnessed the more famous 'birth' of SARS, HIV and Ebola (Jones et al. 2008). Experts consider it a fact that sooner or later a novel influenza strain will appear that will pose a serious public health threat (Giles-Vernick and Craddock 2010). An estimated 175–350 million individuals risk to die when the common influenza virus undergoes a dangerous mutation (Knobler et al. 2005). The tremendous success of public health programs and the increased hygienic standards in the developed world have enormously reduced the incidence of most common infectious diseases (Roush and Murphy 2007). But this also has a perverse effect in that it leaves us with highly susceptible populations. A re-emergence of a virus could easily lead to large scale outbreaks, perhaps even epidemics, in a population that has lost its build-up immunity. A deliberate release of a virus by terrorists remains a viable security threat. Concerns exist that the stocks of the (officially eradicated) smallpox virus that were artificially manufactured for military purposes in the former Soviet Union, may have fallen in dangerous hands after the fall of the communist regime in the early 1990s (Henderson 1999). An organized release of this virus by terrorist organizations could according to experts trigger a global epidemic with the potential impact of a series of nuclear attacks (Selgelid 2003). But also non-deliberate introductions of microbes should be of concern. Changed travel patterns and the free movement of goods and persons in a globalized economy have enabled the spread of viruses across continents in a matter of hours. This increases the risk of outbreaks with potentially serious medical and economic consequences (Luyten and Beutels 2009). There is also another – and perhaps even most important – reason to believe that infectious diseases are likely to remain a serious health problem. The antibiotics used to treat infected patients are becoming less effective since infectious pathogens appear to develop an increasing resistance to their effects (Carlet et al. 2011). This means that the miracle drugs of the twentieth century (such as penicillin) will lose their curative potential for many common diseases, without the prospect of having worthwhile alternatives in development. Arias and Murray conclude that

> it is more difficult than ever to eradicate infections caused by antibiotic-resistant "super-bugs", and the problem is exacerbated by a dry pipeline for new antimicrobials with bactericidal activity against gram-negative bacteria and enterococci. A concerted effort on the part of academic researchers and their institutions, industry, and government is crucial if humans are to maintain the upper hand in this battle against bacteria – a fight with global consequences (Arias and Murray 2009).

The continuing threat of infectious diseases plus the diminished possibilities to cure infections increases the ethical importance of prevention.

5.3 The Role of the State

Authorities can take several preventive measures that are likely to be effective in reducing virus transmission and circulation. But these measures are often ethically controversial because they are difficult to rhyme with a protection of civil liberties. Obligatory screening for diseases, the surveillance of (sexual) activity, forced treatment or compulsory disclosure and tracing of contacts can prevent the spreading of a disease, but these steps also deeply invade the private sphere of individuals. Quarantine measures can be powerful weapons in the hands of governments because they enable to isolate individuals on preventive grounds. Visible symptoms of disease would not be required since for many diseases the infectious period starts well before the appearance of symptoms, and thus before the patient is aware of being infected, sometimes weeks to even months. For instance the infectious period of an influenza episode starts at least a day before the onset of illness (CDC 2011b). In the case of measles, infectiousness starts about 4 days before rashes appear (CDC 2011c). An infection with tuberculosis is associated with several months of infectiousness (CDC 2011a). Public health instruments (like quarantine, surveillance or contact disclosing) can be abused as a pretext for governments to silence opposition and to erode fundamental rights for self-serving purposes.

Compulsory vaccination, another controversial measure, is executed in several countries all over the world. In Belgium for instance recently two parents were sentenced to prison for refusing to have their child vaccinated (Stafford 2008). This remains a drastic policy option that fails to respect the autonomy of individuals. Rarely, a public policy measure (literally) intrudes the individual sphere in such a real and physical way. A senior WHO physician-epidemiologist who was assigned for the last phase of the smallpox eradication campaign in India from 1973 to 1975 described his experience with a compulsory vaccination program in the following way:

> The initial stage in the evolution of a coherent containment policy was marked by an almost military style attack on infected villages. [...] In the hit-and-run excitement of such a campaign,

> women and children were often pulled out from under their beds, from behind doors, from within latrines, etc. People were chased and, when caught, vaccinated. [...] Almost invariably a chase or a forcible vaccination ensued in such circumstances. [...] We considered the villagers to have an understandable but irrational fear of vaccination. [...] We just couldn't let people get smallpox and die needlessly. We went from door to door and when they ran, we chased. When they locked their doors, we broke down their doors and vaccinated (Greenough 1995).

This section indicates how difficult it can be to balance utilitarian public health values against libertarian rights and freedoms. Sometimes preventive measures such as vaccination or the use of preservatives go against deeply-held metaphysical beliefs. This exacerbates the dilemma since in these cases the problem is not a lack of understanding, or as in the fragment above, an "irrational fear", but a divergence in fundamental conceptions of 'the good life' (cfr. infra).

An important question in this respect will be: how to determine the legitimate role of the state in preventing infectious diseases? A distinction must be made between on the one hand those situations where there is a clear necessity to enforce preventive measures, and on the other hand those more average situations where the risks are in line with 'normal' hazards inherent to communal life. In the face of a public health emergency with potentially catastrophic consequences the state is arguably justified to weigh the interests of an individual against those of the public and to deprive citizens of certain liberties. The state may also regulate the implementation of basic forms of prevention that can prevent serious and concrete harm. In several countries legal precedents have occurred in which a person is convicted of inflicting grievous bodily harm for not taking precautionary measures and infecting others with a serious disease. For instance, in 2003 a London jury has found a 37-year old man guilty of infecting two women with the HIV-virus (BBC 2003). Similar cases occurred in 2010 in Germany (BBC 2010) and in 2011 in Belgium (Standaard 2011). In many countries there exist legal obligations for specific professional groups to take precautionary measures in order to avoid epidemics and outbreaks. For instance, in Belgium, since 2005 food handlers are obliged by law to wash their hands after using the toilet (Belgisch Staatsblad 2005). The emergence of these precedents is indicative of the fact that our ethical duty not to spread diseases is increasingly taken serious.

But, in a public health emergency or in the case of a deliberate infection with a life-threatening disease our ethical duties are rather obvious. In more common situations however it seems a bit unclear exactly *how much* effort we can expect from each other. In those normal circumstances, the state's legitimate role is likely to be limited to policies that enable citizens to take preventive measures themselves: informing and educating the population on infectious disease prevention and – as acknowledged in the International Covenant on Economic, Social and Cultural Rights of the United Nations – "to provide immunization against the major infectious diseases of the community" (Hinman 2004). Safeguarding civil liberties in the field of infectious disease prevention will in normal circumstances require confidence in the ability of individuals to make competent ethical decisions, on which preventive measures to take, if any.

5.4 The Scope of Our Moral Duties to Prevent Infectious Disease

The range of possibilities to prevent infectious disease transmission is very large, and the choice either or not to implement them is not only relevant for those individuals who know they are carrying an infectious pathogen, or those who suspect that they are infected. Since the infectious period often begins before a person is aware of being infected this choice is relevant for everyone, at any time (Verweij 2005). Because the consequences of transmitting disease are potentially severe (e.g. even a common cold infection can occasionally be deadly), and because in most countries prevention is not unreasonably costly to the individual (e.g. subsidized vaccines, affordable screening, social security that covers the income loss of staying home when ill, availability of hand-washing facilities, etc.), the following question is morally relevant. How much preventive effort do we owe to each other? Or, how do we justify the fact that we neglect to do whatever we can to safeguard each other from potentially dangerous infections? A maximal level of precaution would imply a behavioral revolution. It would require such a drastic alteration of our customs that afterwards we could hardly label our world as 'social'. We would have to limit physical contact to the bare minimum and restrict public crowding in order to create a world that is as sterile as possible. The inconvenience of such a world however is in itself not a decisive argument to indicate that very strict prevention does not belong to the requirements of justice.

In determining the just scope of our duties to prevent disease we will have to consider the following four nuances. First, how much should we care for our own health? Second, what do we owe to those individuals that cannot protect themselves against infectious diseases? There exist relatively large groups of people who are extra vulnerable to infectious diseases *and* who cannot get vaccinated: those with developing and deteriorated immune systems (newborns, the elderly, pregnant women, the chronically ill, etc.).[1] Third, what do we owe to those who are perfectly able to protect themselves, but who neglect to do so (e.g. unsafe sex practitioners, vaccine refusers, etc.)? And fourth, what do we owe to future generations? Due to decades of immunization many infectious diseases are in large parts of the world reduced to overseeable proportions. One deadly disease, smallpox, has been completely eradicated, and a global effort is being made to eradicate polio (Roberts 2005). If we *are* able to eradicate diseases, do we have a moral obligation to do so? So far, these topics have not received a great deal of attention. I am aware of only three articles that explicitly consider our mutual obligations in the prevention of infectious diseases (Verweij 2005; Harris and Holm 1995; Dawson 2007). I will build further on Verweij's discussion of this subject and explore the questions above from two different perspectives on normative ethics: a deontological and a consequentialist one.

[1] Among those who cannot protect themselves we may also consider the large groups of individuals who *are* able to become vaccinated, but who have no access to vaccines for social, economic or political reasons. But because I am considering the scope of our mutual duties in a situation where prevention *is* available to everyone, I will not deal with this important issue of global justice.

5.4.1 A Deontological Perspective

In a deontological approach to ethics, what makes a choice or an action morally right or wrong depends upon the conformity of our intentions with moral principles or norms. The fact that an act has desirable consequences will not be morally relevant as such. A central element will be the universal applicability of our motives and intentions. We are not allowed to make an opportunistic exception for ourselves. Famous principles in this tradition are the Confucian golden rule, the Kantian categorical imperative or the Christian wisdom 'love thy neighbour as thyself'. Orthogonal to these principles on an individual level is the contractualist account of ethics on a societal level. Here, the different individual principles are bundled in a 'social contract' in which the contracting parties agree on the principles that need to be honored in the world they will be living in. Morally wrong acts are then those acts that would be forbidden by the principles that are agreed upon in the contract. If an act would follow from a certain principle, and that principle can be reasonably rejected by one of the contracting parties, then the act could be labeled as wrong. Central to this approach is thus the fact that we need to take into account the rightful interests of others. We have to be able to justify our actions to the rest of society. However, it would not be unreasonable to hold each other to some extent responsible for the consequences that follow from certain choices. Contemporary accounts of justice are responsibility-sensitive, i.e. our solidarity with others will not be unconditional. Luck-egalitarianism – a central theory in this book – argues that a community has to be solidaristic with those who are struck by bad luck, i.e. those who became victim of a process that was beyond their control, but not with those who became disadvantaged through their own fault. In other words, there is a moral difference between 'brute bad luck' beyond the control of individuals and bad luck that was somehow 'optional'. If we apply a responsibility-sensitive contractualist framework to our mutual obligations in infectious disease prevention, I believe we would come up with the following result.

A first question that must be asked is whether we have a moral duty to protect *ourselves*. Is there a principle in a social contract that would prohibit that someone disregards her own health? I presume the most likely answer will be liberal in the sense that it leaves this to the private sphere of citizens. There are reasons to do so. Certain groups see the absence of illness not as an ultimate goal, not as something included in their conception of the good life. Some of them are religious groups that want to live their life in accordance with 'the divine providence'. They believe that vaccination reveals a lack of trust in God's purposes. Other groups (e.g. the 'anthroposofists') consider certain childhood diseases as a necessary step in the development of a child's character (Woonink 1953). These groups generally remain limited in size but the underlying motive is nonetheless present in many people's attitudes towards the use of a 'technical fix' for a life-style problem. Certain health risks are a consequence of behavioral choices. Vaccination, which can be seen as a 'technical fix', could be considered by some individuals to be an inferior, perhaps even an immoral way of avoiding certain outcomes which in the first place should be avoided by not carrying through certain behaviors. It would be felt somehow as 'shortcutting' nature's way of keeping a spontaneous order. The introduction of vaccines against sexually transmitted diseases, e.g. the human-papillomavirus vaccine for young girls, caused criticisms in larger groups of society because it was believed to promote sexually promiscuous behavior (Balog 2009). Similar discussions occur, or may occur, with the development of vaccines against obesity, cocaine or nicotine addiction (Kantak 2003). A biological risk or limitation that normally regulates our behavior is in these cases overcome by technological progress. Developments like these urge us to reveal our metaphysical views upon the moral value of biological and environmental limitations and ultimately about the place of man in the universe. A majority of individuals would support the point of view that nature has at least *some* moral authority in setting our limits. This can for instance be witnessed in the widespread remorse for the human responsibility for climate change and its consequences. The environment indicates that it cannot cope with our exuberant life-style and many interpret these signals as a moral reproach. A 'technical fix' that could overcome the burden of global warming (e.g. a state-of-the-art construction that would protect our continents from sea-level rising, or a preservation policy for species that would become extinct because of the rising temperature) would by many not be considered as an equally valuable alternative for the required change in lifestyle. Because considerations on the desirability of technological progress truly relate to fundamental conceptions of the good life, the basic freedoms in a social contract are likely to allow individuals to forgo preventive measures (like vaccination) in as far as only *their* health is concerned. Nonetheless few would be able to reasonably argue that a healthy condition is not a desirable good in itself, fundamentally entangled with almost *any* conception of a good life. If so, then this will imply a moral responsibility to avoid those actions that harm someone's proper health, and often a duty to take a certain level of prevention. But forgoing this-or-that specific measure in such-and-such circumstances will be a matter of personal convictions and preferences. Moreover this discussion would also fall beyond our purpose to explore the scope of our *mutual* obligations.

What are our obligations towards those groups that cannot protect themselves against infection, i.e. those with vulnerable immune systems? The choice to forgo precautionary measures would not be justifiable to these groups. It would imply that a majority affords itself a freedom that is incompatible with the freedom of a minority. This would be rejected on reasonable grounds by those groups at risk. A principle that allows individuals to forgo the inconveniences of e.g. wearing mouth masks, washing hands or becoming vaccinated would be rejected by those who face the risks of severe morbidity and mortality. Thomas Scanlon, who has elaborated an influential contractualist theory of justice, states that

> if you are presented with a situation in which you can prevent something very bad from happening, or alleviate someone's dire plight, by making only a slight (or even moderate) sacrifice, then it would be wrong not to do so (Scanlon 1998, p. 224).

However, when prevention is very costly to an individual, it would not be obligatory. Social isolation of a contagious person is perhaps beneficial to other people but remains a burden to that person and his relatives. For many families it would imply an income-loss and a disturbed daily practice. It would therefore be required that individuals are compensated for the personal losses they run when living up to their ethical obligation not to infect others. As Harris and Holm argue

> the reasonableness of expecting people to live up to this obligation [...], depends on society reciprocating the obligation in the form of providing protection and compensation (Harris and Holm 1995).

The same is true with regard to the safety of prevention. Unless a vaccine is shown to be safe, it would not be reasonable to ask that individuals risk their health in order to protect others. But, in a context in which individuals *are* enabled and supported to fulfill their moral duties, where prevention is generally considered to be affordable and safe, demanding from each other to avoid virus transmission would in many cases not be excessive. The only outcome of a social contract that is reasonable to all parties would be one that includes quite demanding preventive efforts for everyone in order to safeguard those who are dependent on the efforts of others. Since even an influenza virus can be lethal in these most vulnerable groups, the solidarity that is owed to them will likely demand more than our current customs.

A different case could however be made for those who can, but neglect to take care for their health. From a luck egalitarian stance, we are obligated to compensate individuals for the bad luck they run through no fault of their own. But we do not have the same moral obligations towards those struck by 'optional' bad luck. When we can hold individuals responsible for not sufficiently protecting their own health, we would not have a duty to take extensive measures in order to prevent them from becoming infected. Without limitations in access to vaccines, and when extensive public health programs are available that inform citizens on how to protect themselves against disease, it could be argued that those who remain unvaccinated make a free and conscious choice to undergo certain health risks. The same may perhaps be true for unsafe sex practitioners. Principally, others are not obliged to take measures in order to protect these individuals. A crucial difficulty will however be to show that individuals can indeed be held responsible for these choices and that the bad luck they ran was truly avoidable. But if we believe that this is the case, then a strict following of principles would lead to a rather limited scope of solidarity (as far as only this group is concerned). Many precautionary measures would become optional when others can in fact protect themselves.

With regards to future generations a deontological perspective may imply the following ambiguous result. If we are not obliged to take care of those who are unwilling to become vaccinated at present time, we would also not have responsibilities towards those at future times. Future generations can equally well take the necessary measures themselves. But, when we are able to eradicate diseases, intergenerational justice may require us to relieve all the vulnerable ones in the future forever from these health risks. However, some considerations must be made. It must be argued that future generations can make a convincing claim in this respect. Does it make a difference whether we cannot justify our principles to our fellow citizens at present time or to those in the future who don't yet exist? Also, it has to be shown that our intentions are not mistaken. Disease eradication is a very difficult task, often a utopian one (Dowdle 1998). If it is unlikely that a disease will ever be eradicated, then honoring an ethical principle to protect the weak will not necessarily imply participation to disease eradication programs.

In summary, if we take a deontological perspective on our mutual obligations to take preventive measures, we may come up with ethical guidelines that differ from those that we are accustomed to in our habits and rules of politeness. Towards groups that are able, but unwilling to take care of their own health, the morally required level of solidarity may fall below the efforts that many of us spontaneously make in order to protect each other against infectious diseases. Towards future generations, our duties are somewhat ambiguous. But there are good reasons to substantially increase the level of prevention in order to protect those that cannot protect themselves. We would not be able to justify the choice *not* to prevent illnesses towards those that will be most at risk. This finding will be most relevant for those diseases against which vaccination is likely to be the only effective way of prevention (because not everyone can get immunized). Since we are not always capable of identifying vulnerable persons, neither to avoid contact with them, a strict obligation to prevent disease will impact our daily lives. The fact that the costs and the benefits are likely to be very unattractive (since a majority will become limited in its freedom for the benefit of a minority) is not an argument in a contractualist framework. Exactly this point, the protection of the 'separateness of persons', is a point where a contractualist account distinguishes itself from its major theoretical rival: a consequentialist account.

5.4.2 A Consequentialist Perspective

A quite different conclusion will be reached when we adopt a consequentialist point of view. This ethical theory holds that the moral value of actions or choices depends solely on the states of affairs they bring about, i.e. their consequences and not the underlying intentions and motivations. In order to determine the morally required course of action, consequentialists must initially specify which outcomes are intrinsically valuable in order to enable a comparison of the instruments that bring them about. Candidates are happiness, wellbeing, welfare, utility, pleasure, love, friendship, etc. Perhaps health has only an instrumental value to reach these ultimate targets, but whichever consequentialist variant one chooses, health will certainly be of quintessential importance. When we translate this ethical perspective to the context of infectious disease prevention, the result would be the following. We are morally obligated to take precautionary measures only when our efforts are of actual influence in the transmission of disease (and ultimately in the creation of say wellbeing). The only question that should be asked is thus 'what difference does it make'? Answers will differ according to the time horizon in which consequences are considered relevant.

In the short term consequentialism prescribes a level of solidarity that corresponds quite well with our daily practice. If a disease is rather rare and preventive efforts cost a lot of effort, then we would not have to implement them. The costs and inconveniences would outweigh the benefits. The opposite would be true for those diseases where the risk is serious and real and where our preventive efforts do make a difference. Then, the benefits are likely to dominate the burden of prevention. But even for virulent and contagious diseases it can from a consequentialist point of view be morally justifiable that we forgo preventive efforts. If a disease is endemic and very contagious, then *my* efforts to stop transmission are futile as long as they are not supported and copied by others. For instance, when I (as Belgian) decide to wear a mouth mask or to stay home from work, this will not stop the spread of the flu virus through Belgium. Others are likely to get infected anyway, and that makes the benefit of my action not very worthwhile. However, in a country like Japan where the wearing of mouth masks belongs to the social customs, my choice *not* to wear one is more likely to have an effect and may therefore be morally wrong. The consequentialist perspective gives us a rational explanation of the cultural dependence of our mutual obligations to prevent disease. Its prescriptions would apply to both current and future generations. If *my* participation to a disease eradication program would lead to beneficial consequences, for instance when humanity has come close to eradication, then I would have a moral duty to participate. If not, then my duty would evaporate.

Our moral obligations will thus entirely depend on the disease characteristics (infectiousness and virulence of the pathogen), and the expected number of infected persons. This is a different result than the one we obtained in a principle-based framework. First, unlike in the latter perspective, it would be of no importance whether the groups at risk are those that cannot protect themselves, or whether these are individuals that do not take responsibility towards their own health. There will be no (or very limited) preoccupation with the most vulnerable groups in society as long as these groups remain small. Since the overall costs and inconveniences of large preventive programs to protect only a handful of unlucky individuals will be rather unattractive, we would not be morally obliged to be solidaristic and to consider the health of worst-off groups. Second, the consequentialist perspective neglects the individual responsibility for health. Even when other persons consent to undergo certain risks (e.g. someone who consents to having unprotected sex or a careless tourist that neglects to take basic vaccinations) an ethical person would have to choose the option that minimizes the transmission of diseases. In that way it does not take other persons serious as autonomous individuals capable of making competent decisions. Or as Peter Strawson would say, it does not adopt a 'reactive attitude' towards others (Strawson 1962). The attitudes and the intentions of those who stand in a relationship to us are considered irrelevant. Moreover, for those diseases where an individual effort *can* make a difference, this 'objective attitude' towards others may lead to the 'over-demandingness problem'. This problem is often stated as a criticism against a consequentialist way of reasoning because individuals always have to aim for the best consequences, even at significant costs for themselves. An example could be found in Peter Singer's essay "Famine, Affluence and Morality" (Singer 1972). As a convinced utilitarian Singer argues that we have a moral duty to donate most of our money to the fight against extreme poverty and famine, because the results in terms of wellbeing of *not* donating and thus spending our money on self-serving purposes will always be inferior to the benefits that can be achieved through development aid. However, when others refuse to contribute, the beneficial effect of my charitable gift will increase (because now there is an increased need) and so will my moral obligation to donate money. When others behave egoistic, my moral duty would become more stringent and that would be over-demanding and unfair. Verweij argues that this problem does not really occur in infectious disease prevention because (cfr. supra) the effect of one person's contribution would often be futile unless it is *supported* by others instead of neglected (Verweij 2005). However, that would only be true for those diseases where we can assume that one individual's preventive efforts are indeed rather futile, i.e. those diseases that are endemic and sufficiently contagious. Many diseases fail to be so, and then the critique of over-demandingness could be valid though (especially when the disease in question is not life-threatening). For instance, someone who carries herpes simplex virus type I (a virus that causes fever blisters mainly around the mouth) would have to refrain from kissing a partner, drinking from common bottles or giving goodnight kisses to children. It is likely that her choice to prevent transmission will highly influence the fact whether her lovers, relatives and friends will ever become a carrier of the virus. Her loss will be outweighed by the fact that these others may become infected, and will in their turn infect others who will infect others and so on…. If these others are more likely to behave careless with regards to transmission of the herpes virus, her moral duties will only increase. As argued before, the fact that other persons consent with these risks is not morally relevant.

Perhaps for certain diseases in the short run the precautionary measures taken by one single individual may not have sufficient effect to create a moral obligation, but in the long run this may be completely different. In the short run our moral obligations depend upon the support we get from others. However in a longer time horizon we can always try to *gain* support so that prevention *does* become effective. Then the question becomes the following. Does a general rule to take certain preventive measures lead to desirable consequences? In the former paragraph we compared the effect of our actions only on the scale of health benefits. Now, on a more aggregate level, we will have to compare the value of public health to other societal goals such as economic welfare or social cohesion. If effective precautionary measures would imply an excessive cost in terms of these other goals, then it would be morally acceptable for a society to forgo them. But there is no universal way to trade off different social goals like welfare, health or social cohesion. Therefore, it may be difficult to determine in an objective way whether a preventive rule is either or not excessive because that will largely depend upon one's social philosophy. In the extreme case, someone who suffers from mysophobia (i.e. an irrational fear of contamination with germs) will be willing to accept a much higher opportunity cost in order to have a reduced transmission of microbes. Nonetheless in many instances it is possible to determine which outcome is generally preferable. An obligation to stay home from work when the seasons change would perhaps prevent transmission of the common cold virus among coworkers, but the economic cost of high absenteeism will be too elevated. The internet is a much safer place to communicate than in a crowded bar, but situations of public crowding may nonetheless be preferable over isolation for all kinds of social reasons. However, it could be that consequentialism in a longer time horizon requires an increased level of prevention compared to our current practice. When we evaluate a preventive rule like say 'compulsory wearing of mouth masks or gloves during the flu-season', the consequentialist may have to choose wearing rather than not wearing them. If such a measure is shown to be effective, the personal and societal benefits of the reduced disease burden may outweigh the burden of actually implementing this behavioral change. Arguably, there are more of these rules to be invented.

In sum, the required scope of prevention in a consequentialist framework will entirely depend upon the net effect of prevention on the resulting aggregate disease burden, and not on characteristics of those individuals at risk. When one person's effort matters, then the moral requirements not to spread disease will generally be elevated. It would be morally wrong to engage in behaviors that foster the transmission of pathogens, even though other persons consent to the risks by not taking preventive measures themselves. When one person's effort does not make much of a difference in the aggregated disease burden then the situation is different. For rare diseases or diseases that only rarely lead to morbidity, the benefit of strict precaution will not outweigh the burden because the potential health benefits would just be too small. For endemic and contagious diseases our moral duties will in the short run depend upon the efforts of others. Only when others follow a certain rule, then I would be morally obliged to do the same thing. If I refuse, then the effect of my choice on the resulting disease burden may be substantial. On the other hand, if no one follows a certain rule, my effort to stop transmission is going to be rather futile because others are likely to become infected anyway. In the long run – when the efforts of others cannot be considered exogenous anymore – the required level of prevention may however increase for these diseases. Forgoing prevention will then only be justified when the trade-off that it implies with regard to other societal goals (like economic welfare or social cohesion) is considered to be excessive.

5.5 Conclusion

There are good reasons to believe that infectious diseases will remain a factor of considerable importance to public health. Moreover, since the curative potential of many antibiotics is declining, their prevention will become relatively more important. Because the transmission dynamics of infectious diseases infiltrate the private sphere of citizens, measures taken by public health authorities will often conflict with protection of civil liberties. Policy makers who aim to reduce the incidence of infectious diseases in the least controversial way will have to count largely on the voluntary cooperation of citizens. These individuals dispose over a wide variety of possibilities to effectively prevent disease transmission but nonetheless few exhaust all options. Considering the harm that can be caused by infectious diseases, this begs the question how much precautionary measures we are mutually obliged to take. In this paper, I explored from two basic ethical perspectives the morally required scope of prevention. Both of them argue that for most diseases an elevated level of prevention is morally required. This level may be stricter than the level that we are habituated to in our current customs and rules of politeness. However, both perspectives also set different priorities and differ in their underlying motivation as to why prevention would be necessary. When we adopt a deontological perspective (and thus focus on the principles that guide our behavior), we end up with a set of mutual obligations that is very solidaristic with vulnerable groups, but less with those who neglect to take care of their own health. Because of the existence of groups that cannot protect themselves against serious health risks, and that rely upon the efforts of others, these others are obliged to implement a high level of prevention. Forgoing possibilities to prevent disease would not be justifiable to these groups. When we adopt a consequentialist point of view and focus on the effects of our actions, we find ourselves in a different situation. In the short run consequentialism will often give a moral justification for our daily practice. If it is worthwhile to take preventive measures, it would be morally required to do so, and that in the name of ourselves, others that cannot protect themselves, others that are unwilling to protect themselves or even future generations. The fact that other persons consent to undergo certain risks, would not bereave us from our responsibilities. If prevention is not worthwhile however, then it would be justified to forgo, even though that will imply serious risks to those with vulnerable immune systems. In the somewhat longer run however consequentialism becomes more demanding because then, the efforts of others are no longer to be considered as exogenous. The required level of prevention will then depend upon the relative value of public health to the other societal goals that must be sacrificed.

References

Arias, C.A., and B.E. Murray. 2009. Antibiotic-resistant bugs in the 21st century – A clinical superchallenge. *The New England Journal of Medicine* 360: 439–443.

Balog, J.E. 2009. The moral justification for a compulsory human papillomavirus vaccination program. *American Journal of Public Health* 99: 616–622.

BBC. 2003. *HIV man guilty of infecting lovers* (Online). Available: http://news.bbc.co.uk/2/hi/uk_news/england/london/3190626.stm. Accessed 07 June 2011.

BBC. 2010. *German girl band star charged in HIV case* (Online). Available: http://news.bbc.co.uk/2/hi/europe/8512933.stmGerman. Accessed 07 June 2011.

Belgisch staatsblad. 2005. *Koninklijk Besluit Betreffende Levensmiddelenhygiëne* (Online). Available: http://www.fasnk.be/legislation/hygiene/denreesalimentaires/_documents/KB-AR_H1.pdf. Accessed 07 June 2011.

Beran, G.W. 2008. Disease and destiny-mystery and mastery. *Preventive Veterinary Medicine* 86: 198–207.

Bryce, J., C. Boschi-Pinto, K. Shibuya, and R.E. Black. 2005. WHO estimates of the causes of death in children. *The Lancet* 365: 1147–1152.

Carlet, J., P. Collignon, D. Goldmann, H. Goossens, I.C. Gyssens, S. Harbarth, V. Jarlier, S.B. Levy, B. N'Doye, D. Pittet, R. Richtmann, W.H. Seto, J.W. Van der Meer, and A. Voss. 2011. Society's failure to protect a precious resource: Antibiotics. *The Lancet* 378(9788): 369–371.

CDC. 2011a. *Effective TB interviewing for contact investigation: Self-study modules* (Online). Available: http://www.cdc.gov/tb/publications/guidestoolkits/interviewing/selfstudy/module1/1_2_3.htm. Accessed 16 Aug 2011.

CDC. 2011b. *How flu spreads* (Online). Available: http://www.cdc.gov/flu/about/disease/spread.htm. Accessed 15 Aug 2011.

CDC. 2011c. *Transmission of measles* (Online) Available: http://www.cdc.gov/measles/about/transmission.html. Accessed 15 Aug 2011.

Dawson, A. 2007. What are the moral obligations of the traveller in relation to vaccination? *Travel Medicine and Infectious Disease* 5: 90–96.

Dowdle, W.R. 1998. The principles of disease elimination and eradication. *Bulletin of the World Health Organization* 76(suppl. 2): 22–25.

Giles-Vernick, T., and S. Craddock. 2010. *Influenza and public health: Learning from past pandemics*. London: Earthscan.

Greenough, P. 1995. Intimidation, coercion and resistance in the final stages of the South Asian smallpox eradication campaign 1973–1975. *Social Science & Medicine* 41: 633–645.

Harris, J., and S. Holm. 1995. Is there a moral obligation not to infect others? *British Medical Journal* 311: 1215–1217.

Henderson, D.A. 1999. The looming threat of bioterrorism. *Science* 283: 1279–1282.

Henderson, D.A., L.L. Borio, and J.D. Grabenstein. 2008. Smallpox and vaccinia. In *Vaccines*, ed. S. Plotkin, P. Offit, and W. Orenstein. Philadelphia: Elsevier.

Hinman, A.R. 2004. Immunization, equity, and human rights. *American Journal of Preventive Medicine* 26: 84–88.

Jefferson, T., R. Foxlee, C. Del Mar, L. Dooley, E. Ferroni, B. Hewak, A. Prabhala, S. Nair, and A. Rivetti. 2008. Physical interventions to interrupt or reduce the spread of respiratory viruses: Systematic review. *British Medical Journal* 336: 77–80.

Johnson, N.P., and J. Mueller. 2002. Updating the accounts: Global mortality of the 1918–1920 "Spanish" influenza pandemic. *Bulletin of the History of Medicine* 76: 105–115.

Jones, K.E., N.G. Patel, M.A. Levy, A. Storeygard, D. Balk, J.L. Gittleman, and P. Daszak. 2008. Global trends in emerging infectious diseases. *Nature* 451: 990–993.

Kantak, K.M. 2003. Vaccines against drugs of abuse: A viable treatment option? *Drugs* 63: 341–352.

Knobler, S.L., A. Mack, A. Mahmoud, and S.M. Lemon (eds.). 2005. *Institutes of medicine: The threat of pandemic influenza: Are we ready?* Washington, DC: National Academies Press.

Luyten, J., and P. Beutels. 2009. Costing infectious disease outbreaks for economic evaluation: A review for hepatitis A. *PharmacoEconomics* 27: 379–389.

Mackenbach, J.P. 1996. The contribution of medical care to mortality decline: McKeown revisited. *Journal of Clinical Epidemiology* 49: 1207–1213.

McKeown, T. 1976. *The role of medicine: Dream, mirage, or nemesis?* London: Nuffield Provincial Hospitals Trust.

Mitka, M. 2007. Face masks, respirators might help during pandemic flu outbreak. *Journal of the American Medical Association* 297: 2338.

Norkin, L.C. 2010. *Virology: Molecular biology and pathogenesis*. Washington, DC: American Society for Microbiology Press.

Patz, J.A., D. Campbell-Lendrum, T. Holloway, and J.A. Foley. 2005. Impact of regional climate change on human health. *Nature* 438: 310–317.

Roberts, L. 2005. Infectious disease. Polio eradication effort adds new weapon to its armory. *Science* 307: 190.

Roush, S.W., and T.V. Murphy. 2007. Historical comparisons of morbidity and mortality for vaccine-preventable diseases in the United States. *Journal of the American Medical Association* 298: 2155–2163.

Scanlon, T.M. 1998. *What we owe to each other*. Cambridge: Harvard University Press.

Selgelid, M.J. 2003. Smallpox revisited? *The American Journal of Bioethics* 3(1): W5–W11.

Selgelid, M.J. 2004. Bioterrorism and smallpox planning: Information and voluntary vaccination. *Journal of Medical Ethics* 30: 558–560.

Selgelid, M.J. 2005. Ethics and infectious disease. *Bioethics* 19: 272–289.

Singer, P. 1972. Famine, affluence, and morality. *Philosophy & Public Affairs* 1: 229–243.

Stafford, N. 2008. Belgian parents are sentenced to prison for not vaccinating children. *British Medical Journal* 336: 348.

Standaard, D. 2011. *Celstraf voor Opzettelijke Hiv-besmetting* (Online). Available: http://www.standaard.be/artikel/detail.aspx?artikelid=D23B88ES. Accessed 31 May 2011.

Strawson, P. 1962. Freedom and resentment. *Proceedings of the British Academy* 48: 1–25.

Verweij, M. 2005. Obligatory precautions against infection. *Bioethics* 19: 323–335.

WHO. 2009a. *Fact sheet: Influenza (seasonal)* (Online). Available: http://www.who.int/mediacentre/factsheets/fs211/en/. Accessed 31 May 2011.

WHO. 2009b. *Global summary of the AIDS epidemic* (Online). Available: http://www.who.int/hiv/data/2009_global_summary.png. Accessed 31 May 2011.

WHO. 2009c. *Tuberculosis fact sheet* (Online). Available: http://www.who.int/mediacentre/factsheets/fs104/en/. Accessed 31 May 2011.

WHO. 2011. *Fact sheet: The top ten causes of death* (Online). Available: http://www.who.int/mediacentre/factsheets/fs310.pdf. Accessed 31 May 2011.

Wilkinson, R., and M. Marmot. 2003. *Social determinants of health: The solid facts*. Copenhagen: WHO.

Williamson, E.D., A.J. Simpson, and R.W. Titball. 2008. Plague vaccines. In *Vaccines*, ed. S. Plotkin, P. Offit, and W. Orenstein. Philadelphia: Elsevier.

Woonink, F. 1953. *Bezwaren tegen Vaccinaties: Het Perspectief van de Weigeraar*. Bithoven: Rijksinstituut voor Volksgezondheid en Milieu.

Chapter 6
Justice and Responsibility in Health Care: General Discussion and Conclusion of Part I

Antoon Vandevelde

6.1 Introduction

Most contributions to the first part of this book – with the exception of Jeroen Luyten's article, which focuses on the difference between deontological and consequentialist reasons for obligatory vaccination – defend some form of egalitarian justice. This is, however, both an evident point of departure and a highly contested issue.

In this short conclusion I will try to indicate the most salient features of egalitarian justice as it applies in the field of health and health care.

6.2 Equality as Starting Point

No matter how greatly different individuals are, whether they are strong or weak, intelligent or stupid, rich or poor, powerful or dependent, healthy or chronically ill, disabled or able-bodied, basically, they are all human beings, endowed with equal dignity. Now, if we put aside the issue of animal rights, this means, in principle, that equal concern and respect should be shown to all human persons.

However, in actual reality, we are far removed from that mark. We know that human rights can only be enforced and realized by particular institutions and that these tend to protect primarily their own members, the insiders, not the outsiders. As the quality of these institutions is very unequal, it is sheer luck whether one is born in a society (or in a family) that grants its members maximal opportunities to develop their basic capabilities, or in a society (or family) that refuses to do so. In reality, we discover much inequality between human beings.

A. Vandevelde (✉)
Institute of Philosophy, Catholic University of Leuven,
Kardinaal Mercierplein 2, box 3200, 3000 Leuven, Belgium
e-mail: antoon.vandevelde@hiw.kuleuven.be

Y. Denier et al. (eds.), *Justice, Luck & Responsibility in Health Care*,
Library of Ethics and Applied Philosophy 30, DOI 10.1007/978-94-007-5335-8_6,

6.3 "Why Are You Entitled to Have More Than Me?"

Suppose that one day, someone who has less than me approaches me and asks the question: "Why do you have so much more than me?" This is a just question. For after all, when looking at our *prima facie* principles, we are very much committed to the value of equality. However, in some instances I may tend to think that I am entitled to have (much) more than this person, because in general, two divergences from strict equality are accepted by most ethicists.

I may answer to him: "I am entitled to have more than you for two reasons: The inequality between us can be justified (1) if you would have less if there was no inequality and (2) if your relatively unfavorable situation is due to your own fault.

6.3.1 Efficiency Considerations

First, inequality is permitted in order to avoid leveling down. If everybody would earn the same income, probably only a minority of intrinsically motivated people would work hard. There would be a huge loss of efficiency in society. It would be poverty, rather than wealth that we distribute evenly. Hence inequality of income and wealth is permitted if and only if it maximally improves the fate of the least advantaged. This is the rationale behind John Rawls's Maximin Principle (Rawls 1971, 1999).

Do efficiency considerations also justify inequalities in health and access to health care? This is less obvious. We tend to think that, at some very basic level, all human beings are equally confronted with vulnerability and mortality and that society should respect the human condition at least by providing equal access to health care to all human persons. However equal access to health care is no guarantee for equal health. Take the example of the difference in life expectancy between men and women. We can try to correct this insofar as it is a consequence of the more risky life style adopted by most men, and clearly, there is some scope for health information campaign policy. However, differential survival rates between men and women are mainly due to social and natural determinants that are not easily corrected. In such cases, a differential treatment can be justified.

Indeed, the Aristotelian principle of distributive justice makes clear that equality implies that *equal cases should be treated equally and unequal cases should be treated unequally* (*Nichomachean Ethics*, Book V in Aristotle (2000)). In the case of disabled persons for instance, it may be impossible to correct nature, but then we try to soften or even eliminate the consequences of this inequality. We give additional support to handicapped people in order to permit them to achieve the most important basic capabilities. However, in the case of the difference in life expectancy between men and women we tend to think that a differential treatment is inappropriate. Either it would lead to leveling down of women's health, or it would necessitate a huge investment in order to improve exclusively men's health. The first alternative is clearly unattractive. We do not want to worsen the situation of half of mankind without improving the situation of the other half. The second alternative is no better because – apart from the information campaign we mentioned above – more important gains in health for the general population can be reached without such an exclusive targeting on male population. Hence, inequality in health between men and women does not justify inequality in access to health care. It is a form of inequality that can be justified in an overall scheme of distribution of opportunities and assets that is broadly inspired by egalitarian ideals.

Another example of acceptable inequality on the basis of the search for maximal efficiency (for the least well-off) can be found in the provision of new pharmaceuticals and new medical treatments. Egalitarianism could mean that these can only be introduced on condition that they can be provided to all patients who could profit from them. Hence, it would be unjust to apply new treatments as long as they are not accessible to all, i.e. as long as they are not integrated into the obligatory package of universal health insurance. However general provision of new treatments and new pharmaceuticals can probably be achieved much earlier if, for a certain period of time, we permit them to be provided at expensive prices, only to those who can afford them. After some time, when expenditures for research and development are more or less paid back, the treatment could be reimbursed by general health insurance. Moreover, the whole process should be thoroughly monitored by social institutions in order to make sure that the right type of efficiency is being aimed at.

6.3.2 *Individual Responsibility?*

"Am I entitled to have more than you?" In my answer to the poor person I may use individual responsibility as the basis for justification: "Maybe I work harder than you. If I make more efforts than you, why couldn't I have more?"

Inequalities based on some form of merit are supposed to be just(ified). They do not need compensation. Arbitrary inequalities on the other hand for instance between citizens of poor and rich countries – are to be compensated. Chance or choice? It makes a difference from an egalitarian perspective. Responsibility-sensitive egalitarianism should create equality of opportunities rather than equality of outcomes. It should offer people the opportunity to develop fully their capabilities. Whether people make good use of these opportunities is their own responsibility.

However, application of the cut between chance and choice to the sphere of health and health care is tricky. Of course, some inequalities in health are the result of bad choices. Some people are obviously not responsive to sound health advice. Their bad health is caused by an imprudent life style and this is a matter of personal responsibility. From a liberal, anti-perfectionist perspective, society should inform people about health risks, but should not compensate people for their stupid choices.

However, many authors have shown that it is difficult in actual practice to disentangle choice and circumstances. Most ethicists are not inclined to go into deep metaphysical considerations about freedom and determinism. They rather try to find a practical thumb rule, like Shlomi Segall's proposal: "an individual is responsible for an outcome if it would be unreasonable for society to expect the individual to avoid it" (Segall 2010, p. 20). However, like Daniel Hausman shows in his article in this volume, the appeal to reasonableness is far from solving all problems in this respect.

Many of our choices seem to be determined by circumstances that we do not control. One of the most striking examples of this phenomenon in the sphere of health is the social gradient Michael Marmot discovered in his Whitehall Study (Marmot 2004). Marmot found that life expectancy and the occurrence of health problems among British civil servants whose health condition has been followed during 25 years reflects almost exactly the social hierarchy on the work place and in remuneration. We knew already for a long time that poverty makes sick, but these civil servants were not poor. They were all white collar workers, in stable employment. Apparently, it is not just poverty, but inequality in itself that makes sick. Marmot wages the hypothesis that the social gradient in mortality and in morbidity that he discovers among British civil servants is to a large extent determined by the degree of control they have on their environment. A lower place in the social hierarchy simply means a lack of control and hence a lack of free choice. Responsibility-sensitive justice cannot blame these people, simply because their health is determined by circumstances beyond their control. To the extent that society can hardly function without some form of social hierarchy, it is predictable that public policy can only mitigate, but never eliminate the ensuing inequality of health.

Luck egalitarianism is the ethical theory that tries most consistently to track individual responsibilities. However it has to face the abandonment objection (Anderson 1999). If someone gets into a life-threatening situation due to his own imprudence, should we then abandon him to his fate? Our spontaneous intuition revolts against this suggestion. Even Shlomi Segall, the most audacious defender of luck egalitarianism in recent philosophical literature, admits that we cannot refuse to help the smoker with lung cancer or the drunken driver who has been injured in an accident. When our most fundamental needs are at stake, the question of individual responsibility does not apply anymore. Of course, this concession severely restricts the scope of luck egalitarianism, as it only applies beyond a certain threshold of basic needs.

6.4 Conclusion

Ultimately, the policy conclusions of the various theories of Norman Daniels, Shlomi Segall and Ronald Dworkin concerning the provision of health care diverge only marginally (Daniels 2008; Segall 2010; Dworkin 2000). All of them agree that smokers with health problems should not be abandoned, but that they should be made to pay for their unhealthy life style through high taxes on tobacco. Also, all of them seem to advocate a more or less generous system of compulsory health insurance, eventually to be supplemented by optional private insurances. Maybe this convergence is not so surprising, as they all refer to a form of egalitarianism that is not merely formal.

However the rise of very expensive forms of individualized medicine in the near future will challenge these theories of egalitarian justice ever more seriously. Probably the hardest choices about the use of scarce resources in health care will concern medical decisions at the beginning and at the end of life. Already at this moment, prenatal genetic diagnosis makes it possible to predict chromosomal deficiencies of the baby to be born. Does egalitarian justice require solidarity with parents who, knowingly and willingly, choose to give birth to a handicapped baby? And what does justice require towards the end of life? Medicine has become capable to delay natural death for a very long period, at a considerable financial cost for society and with important emotional and (often) financial consequences for the family. Do we as individuals become morally required to take up responsibility for the moment we will die? Is there, in some occasions, a duty to die? These are the issues that are discussed in the second part of this volume.

References

Anderson, E. 1999. What is the point of equality? *Ethics* 109: 287–337.

Aristotle. 2000. *Nichomachean ethics*. Trans. and ed. R. Crisp. Cambridge: Cambridge University Press.

Daniels, N. 2008. *Just health – Meeting health needs fairly*. Cambridge: Cambridge University Press.

Dworkin, R. 2000. Justice and the high cost of health. In Id., *Sovereign virtue – The theory and practice of equality*, 307–319. Cambridge: Harvard University Press.

Marmot, M. 2004. Social causes of social inequalities in health. In *Public health, ethics, and equity*, ed. S. Anand, F. Peter, and A. Sen, 37–62. Oxford: Oxford University Press.

Rawls, J. 1971. *A theory of justice*. Cambridge: Harvard University Press.

Rawls, J. 1999. *A theory of justice* (rev. ed.). Cambridge: The Belknap Press of Harvard University Press.

Segall, S. 2010. *Health, luck and justice*. Princeton: Princeton University Press.

Part II
Ethics of End-of-Life Care

Chapter 7
Is There a Duty to Die in Europe? If Not Now, When?

John Hardwig

7.1 Introduction

We have invented a new kind of death in the last 60 years. This new kind of death makes a profound difference – ethically, legally, socially, theologically and philosophically – and urges us to reflect on the implications of this new death. Some 15 years ago, I posed the question "Is There a Duty to Die?" (Hardwig 1997) to which I argued that there is.

I think there has been a duty to die for millennia. But within wealthier societies in more recent times, it has usually been quite rare, requiring very unusual circumstances. One thinks of a captured secret agent who is afraid that under torture she will give up too much information, or of Captain Oates, a member of Scott's expedition to the South Pole, who walked out into a raging blizzard when he became too ill to continue. Both commit suicide and arguably both may have had a duty to do so. However, I believe that our new kind of death makes – or will soon make – a duty to die much more common. I think there is a fairly good chance that I myself will one day face a duty to die. If I do, I hope that I will be able to end my life as I have tried to live it – responsibly, and both loyal to and considerate of my loved ones.

My earlier essay is, however, very contextual. It presupposes the context of the contemporary United States and the U.S. healthcare system. I do not know enough about European healthcare systems to know whether the argument of that paper is generalizable to European contexts, though I suspect that much of it is. In the present paper, after presenting my argument in favor of a duty to die, I offer some factors that strike me as probably applicable across advanced healthcare systems, either now or in the very near future. But that will be as far as I can take the argument.

J. Hardwig (✉)
Department of Philosophy, University of Tennessee,
Knoxville, TN 37996-0480, USA
e-mail: jhardwig@utk.edu

Y. Denier et al. (eds.), *Justice, Luck & Responsibility in Health Care*,
Library of Ethics and Applied Philosophy 30, DOI 10.1007/978-94-007-5335-8_7,

I must leave it to those more familiar with healthcare systems in Europe to determine whether there is a duty to die in Belgium, in France, in Germany, etc.

7.2 The Ethics of Contexts and Ethics Within a Context

I will be considering personal responsibility for individual choices, not the design or reform of healthcare systems. Individual choices always presuppose a context and personal responsibility varies with the context. People who think about how to make healthcare systems ethically better are thinking about what I have called *the ethics of contexts.* Making changes in a healthcare system changes the contexts in which people make decisions and this often changes the responsibilities that individuals covered by that healthcare system have. Thinking about an optimally just healthcare system is an important endeavor, obviously, and the responsibilities people would face within such a system is one small piece of that enterprise.

But here I want us to consider our individual responsibilities as we face the end of our lives *in our given context.* As an agent, the context is a given for me; there is little I can do to change that context within the timeframe in which I must act. So I must make my moral decisions within that context. Granted, the context *itself* may be grossly unethical. I believe that many elements of the healthcare system in the United States *are* unethical. But I cannot normally free myself from my responsibilities by protesting: "this entire context is unethical – I shouldn't be in this situation in the first place." That may well be true, but it is irrelevant because I do find myself in this situation and my responsibilities are defined, in part, by it.

The fact that I am focusing on personal responsibility means that I am not talking about a social policy of any kind, certainly not a policy of involuntary euthanasia. My argument also cannot be used to support a duty to die on the part of the demented, the mentally handicapped or children. Those who are not competent adults are not capable of having a duty to die. I might mention in passing, however, that I support policies that permit advance directives requesting euthanasia. That, on my view, could be an attempt by a competent adult to ensure that his life will end responsibly, even if he becomes incompetent to make decisions for himself.

Two further points of clarification: First, I restrict the scope of my argument to the elderly. As Daniel Callahan has pointed out, the death of a 27 or 33-year old is tragic in the way that the death of an 82 or 87-year old is not (Callahan 2009). Although a 27 or 33-year old can also have a duty to die, such cases are much less common, much more troubling and require more by way of justification. Second, I used the expression "duty to die" because Richard Lamm, a former governor of the U.S. State of Colorado, was once quoted as saying that old people have a duty to die and get out of the way (*New York Times* 1984). That remark was widely publicized. Without thinking the implications through carefully enough, I simply repeated the governor's expression because it had currency. I will continue to use that expression here. But a "responsibility to die" would be a better expression – I do not think that anyone has a moral right that would be violated if I failed to live up to my duty to die. "Responsibility" is also just a better word, rooted as it is in the verb, "to respond." Ethics, on my view, is more about responding thoughtfully and caringly to situations than it is about following abstract rules of conduct.

I am trying to think about how to face the end of my life responsibly and a responsible ending may, I believe, include making sure that I do not live too long. A duty to die is based on harms I will impose on my loved ones if I continue to live. My argument, then, is about personal ethics, about moral responsibility within a situation or context. In the terms of my argument, the duty to die is a very intimate responsibility, grounded in the responsibility to try to shelter one's family and loved ones from great burdens.

7.3 Our New Kind of Death

When I was a boy, I was afraid of death. And the deaths I feared had three characteristic features: I was afraid that it would be unexpected, that it would be quick and that it would come too soon. Death might hit me "completely out of the blue" and it could even "all be over in the blink of an eye." I will call deaths of these kinds "traditional death." This is the death that has traditionally fueled both popular imagination and theoretical reflection. There are many tales, parables and prayers about this kind of death.

Throughout history, when people died of infectious diseases, of accidents, in war or in childbirth, this is the kind of death one usually got. These deaths were not often predictable. And, though there have always been exceptions (e.g., tuberculosis), one's terminal illness usually lasted a few days or weeks at most, from onset to death, or at least to delirious non-comprehension. The fear then was that death would come as an interruption: one's life could be cut off without warning, leaving potentialities unrealized, plans half-finished, dreams unfulfilled and young children orphaned. The fear of being bedridden for years and years did not loom large then – someone who was bedridden for any length of time usually caught pneumonia and insofar as pneumonias could not be treated, they died.

Just a little over 100 years ago, Sir William Osler, sometimes referred to as the father of modern medicine, said that pneumonia is "the friend of the aged" (Osler 1898). In the U.S., it was popularly known as "the old man's friend." But we have killed the old man's friend, primarily since World War II.[1] Physicians tell me that it is largely antibiotics and the respirator that have wrought the change from traditional death to our new kind of death.

Our new kind of death is, then, the result of the *successes,* not the failures, of contemporary medicine and we are all glad to have that medicine. I certainly am.

[1] In fact, we have not quite killed the old man's friend – the combination of pneumonia and influenza is still the fourth leading cause of death among those 75 and older (Yoshikawa 1983).

But like many other technological advances, our new kind of death leaves us facing tremendous ethical challenges. We are largely unprepared – morally, legally, theologically, philosophically and socially – for our new kind of death. Moreover, in terms of the evolution of a culture, World War II is very recent.

Of course, I may still get the traditional death – sudden and unexpected – I feared as a young boy. But the odds are against it. Perhaps more importantly, I can no longer reasonably fear a death that comes too soon. At 71, I am simply too old for that to be a reasonable fear. And death is now normally *far* from unexpected. A noted geriatrician and bioethicist, Joanne Lynn, once remarked that the average American now knows 3 years in advance what she or he will die of. And, Dr. Lynn went on to say that the average American male will be debilitated for 5 years before he dies; the average American female will be debilitated for 8 years before she dies.

Three, five, eight. Those are awe-inspiring numbers. We now live in the shadow of death for a very long time. And we should expect all of Dr. Lynn's numbers to be even larger by the time we come to the end of our lives. Better diagnostic tools will enable us to know earlier what we will die of; better treatments will permit us to live with terminal illnesses much longer. Consider just one example: We now have diagnostic tests that enable us to diagnose Alzheimer's years before any of the symptoms are observable. And it's not hard to imagine that someone will come up with a drug that would slow the progression of Alzheimer's by 50%. What a wonderful medicine that would be! But then, instead of dying of Alzheimer's over an 8–15 year period, we could live for 15 or 20 years with Alzheimer's and we could have known for 15 or 20 years before that that we would eventually get Alzheimer's.

The success of our life-prolonging medicine has brought with it a new fear, the fear that death will come too late. When I give talks about death and dying to non-academic audiences, I often start by explaining the traditional fear that death would come too soon. Then I ask, how many of you are afraid that death will come too *late*? Usually, about half of the audience raises their hands in public acknowledgement of this fear. Many of us now fear that death will come long after we have completed our life-plans, long after we know what to do with ourselves, long after we have lost all of our friends, long after we even are ourselves (between 40 and 60% of those over 80 have dementia). Barring a sudden death or sudden incapacity from a massive stroke or some such, we will have to face very difficult decisions as we approach the end of our lives. We will need to strategize ways to avoid a death that comes too late. We may have to take very active steps if we are to avoid a death that comes too late.

7.4 Avoiding a Death That Comes Too Late – A Good Death and a Responsible Death

When death comes too soon, the tragedy is often, even usually, a double tragedy. Consider a 32-year old mother of two small children whose career is just beginning to blossom when she learns that she has a terminal cancer. Such a death is a tragedy both for the woman who is dying and also for her loved ones. We grieve both for her – for her uncompleted projects and plans, for the experiences she might have had, for what she might have become – and for her family and loved ones who must now go on without her. Her death is a tragedy for them, too – especially for her husband and her young children, but also for her parents and close friends.

Similarly, when death comes too late, the tragedy is also often double, a tragedy both for the one who is not yet dying and also for her family and loved ones. A death that comes too late is often tragically burdensome for the person who must endure (or *believes* she must endure) years of a debilitated existence and also for her close friends and family who must support her through these years when she is unable to care for herself.

My mother and one of her sisters both spent the last years of their lives sitting by the side of their beds in very nice nursing homes 3,000 km from each other. Neither was mentally impaired, and neither suffered great pain or other physical discomforts, though my aunt was nearly blind. Both my mother and my aunt found such an existence unbearable. My mother said over and over, "Why does this have to take so long? I'm ready to go – I've been ready to go for *years.* Why does this have to take so long?" The suffering of both of these women was exacerbated by the fact that neither had a terminal illness. Because they had no life-threatening illnesses, there was no end in sight. They had lived their lives, and both suffered from an overwhelming sense of uselessness and purposelessness. They were ready to die but death was nowhere in sight. I believe those years in a nursing home probably even cost my mother her life-long Christian faith.

In the cases of my mother and aunt, the burdens of a death that comes too late were largely confined to themselves. Both had outlived most of their friends and had lost contact with the others as infirmity decreased mobility, making distance an increasing challenge and finally, an insurmountable barrier. Their children were grown and had scattered across the U.S. Neither of these women's families was unduly burdened by the responsibility of caring for them. The burdens of a death that came too late fell almost exclusively on themselves. I call the attempt to avoid the *individual* tragedy of a death that comes too late the *art* of dying and have written a little about it (Hardwig 2009). Most of the generation that is dying now did not expect to have to strategize to ensure that their deaths would come soon enough and they were often unprepared to meet this challenge. My aunt eventually found her way out by refusing to eat and she was fortunate enough to be in a nursing home that supported her in that decision. My mother, however, was trapped by her religious upbringing. She had been raised to believe that ending your own life is "the worst thing you can do." Her religion let her down at the end; it was inadequate to that challenge of a death that came too late.[2]

[2] There are many versions of Christianity, of course, but my mother's case may not be unusual. A hospital chaplain I worked with maintains that none of the traditional religions is of any help to us in dying – they were, he claims, formulated to deal with deaths that are very different from those we now face.

If the generation that is dying now is unprepared, my generation should not be. Most people my age carry searing family stories about a family member who died far too late. We know very well that the best death is not the one that can be put off longest and that the last years of life can go very badly if we stay alive too long. Nevertheless, the art of dying will be a very difficult art to develop and many of us will be pretty much on our own in trying to avoid such a death. Our ministers and doctors, our family and friends, are often unwilling to help us even *think* about avoiding a death that comes too late, much less providing help in activities to ensure that we die sooner rather than later. If we are planning to do something to end our lives, many of them would rather not know about it. Although I won't see it, of course, it will be very interesting to see whether my generation has learned enough from our experiences of deaths that came too late to develop the art of dying at something much closer to the right time – neither too soon nor too late.

7.5 Facing the End of Life Responsibly

I mention the *art* of dying mainly to distinguish it from the *ethics* of dying. The art of dying is primarily a matter of prudence and discernment; it is the skill of arranging for an end that is good for the person who is approaching the end of life. But our new kind of death also forces upon us troubling questions about ending life responsibly. When death came unpredictably and fairly quickly, there was little need for talk of responsibility. And a death that comes too soon is *morally* simpler, no matter how emotionally and even spiritually difficult it may be. We take our loved one to the hospital and the doctors do what they can to avoid or postpone death. And when they can do no more, there is moral solace in knowing that we all did what we could. We grieve with the survivors and then we try to move on. But we move on without a burden of guilt or gnawing moral questions about whether we did the right thing.

Ethics at the end of life is, as I understand it, primarily other-directed. Those who are still in positions of power and public responsibility will have *many* others to consider as they approach death, but for most of us, ethics at the end of life needs to consider only the interests of family and close friends. The *ethics* of dying grows out of recognition that the lives of close friends and family are interwoven. Because the lives of others I care deeply for will be dramatically impacted by choices I make at the end of life, I ought not to make decisions based simply on what I want for myself. That would be irresponsible – inconsiderate and selfish in the extreme.

The search for a responsible ending focuses on the impact of our last years on our family and loved ones. When we can no long take care of ourselves, our care must be provided or paid by someone, and our ongoing medical treatment must also be paid for by someone. If family caregiving is desired or sought or required, the rest of the family will need to make major adjustments in their lives to take care of us.

Perhaps I need to emphasize that I am not talking only or even primarily about *medical* resources. Even if I do not consume vast quantities of medical resources at the end of my life, I will likely consume vast family caregiving resources. The care I require could easily overwhelm the "caring capacity" of my partner or my sons' families, forcing them to neglect or give short-shrift to their other responsibilities and to neglect care for themselves.

A literature is beginning to accumulate about the effects of long-term caregiving on family caregivers. The famous SUPPORT study was one of the first to document lifestyle changes and burdens of end-of-life care in the U.S. (Covinsky et al. 1994). The SUPPORT study included only patients whose APACHE score predicted they had less than 6 months to live. When these patients survived their initial hospitalization and were discharged back home, the study found:

- 1/3 required considerable family caregiving;
- in 20% of these families, one family member quit work or made some other major lifestyle change (e.g., relocate to a different city);
- 1/3 of these families lost all of their savings; and
- 30% of these families lost a major source of income.

There is now a burgeoning literature on the burdens of family caregiving. Careers are lost and savings wiped out by caregiving, of course. When caregiving becomes extensive – and many elderly persons eventually require care 24 h/day, 7 days/week – family caregivers usually become depressed. They lose hope. Their friendships vanish because there is no longer time for them. They suffer physical injuries from the physical requirements of caregiving. They start neglecting their own health (e.g., no longer make or keep appointments with their own physicians) and their health declines. Health outcomes are worse for family caregivers who must provide more than a small amount of caregiving.

Caregiving may even have mortal consequences. The most dramatic finding I am aware of comes from a study that compared 80-year olds who were caregivers for their spouses with 80-year olds who were not. In addition to age, health, economic status, sex, education and other stressful life events were controlled for. At the end of the 4½ year study, the caregivers who reported that caregiving was stressful were 63% more likely to have died than the non-caregivers (Schulz and Beach 1999).[3] And this study is likely to have *underestimated* the risk of morality for a number of reasons (Kiecolt-Glaser and Glaser 1999). Caregiving is an independent risk for mortality. I might unintentionally kill my wife just by trying to prolong my life. How could I do that to her?

[3] See also Brown et al. (2009). This study found a decreased risk of mortality for elderly spouses who were providing fewer than 14 h/week of caregiving. These are, however, very modest caregiving requirements and the authors hypothesize that their findings might not apply to caregivers providing more intensive caregiving.

7.6 The Argument for a Duty to Die

My argument for a duty to die is simple:

1. Many medical treatment decisions have a dramatic impact not only on the life of the patient, but also on the lives of the patient's family and loved ones. When family must provide care for a chronically-ill, debilitated or demented elderly family member (either through purchasing it or by delivering it), the lives of all are usually affected in important and long-lasting ways.
2. Therefore, a patient-centered bioethics must be abandoned. A patient-centered bioethics makes treatment decisions by asking "What does the patient want?" or "What is best for the patient?" But there is no good reason for ignoring the legitimate interests of other family members whose lives will also be affected by medical treatment decisions. Medical treatment decisions, like all major decisions within a family, should be made by considering what is best for all concerned.
3. Although families have a responsibility to care for chronically ill or debilitated elderly family members, the elderly also have responsibilities to their loved ones. These include the responsibility to try to protect the well-being of their families. In sickness as in health, it is often wrong for a family member to choose what she wants for herself or what is best for her.
4. There are some burdens that are too great to legitimately expect, ask, or even allow others in one's family to bear.
5. In many cases, there is no way to continue to live without requiring one's family members to bear such burdens.
6. In such cases, one still has a duty to try to protect one's family from those burdens.
7. This duty can include the duty to refuse life-prolonging medical treatment. But it can also include the duty to end one's life in the absence of any terminal illness at all.

This seems clear and obvious to me. But some points in this argument may be worth emphasizing: I am not denying that family members and close friends of a debilitated or ill elderly person have a duty both to care and to provide for an elderly relative. My claim is that this responsibility is not unlimited and that family responsibility at the end of life is a two-way street: the debilitated elderly family member also has responsibilities to his family. Family responsibility for a debilitated elderly family member cannot be unlimited because it must be weighed against other responsibilities in a family caregiver's life and even against a family caregiver's completely legitimate claim to a life of her own – a claim to her own autonomy, to friendships and other sources of happiness, and even to some rest and recreation.[4]

If we choose to do our ethical thinking in terms of rights, my claim is that the rest of the family also has rights and that they are not automatically trumped or

[4] Incidentally, most studies have found that respite care is not sufficient to significantly alleviate the burdens of family caregiving (Shoenmakers et al. 2010; Mason et al. 2007).

invalidated by the needs of a debilitated or chronically-ill elderly family member. Put in terms of family and friends helping each other bear life's burdens, ethics at the end of life is not simply a matter of calculating what is best for an elderly family member. That kind of moral calculus would implicitly reduce the rest of the family to means to her ends.

Finally, absent mental illness or senility, chronic illness or debility does not obliterate moral agency. When I become old and feeble, I will still have responsibilities, including some that grow out of my increasing incapacity, including perhaps the loss of the ability to take care of my basic everyday needs. The view that the elderly still have serious moral responsibilities is, I submit, part of affirming their dignity. For Kant, at least, human dignity grows out of the capacity for moral responsibility. If there is anything importantly correct about that view, it is an assault on the dignity of the elderly to claim that the chronic illnesses or physical disabilities most of us will encounter at the end of life remove all significant moral responsibilities from us.

This is one of the silver linings that comes with what may be a weighty moral responsibility to end my life: I am still a moral agent, capable of important decisions and actions; I am still part of a moral community, connected to others, to family and loved ones. This connection is itself a silver lining, I believe, and it is capable of endowing the end of life with meaning. At the end of life, we *must* see ourselves as connected to something valuable that will outlast us, on pain of complete meaninglessness.

7.7 A Case Involving Issues of Justice in the Family

I offer one more consideration in support of a duty to die: death is neither the greatest evil nor the greatest burden. In fact, viewed from an "over-a-lifetime perspective" rather than a "slice of time perspective,"[5] the burdens to family members of providing care for a patient can easily be far greater than the burdens to the patient of foregoing this care. Consider the following case, a case with which I was familiar:

> An 87-year-old woman was dying of congestive heart failure. Her APACHE score predicted that she had less than a 50 percent chance to live for another six months. She was lucid, assertive, and terrified of death. She very much wanted to live and kept opting for rehospitalization and the most aggressive life-prolonging treatment available. That treatment successfully prolonged her life (though with increasing debility) for nearly two years. Her 55-year-old daughter was her only remaining family, her sole caregiver, and the main source of her financial support. The daughter duly cared for her mother. But before her mother died, her illness had cost the daughter all of her savings, her home, her job, and her career.

Consider which is the greater burden, the burden would you more hope to avoid: (a) to lose a 50% chance of 6 more months of life at age 87? Or (b) to lose all your savings, your home, your job and your career at age 55?

[5] I borrow this terminology from Veatch (1988).

To most people, the answer is very clear: (b) is the burden one hopes most to be able to avoid. And with reason: lost savings cannot be recouped starting at age 55. New careers are also difficult to establish then; indeed, it is difficult for many to even find a financially comparable job at that age. Home loans are almost impossible to arrange at that age, especially with no savings. So, the rest of the daughter's life will be significantly affected by her mother's decisions about her healthcare. My argument in favor of a duty to die might, then, also be cast in terms of justice within the family. At least this: on most people's assessment, the mother's decisions impose greater burdens on her daughter to avoid lesser burdens for herself. When we consider questions of justice and health care, it is morally myopic to overlook fairness to family caregivers.

7.8 Deciding Who Has a Duty to Die

A very weighty problem of moral judgment that has not yet been answered is: "Who has a duty to die? And when?" There will not, I think, be simple, universally-applicable answers to such questions. Answers will have to be very particular and individualized, depending on the person, on the situation of her family, on the relationships within the family, etc. That having been said, the following ten considerations nevertheless deserve reflection[6]:

1. There is more likely to be a duty to die when prolonging your life will impose greater burdens – emotional burdens, extensive caregiving, disruption of life plans, and financial hardship – on your family and loved ones. This is the fundamental insight underlying a duty to die. In determining what is "too much of a burden," an "over-a-lifetime perspective" rather than a "slice of time perspective" is appropriate
2. A duty to die is more likely if your loved ones' lives have already been difficult or impoverished (not just financially) – if they have had only a small share of the good things that life has to offer (especially if through no fault of their own).
3. There is more likely to be a duty to die to the extent that your loved ones have already made great contributions – perhaps even sacrifices – to make your life a good one, especially if you have not made similar sacrifices for their well-being or for the well-being of other members of your family.
4. A duty to die is more likely to the extent that you have already lived a full and rich life. You have already had a full share of the good things life offers.
5. Even if one has not lived a full and rich life, there is more likely to be a duty to die as one grows older. As we age, we give up less by giving up our lives, if only because we will sacrifice fewer years of life and a smaller portion of our life plans.

[6] With only slight modifications, this is the list of considerations previously published in Hardwig (1997).

6. To the extent that you can make a good adjustment to illness or handicapping condition, there is less likely to be a duty to die. A good adjustment means that less sacrifice will be required of loved ones and there is more compensating interaction for them.[7]
7. There is less likely to be a duty to die if you can still make significant contributions to others, especially to members of your family. The burdens to family members are not only or even primarily financial, neither are contributions to them. However, the old and those who have terminal illnesses must bear in mind that the loss their family and loved ones will feel when they die cannot be avoided, only postponed.
8. There is more likely to be a duty to die to the extent that the part of you that is loved will soon be gone or seriously compromised. There is also more duty to die when you are no longer capable of giving love. Part of the horror of Alzheimer's or Huntington's, again, is that it destroys the person we loved, leaving a stranger and eventually only a shell behind. By contrast, someone can be seriously debilitated and yet clearly still be the person we love.
9. There is more likely to be a duty to die to the extent that you have lived a relatively lavish lifestyle instead of saving for illness or old age.
10. Greater ties of deep affection and loyalty increase the likelihood of a duty to die. As far as my present argument goes, there is no duty to die for anyone who is all alone at the end of life. But perhaps somewhat paradoxically, there is a greater duty to die for those who have families bound together by deep ties of affection, loyalty to each other and/or a strong sense of familial responsibility. If I outlive my partner, and I knew my sons had no concern about what happens to me and would not try to help me at the end of my life, I would no longer have to consider how to die responsibly. There would then be no one whose life would be significantly impacted by how I lived or died.

7.9 Factors that Might Increase the Duty to Die in Europe

Finally, we come to the question of whether any of this is applicable in European contexts. Different healthcare and social welfare systems bring with them different personal responsibilities. To some extent, the citizens of all democracies face decisions about how much social insurance to provide against life's misfortunes and whether to discharge collectively or individually our responsibilities to provide for the needs of the less fortunate. We must be careful here, however: the less fortunate may not be the debilitated elderly. As we have seen, they may be the *family* of the elderly.

[7] Still, we must also recognize that some diseases – Alzheimer's or Huntington's chorea – will eventually take their toll on our loved ones no matter how courageously, resolutely, even cheerfully we might manage to face that illness.

The culture of the United States has always had a strong individualistic streak and it seems that we are now moving toward an even greater emphasis on individual responsibility. Americans aren't much on solidarity. By contrast, most European countries support a much stronger social safety net. If I am correct, the American healthcare, welfare and retirement systems make a duty to die much more common today in the U.S. than it is in most Western European countries. That is one of the generally unnoticed features of a commitment to individual responsibility. With a weaker social safety net, the burdens of old age fall much more unevenly and heavily on some individuals and families than on others.

I believe a duty to die emerged earlier in the U.S. due to our individualistic culture, our fascination with high-tech medicine, and the quirks and defects of our healthcare system. But the data suggest that European countries will soon face the kinds of healthcare cost problems that prevail in the U.S. today: Though most European countries spend a far smaller percentage of their GDP on healthcare (and get better health outcomes for their expenditures), I do not think there is *any* highly-developed country in which healthcare does not consume an increasing percentage of GDP. Thus, the problem of increasingly expensive healthcare is not limited to the U.S. nor is it due entirely to the failures of the American healthcare system. Obviously, no country can devote an increasing percentage of its GDP to healthcare indefinitely.

So I doubt that a fairly widespread duty to die is due solely to the peculiarities of the United States and its healthcare system. But the question in most European contexts is not so much whether a duty to die is common right now. Rather, it is whether the healthcare and pension systems now in place can be sustained at a level that would prevent a fairly common duty to die from arising in Europe, as well.

I conclude this paper by listing four factors that have increased the duty to die in the United States. I think most are generalizable to other advanced healthcare systems. If not yet, then quite soon, I would think.

7.9.1 Our New Kind of Death

Our new kind of death, wrought by medical progress and better public health, is the primary cause of a fairly widespread duty to die. Elderly people who are debilitated or who suffer from chronic illnesses for many years prior to death need a lot of personal care. Often, too, there will also be frequent hospitalizations for intensive treatment to deal with health crises, followed by discharge and a period of increased dependency after discharge. Although such individuals may face difficult moral decisions resulting from their fragility and incapacity, we are the lucky ones. Those less fortunate died much earlier.

This new kind of death is, of course, prevalent not only in the United States; if is found throughout Europe. I think it will pose increasingly difficult problems for the allocation of resources. Although I am more concerned here with family resources than a country's resources, all countries' pooled healthcare resources will be strained by the new death. I expect our new kind of old age and dying will make the duty to die much more common throughout Europe. We can no longer pursue a healthcare system that is dedicated to prolonging life as long as we can do so, provided only that the patient wants the life-prolonging treatment. That is or soon will be unaffordable.[8] We simply have to ration healthcare.

The problem of our new kind of death is exacerbated in many European countries by an aging population created by longer life expectancies and a declining birthrate. The combination of these two demographic factors results in a much smaller number of working people who must support the social safety net for the elderly. A United Nations report issued in 2009 estimated that "by 2050, the number of persons in the working ages per older person is projected to be 2.2 in the more developed regions [of the world], implying a decrease of 48% relative to 2009" (United Nations 2009).

7.9.2 *Impossible Affordability*

Ongoing medical progress is a related cause of an increasingly frequent duty to die. I believe that medical science can keep on discovering or inventing new and better treatments, treatments that will continue to be very attractive to people with chronic illnesses or simply degeneration due to aging. The new and better treatments will only rarely be less expensive than the older treatments they replace. Moreover, I think medical science will continue to be able to invent/discover new treatments much faster than we can grow our economies to pay for them.[9]

This, I think, will prove to be true for any country's economy. Granted, many medications and treatments are developed primarily as attempts to capture a share of a profitable market or to extend the patent life and profitability of existing treatments. But putting those aside, I expect developments that do represent better healthcare and that are genuinely desired by the patients with the relevant illnesses or conditions to outstrip our ability to pay for them.

On the other hand, a duty to die could probably be *decreased* by government or private insurer decisions not to pay for these new treatments or to ration them by age. If we stop paying for improved medical technologies and treatments, or to limit the population in which these new developments will be used, there will be less incentive to develop them. Or, better treatments will still be on the market, but not available for those participating in a given insurance plan.

An age-based system of rationing healthcare would probably result in fewer elderly people living with chronic illnesses or in a debilitated state. I would support

[8] The London School of Economics published a report about dementia in 2009 that stated, "There are currently 700,000 people in the UK with dementia. By 2021, the figure is expected to rise to 940,110, before reaching 1,735,087 in 2051" (Disabled World 2009).

[9] An assumption is evident at this point: I am assuming that there will be no "cure" for aging, at least not in our lifetimes, or that if there is a cure, it will be very expensive. There will not, I assume, be the equivalent of the Salk polio vaccine for aging.

age-based rationing for reasons carefully developed by Norman Daniels (1985, 2008) and Daniel Callahan (1995), among others. It is worth noting that age-based rationing would probably *decrease* the number of people facing a duty to die. But this "relief" from a duty to die would come at the expense of an earlier death for many elderly persons.

In the United States, all of these measures to stem the tide of medical progress would be extremely difficult or impossible even to discuss publicly, much less to enact. Tremendous social pressure to make new treatments available to desperate patients is generated even before these treatments have been proven successful. Additionally, the internet has contributed in a major way to this development by making it much easier for patients to find out what new treatments have been developed and also by making it much easier to organize advocacy groups for patients with specific illnesses. Hopefully, European countries will be able to have a more reasoned and realistic discussion about the need to limit healthcare expenditures and the justice of age-based rationing of scarce healthcare resources.

7.9.3 The Ethics of Patient Autonomy and Patient Responsibility

Perhaps the emphasis on patient autonomy in American bioethics is also symptomatic of our individualistic culture. In any case, bioethicists in the U.S. have argued quite successfully against physician paternalism and against an ethics based on a *telos* supplied by medicine or medical science. The argument, in brief, went like this: all medical treatment decisions presuppose value judgments and the values guiding a choice among the available alternatives should be the patient's values, not the professional aims of medicine or the goals of medical science. "It's her body; it's her life, so she should choose what will be done to her." Most American doctors have by now absorbed this ethic of patient autonomy.

But bioethicists, physicians and patients seem not to have noticed that responsibility comes with autonomy and the right to control your own medical treatment. Probably we are all more receptive to the idea that we have the right to choose than we are to the responsibilities that come with our choices. But the power to choose is always accompanied by responsibility. So, the doctrine of patient autonomy has the unintended consequence of saddling seriously ill, frightened and debilitated people with very weighty moral responsibilities. Including, I believe, a duty to decline further life-prolonging treatments and to die as a result. However, the *responsibilities* of patients are routinely ignored in American hospitals; patients are very rarely encouraged to think about what their healthcare decisions will mean for their families and loved ones. This, too, places additional responsibility on the shoulders of patients – "If I don't consider the well-being of my loved ones, no one is going to."

Imagine, by contrast, a much more paternalistic medicine. To the extent that paternalism dominates healthcare, *physicians* and healthcare planners bear the moral responsibility for the healthcare we get. So, there are or could be healthcare systems in which doctors simply refuse even to offer treatments to elderly people when they know such treatment would result in undue burdens on their families: "We shouldn't hospitalize her and attempt to pull her through the present crisis because her family simply can't afford it and the care she will require if she survives. Even if they might be able to afford it, they shouldn't try. Caring for her would usurp too many other more important family goals."

I have been told that many European healthcare systems are somewhat more like this. To an American ear, that kind of paternalism sounds outrageous: What could possibly justify my doctor – or worse, some bureaucrat – making decisions about what kind of healthcare I should get at the end of my life? But the point here is not whether this kind of paternalism is justified. The point is the simpler one that *IF* my doctor made such decisions as I approached the end of life, then *she,* not I, would bear the moral responsibility for the consequences of my healthcare for my family and loved ones. Her decision to limit my care in accord with what is best for my entire family would free me from the moral responsibility of considering that, provided that she had done a good job in assessing what's best for my family. I would then be much less likely to have a duty to die; my doctor would have already have taken care of ensuring that death did not come too late for me.

7.9.4 "Outsourcing" More Care to Families

In the United States, insurers, both public and private, have tried to reduce their costs by limiting the reimbursement to doctors and hospitals for care of their patients. Hospitals are increasingly paid a fixed sum for providing care for patients with a given diagnosis. The hospital benefits financially if it can provide care for a patient for less than that amount. Similar incentives for hospitals are, I believe, also in place in Europe. This is a good thing in that it encourages hospitals to be more efficient and to try to eliminate expensive but only marginally-beneficial treatments. But one of the ways in which American insurers and hospitals have reduced their costs is to "outsource" to unpaid family members a lot of care that they used to deliver. This phenomenon is known as "discharging quicker and sicker." Obviously, the more involved and caring the family, the more care hospitals can require them to give – "this patient has a good support system" doctors and discharge planners often say. But families are not merely patient support systems and it is unethical to treat them as mere means to the interests of patients.

Caring families are assigned the task of providing not only routine nursing care, but increasingly-sophisticated treatments as well, including using wound vacuums, tending to Hickman catheters for IV antibiotics and feeding tubes, repacking wound dressings, and sometimes even caring for patients on ventilators. By contrast, patients with "bad" families – families the hospital staff does not trust – will remain in the hospital for much longer or be discharged to other healthcare institutions. Some families are not trusted to deliver needed care to patients, others are believed likely to steal the patient's medications for their own use or for resale, etc.

Forcing families to provide more of the caregiving has major ethical downsides. I have already noted the financial, caregiving, and even health-related strains this practice puts on patients' families. It is clearly unfair to "good" families. Loyal, caring families are required to deliver much more care than dysfunctional, callous or antagonistic families. There is also an important issue of gender justice (at least in the U.S.), because it is usually women who provide this uncompensated caregiving even if the elderly family member who needs the care is the husband's relative.

But even with all of these ethical negatives, we might still want our healthcare systems to do just this. For one thing, most people would rather be in their own homes when they are ill. For another, given adequate training, a loving family member may well provide better care than the more impersonal institutional staff. For both reasons, most patients would probably rather be sent home to be cared for by family members. But perhaps most relevant to a comparison of alternative healthcare systems is this: If, due to budget limitations, our healthcare systems are straining to provide state-of-the-art care for everyone covered by the system, we might want these systems to require families to provide as much care as they will provide, so as to use the available funding to cover medicines and treatments that families cannot provide.[10] However, by pursuing policies that have the effect of burdening families with more long-term care of the elderly, a healthcare system increases the incidence of a duty to die of those covered by that system.

7.10 Conclusion

These, then, are four factors that increase the likelihood that we will face a duty to die at the end of our lives. I believe that all are or soon will be applicable to varying degrees in European healthcare systems. If so, a duty to die will become much more common in Europe in the near future. I would expect many Europeans living today to face the issue of how to end their lives responsibly. A responsible ending will, for many, include a duty to die.

Institutional arrangements can, however, only increase or diminish the incidence of a duty to die. Institutional arrangements can never completely eliminate it. A duty to die is also shaped, as we have seen, by the history and the domestic "policies" of an individual family and thus can also be created at the intimate, personal level of one's own family. Those who have insisted "don't ever put me in a nursing home" have thereby increased the likelihood that they will face a duty to die.

So, even if long-term care is not being outsourced to families by the healthcare system under which one lives, one may have created a duty to die for oneself by

[10] To some extent, outsourcing healthcare to families is already happening in Europe, too. Again, using the U.K. as our example: "The research by the London School of Economics and Institute of Psychiatry said that caring for one person with late-onset dementia costs an average of 25,472 pounds per year. At the present time, the bulk of this cost is met by the person with dementia and their families" (Disabled World 2009).

insistence that nursing home care is unacceptable. Too much emphasis on the responsibility of children to care for their parents when they are old and frail could also create a duty to die on the individual level. Finally, institutional safety nets will never cover all of the difficulties that can befall families and loved ones. For these reasons, institutional provisions will never completely eliminate the necessity to face the end of one's life responsibly.

Nor should any society try to completely eliminate a duty to die – an attempt to do so would represent a horrible misallocation of resources. No healthcare system will be able to meet all of the healthcare needs of all its citizens indefinitely into the future. An attempt to do so would warp the culture of that society unconscionably, shortchanging other needs like education, public safety, maintaining the infrastructure, supporting the arts, etc. A sane society will not sacrifice all other goods on the altar of providing the longest lives and best healthcare that is technically possible.

In sum, I expect many Europeans living today to face the issue of how to end their lives responsibly. A responsible ending will, for many, include a duty to die. If this sounds just horrible, I can only urge all of us to remember that the duty to die is just the other side of the better health and longer lives we have been privileged to receive.

References

Brown, S.L., D.L. Smith, R. Schulz, M.U. Kabeto, P.A. Ubel, M. Poulin, J. Yi, C. Kim, and K.M. Langa. 2009. Caregiving behavior is associated with decreased mortality risk. *Psychological Science* 20(4): 488–494.

Callahan, D. 1995. *Setting limits: Medical goals in an aging society*. Washington, DC: Georgetown University Press.

Callahan, D. 2009. *Taming the beloved beast*. Princeton: Princeton University Press.

Covinsky, K.E., et al. 1994. The impact of serious illness on patients' families. *Journal of the American Medical Association* 272: 839–844.

Daniels, N. 1985. *Just health care*. Cambridge: Cambridge University Press.

Daniels, N. 2008. *Setting limits fairly: Learning to share resources for health*. Oxford: Oxford University Press.

Disabled World. 2009. *1.7 million will have dementia by 2051*. http://www.disabled-world.com/health/aging/dementia/uk-dementia-statistics.php#ixzz1OydMf0R7. Accessed 1 Sept 2011.

Hardwig, J. 1997. Is there a duty to die? *The Hastings Center Report* 27(2): 34–42.

Hardwig, J. 2009. Going to meet death – The art of dying in the 21st century. *The Hastings Center Report* 39(4): 37–45.

Kiecolt-Glaser, J.K., and R. Glaser. 1999. Chronic stress and mortality among older adults. *Journal of the American Medical Association* 282: 2259–2260.

Mason, A., H. Wheatherly, K. Spilsbury, S. Golder, H. Arksey, J. Adamson, and M. Drummond. 2007. The effectiveness and cost-effectiveness of respite for caregivers of frail older people. *Journal of the American Geriatrics Society* 55(2): 290–299.

New York Times. 1984. Gov. Lamm asserts elderly, if very ill, have 'duty to die'. http://www.nytimes.com/1984/03/29/us/gov-lamm-asserts-elderly-if-very-ill-have-duty-to-die.html?scp=2&sq=Richard%20Lamm&st=cse 29 March 1984. Accessed 1 Sept 2011.

Osler, W. 1898. *Principles and practice of medicine designed for the use of practitioners and students of medicine*. New York: D Appleton.

Schulz, R., and S.R. Beach. 1999. Caregiving as a risk factor for mortality. *Journal of the American Medical Association* 282: 2215–2219.

Shoenmakers, B., F. Buntinx, and J. DeLepeleire. 2010. Supporting the dementia family caregiver: The effect of home care intervention on general well-being. *Aging & Mental Health* 14(1): 44–56.

United Nations Department of Economic and Social Affairs/Population Division. 2009. *World population ageing.* http://www.un.org/esa/population/publications/WPA2009/WPA2009_WorkingPaper.pdf. Accessed 1 Sept 2011.

Veatch, R.M. 1988. Justice and the economics of terminal illness. *The Hastings Center Report* 18(4): 34–40.

Yoshikawa, T.T. 1983. Geriatric infectious diseases: An emerging problem. *Journal of the American Geriatrics Society* 31: 34–39.

Chapter 8
The Duty to Care: Democratic Equality and Responsibility for End-of-Life Health Care

Martin Gunderson

8.1 Introduction

All forms of egalitarianism have important implications for health care. In her classic essay, "What is the Point of Equality?" Elizabeth Anderson sketches a version of egalitarianism that she calls "democratic equality" (Anderson 1999). I argue that Anderson's theory of democratic equality, when suitably modified, is more plausible than her luck egalitarian critics have claimed and that it has important implications for health care generally and end-of-life care in particular. Anderson's Democratic equality is able to account for some of the main insights of luck egalitarianism while avoiding its counter-intuitive implications. In addition, democratic equality can explain the role of responsibility in health care while providing a justification of universal health care regardless of prior choices made by those needing health care. In this respect, democratic equality justifies a duty on the part of society to provide care for citizens throughout their lives while setting limits on the scope of the duty. At the same time democratic equality justifies a duty to care for one's own health.

8.2 Democratic Equality

8.2.1 *Anderson's Version*

Elizabeth Anderson defends an egalitarian view that is based on the equal moral status of persons and directed against hierarchies of moral worth (Anderson 1999,

M. Gunderson (✉)
Department of Philosophy, Macalester College, Saint Paul, Minnesota MN 55105, USA
e-mail: gunderson@macalester.edu

Y. Denier et al. (eds.), *Justice, Luck & Responsibility in Health Care*,
Library of Ethics and Applied Philosophy 30, DOI 10.1007/978-94-007-5335-8_8,

p. 312). On the positive side this means that all competent adults are equally moral agents who are capable of exercising moral responsibility and cooperating in accord with principles of justice. Negatively this means that "…distinctions of moral worth based on birth or social identity – on family membership, inherited social status, race, ethnicity, gender, or genes" are to be repudiated (Anderson 1999, p. 312). To respect people is to treat them as moral equals, and this has implications for how we justify our actions. Anderson spells out what this means in terms of a principle of interpersonal justification according to which

> "…democratic equality regards two people as equal when each accepts the obligation to justify their actions by principles acceptable to the other, and in which they take mutual consultation, reciprocation, and recognition for granted" (Anderson 1999, p. 313).

Interpersonal justification requires that people have a voice in how they are treated and access to participation in the creation of policy by which they will be governed. This in turn requires that people have the capabilities that enable such participation. In short, respect for persons as moral equals engaged in interpersonal justification provides compelling reason for society to guarantee those capabilities "…necessary to enable them to avoid or escape entanglement in oppressive social relationships…[and] necessary for functioning as an equal citizen in a democratic state" (Anderson 1999, p. 316). Anderson uses the term "capabilities" in the technical sense spelled out by Amartya Sen and Martha Nussbaum in their capabilities approach (Nussbaum 2000, 2011 and Sen 1984, 1992). Capabilities can be briefly described as opportunities for being in certain states (e.g., being healthy) and doing various things (e.g., participating in government) (Nussbaum 2011, p. 20). Capabilities give one effective access to goods and abilities, though one is at liberty to decide whether to take advantage of the goods and abilities to which one has access. This is important because it preserves liberty and constrains government paternalism. It is particularly important for Anderson who claims, "Democratic equality guarantees all law-abiding citizens effective access to the social conditions of their freedom at all times" (Anderson 1999, p. 289).

The capabilities include meaningful access to goods, resources and services necessary for being a political agent such as voting and petitioning the government as well as capabilities necessary for participation as an equal in civil society (Anderson 1999, p. 317). Moreover, these are also capabilities necessary for the exercise of responsible agency (Anderson 1999, p. 328). In particular, the relevant capabilities necessary for functioning as an equal citizen include "…effective access to the means of sustaining one's biological existence – food, shelter, clothing, medical care…" (Anderson 1999, p. 317). These capabilities are guaranteed over the course of a person's life regardless of the choices made by the person, so long as the choices do not violate the criminal law (Anderson 1999, p. 314). Presumably even criminals lose only those capabilities necessary for a just punishment and not capabilities such as health and adequate diet. It is also worth noting that Anderson's capabilities approach has built in limits, since democratic equality "…guarantees only a set of capabilities necessary to functioning as a free and equal citizen and avoiding oppression" (Anderson 1999, p. 327).

Elizabeth Anderson is working in the tradition of Rawls's theory of justice. In Sections 12 and 13 of *A Theory of Justice* Rawls defends a notion of democratic equality, which he characterizes as combining the difference principle with the principle of fair opportunity (Rawls 1971). I focus on Anderson's version of democratic equality, however, because it enables us to avoid the raft of objections that have been given to Rawls's difference principle and his restriction of democratic equality to free and equal people in democracies. In addition, Anderson's approach is appealing in its relative simplicity compared with Rawls's theory.

8.2.2 Modified Version of Anderson's Version

Anderson's version of democratic equality rests on the notions of moral equality, a principle of interpersonal justification, and the capabilities approach. These need to be clarified, modified or expanded. Anderson holds that competent adults are morally equal and characterizes competence in terms of the ability to exercise moral responsibility and cooperate in accord with principles of justice. If democratic equality is to result in a plausible defense of universal healthcare it must be modified to include future moral agents such as children and those who are temporarily incompetent such as persons in a coma with the possibility of recovery. It should also be noted that people are more or less capable of exercising responsibility and cooperation. As a result, it should not be assumed that all are equally capable of exercising moral agency by taking responsibility and cooperating on the basis of principles of justice. Hence moral equality should be thought of in terms of respecting the equal moral status of those who are or will be capable of exercising moral agency to whatever degree.

The difficulty of determining degrees of responsibility or of setting a minimum level of responsible agency poses a serious problem for any egalitarian theory, including luck egalitarianism, which bases distribution on responsibility (Carter 2011, pp. 543–548). As Ian Carter points out, Anderson and egalitarianism generally need a more detailed account of moral equality than they provide (Carter 2011, pp. 542–543). For our purposes, however, it is enough to note that democratic equality avoids this problem in the case of health care because it does not set the access provided by the relevant capabilities on the basis of how responsible particular individuals are.

Those who struggle to exercise responsibility and to cooperate are well served by accepting a principle of interpersonal justification, but how should such a principle be described? As it stands, Anderson's principle of interpersonal justification is too rigid and open to obvious objections. Reasonable critics such as Shlomi Segall and Lansing Pollack have made it clear that they do not accept her justifications, and Anderson's position seems commit her to dismissing such critics as simply unreasonable (Brown 2005, p. 314; Pollock 2001, p. 255; Segall 2010, pp. 27–47). In certain situations it may in fact simply be impossible to come up with justifications that all others would accept, even taking for granted reciprocation, consultation and recognition. We would be better off interpreting the principle of interpersonal justification along contractualist lines to require that people make a good faith effort to come up with justifications that are acceptable to others, provided others are reasonable in the sense of being willing to do the same and, when that is not possible, to offer justifications for adopting a decision procedure others could reasonably accept as fair. In some cases such a decision procedure could be majority vote within the constraints of certain civil rights. In other cases it might be having a voice in decisions to be made by an administrative regulatory body or presenting arguments in litigation to a jury of one's peers.

At the level of national policy, I interpret this to mean that legislators and regulators must adopt procedures that allow citizens to have a meaningful voice in legislation and in addition that they must attempt in good faith to justify the laws and regulations that are passed on the basis of background principles – in some cases quite abstract – that are acceptable to reasonable persons subject to the laws and policies even if they do not in fact agree with the way those principles are applied. There may, after all, be intractable disagreement about how to weigh competing values or how to apply them (Daniels 2008, pp. 117–133). For example, policy makers may justify a compulsory vaccination program to protect against human papillomavirus on the basis of health needs and enhanced individual autonomy, even though some may think that the autonomous choice of parents to refuse vaccination for their children should be given more weight. To demand actual agreement on application of principles would make it virtually impossible in a pluralist society to pass laws and regulations.

What Anderson says about capabilities can also be put in terms of rights (Nussbaum 1997). Just as right-holders can decide whether or not to stand on or claim a right, competent adults who are guaranteed capabilities can decide whether or not to take advantage of the access afforded. Moreover, the capabilities guaranteed by democratic equality are just the sort of vital interests that merit the protection of rights – high priority norms that trump competing interests. Anderson speaks in terms of state guaranteed capabilities and does not apply her theory globally. Nonetheless, since all states ought to guarantee these capabilities, on democratic equality, the capabilities are global in scope and the analogous rights can be characterized as human rights. The capabilities will be specified in different ways by different nations depending on available resources and culture, but this is no less true of human rights. Thus, democratic equality provides a defense of human rights that protect civic and political participation in society.

8.3 Implications for Health Care

Democratic equality has obvious implications for health care though they are not spelled out in detail by Anderson. Certainly poor health can become so severe that one is no longer able to function as a free and equal citizen. This is true of both mental and physical health. Severe depression, for instance, makes it difficult to engage in the highly social enterprise of being a free citizen. Injury, disease and various physical maladies can also reach a level at which it is difficult or impossible to be socially active in one's community. Hence, democratic equality justifies guaranteeing meaningful access to health care or, in other words, a right to meaningful access to health and health care. Individuals are responsible for choosing whether to take advantage of this access or refuse offered treatment. Democratic equality preserves the right of competent persons to refuse medical treatment.

In light of the criticisms of luck egalitarianism offered by Anderson and the criticisms of democratic equality given by luck egalitarians, it is helpful to contrast democratic equality with luck egalitarianism regarding the entitlement to health care. While there are different versions of luck egalitarianism, I will focus on the version given by Shlomi Segall, which he then supplements with other principles of justice. Luck egalitarianism, on Segall's interpretation, is the view that "it is unjust for individuals to be worse off than others due to outcomes that it would have been unreasonable to expect them to avoid" (Segall 2010, p. 13). These outcome inequalities are the sole concern of distributive justice, and society has reason to mitigate them (Segall 2010, p. 14 and ch. 8). On the other hand, strict luck egalitarianism provides no reason to help those who are worse off than others because of unreasonable choices they made. Strict luck egalitarianism contrasts with moderate or pluralist luck egalitarianism that combines luck egalitarianism with other principles of justice (Brown 2005, pp. 307–308). The strength of luck egalitarianism is that it accounts for the way in which those who voluntarily take unreasonable risks are responsible for the ensuing burdens they suffer and the unfairness of imposing those burdens on others who have acted reasonably. A major weakness of strict luck egalitarianism, however, is that it provides no reason to aid those who suffer, however severely, as the result of their own unreasonable choices.

Shlomi Segall attempts to avoid this weakness by adopting a pluralist position and supplementing strict luck egalitarianism with the principle that the vital needs of people such as health care ought to be met (Segall 2010, pp. 68–69). Although Segall refers to this as a sufficientarian principle in Chap. 4, he also adopts a prioritarian approach to health care in Chap. 8 where he defends a modified version of luck egalitarianism that he calls luck egalitarian prioritarianism that prioritizes those who are worse off among those equally warranting assistance on grounds of luck egalitarianism (Segall 2010, pp. 112–113). According to Segall, the needs-based principle follows from the equal moral worth of individuals (Segall 2010, pp. 68–69). It also follows from the principle of equal moral worth that it is unfair for people to suffer the bad consequences of brute luck, though it does not follow, according to Segall, that the ill effects of option luck should never be mitigated. This allows the distributive principle of meeting needs to be applied in the case of option luck without undercutting luck egalitarianism, according to Segall.

I have two concerns. The first is an issue raised by Kristin Voight (2007). On the luck egalitarian principle of distribution, it appears to be fair that some suffer the ill consequences of their option luck. But then, as Kristin Voight argues, this fair distribution is upset by a sufficientarian principle of meeting basic needs (Voight 2007, pp. 403–405). An egalitarian account that did not produce such a conflict would have an advantage, and this, I shall argue shortly, is the case with democratic equality. My second concern is that it is not clear why an adequately justified needs-based principle requires supplementation with luck egalitarianism at all. A well-justified needs-based distributive principle seems to adequately account for the bad fortune that society can justifiably be required to alleviate. To require compensation when needs are not at issue runs into the sort of counter-examples often raised against luck egalitarianism such as people who have unattractive features that could be corrected by plastic surgery (Daniels 2008, p. 72). Even if having unattractive features is unfair brute luck in some cosmic sense, it is not the sort of thing that requires inclusion in a universal health care system. Segall discusses such cases and argues that if a feature such as breasts that are too small creates serious problems of self-esteem it should be covered (Segall 2010, pp. 130–131). But in that case it could as easily be argued that it should be covered as a basic necessity in a particular culture.

It is interesting to note that Alexander Brown defends luck egalitarianism by adopting a pluralist or moderate luck egalitarian position that supplements strict luck egalitarianism with democratic equality (Brown 2005, p. 331). The problem with this approach is that democratic equality seems to be doing all the work. On Brown's version, strict luck egalitarianism is not so much supplemented as sidestepped. So why not simply accept democratic equality and be done with it?

Brown's answer is that luck egalitarianism is needed to capture our intuitions about responsibility (Brown 2005, pp. 314–319). I believe, however, that democratic equality can better capture our intuitions about responsibility. There are, of course, different senses of "responsibility" (Dworkin 2011, p. 103). We can be responsible for harm in the sense that we are morally culpable and can be blamed for the harm. In a different sense of "responsibility" we can be justifiably required to bear the burden of the harms that result from our conduct. Even regarding capabilities that are guaranteed, and hence for which people are not fully liable in the second sense of responsible, democratic equality need not deny that those who voluntarily take unreasonable risks are morally responsible in the sense of being culpable for the burdens they suffer themselves and impose on others. Nor does democratic equality deny that it is unfair for the imprudent to impose those burdens on others. Those who voluntarily engage in unreasonably risky activities are free riders on the prudence of others who ultimately need to care for them. The imprudent therefore engage in a subtle form of exploitation.

Democratic equality provides reason to mitigate this, even if the imprudent are guaranteed a certain level of access to health care. Hence, as is true with some forms of luck egalitarianism, democratic equality would also permit taxing certain dangerous products and imposing fees on risky activities as a way of alleviating the potential for exploitation of those who would otherwise bear the full burden of the harm that results. Along these lines Elizabeth Anderson claims that we can prohibit people from building in fire prone areas (Anderson 1999, p. 323, nt. 82). This does not require examination of the motives of individuals, as fees and taxes can be placed on dangerous products (e.g., firearms and cigarettes) and dangerous activities (e.g., mountain climbing and professional boxing). At the same time democratic equality places reasonable limits on responsibility for one's health care. While holding the imprudent morally responsible and even responsible for reasonable costs of their care, it nonetheless guarantees a level of care when those who are burdened cannot afford the costs. To that extent people are not held fully liable for the harm they suffer. Democratic equality also holds individuals responsible for the cost of medical treatment that is not necessary for participation in society as free and equal citizens.

As a result, democratic equality provides a reason for individuals to care for themselves and to find ways to cover the cost of the unreasonable risks that they take. Democratic equality therefore provides both a reason for society to care for its members by providing them with guaranteed access to health care necessary for participation in society as free and equal citizens and a reason for individuals to take advantage of the available access and to care for their own health by not taking unreasonable risks.

This gives democratic equality a way to mitigate the leveling down objection that vexes some forms of egalitarianism. Democratic equality is compatible with significant inequalities in health care, as people decide whether to take advantage of their guaranteed access to health care and whether to devote private resources to health care beyond what is guaranteed. Democratic equality does not value equality for its own sake and hence does not require equality in health or health care unless the inequality is so great that it supports oppressive hierarchies. As Segall notes in a context not related to democratic equality, if some are so ill as to be unable to participate in democracy, making others equally ill does not serve the cause of democracy (Segall 2010, p. 118).

On the other hand, some forms of leveling down such as progressive income tax and luxury tax may be required to preserve the capabilities necessary for free and equal citizenship such as meaningful access to health care (Anderson 1999, p. 326). But, these are justifiable. As people profit or suffer losses from reasonable choices inequalities in society can grow to levels that adversely affect the health and well-being of all. Recent work on public health and the health gradient provides a good illustration of this. Social, economic, and environmental conditions have a tremendous impact on health. Richard Wilkinson and Kate Pickett argue in their recent book, *The Spirit Level*, that the health gradient, including life expectancy, parallels the degree of socioeconomic inequality (Wilkinson and Pickett 2009). They claim that the research provides evidence that it is inequality itself that leads to a variety of social ills such as crime, obesity, various sorts of mental and physical ill health and lowered life expectancy (Wilkinson and Pickett 2009, ch. 2). In addition, those who occupy a lower socioeconomic position have poorer health and a shorter life expectancy than those who occupy higher levels (Wilkinson and Pickett 2009, ch. 6). Wilkinson and Pickett explore various possible causal mechanisms to explain this such as levels of stress generated by inequalities and argue that reducing the degree of inequality would reduce the differences in health and life expectancies and benefit people at all levels of the socioeconomic gradient (Wilkinson and Pickett 2009, ch. 16). Democratic inequality captures our intuitions about why this is problematic and suggests a reason why these inequalities should be reduced. The inequalities that produce differences in health status and social problems including lack of education and violence impede free and equal participation in the life of the community. It follows that democratic equality provides reason to reduce the level of socioeconomic inequality in a society when necessary to secure guaranteed capabilities include a right to health and health care.

An advantage of democratic equality over luck egalitarianism therefore is that it both captures our intuitions regarding responsibility for one's own care and avoids major problems such as tolerance for destructive inequalities based on option luck and abandonment of the imprudent.

8.4 Possible Objections

Luck egalitarians, however, have raised important objections to Anderson's democratic equality that are especially relevant to health care and end-of-life treatment. While democratic equality justifies a right to meaningful access to health care, it is arguable that such a right would have a severely limited scope. It might, for example, be argued that it is unclear on the basis of Anderson's version of democratic equality why incompetent adults and children should have a right to health care. Anderson bases democratic equality on the equality of competent adults as equal moral agents, but there are those so severely incompetent that they will never be able to participate in the community as free and equal citizens. While medication can mitigate the suffering of these people, it will not restore them to moral agency or enable them to participate in society as free and equal citizens. Anderson's democratic equality seems to have escaped the objection of abandoning the imprudent only to be faced with the objection of abandoning the incompetent.

As previously noted, it is best to modify Anderson's version of moral equality to cover moral agents generally as well as future moral agents. Another consideration is that people are more or less competent and they may be competent in some areas while lacking competence in other areas. Thus, a person may be able to participate in civic society in various ways while being incompetent to hold a steady job. In addition, people may drift in and out of competence in a particular area. As a result, it is often difficult to distinguish competent from incompetent persons. History is replete with cases of discrimination against competent adults who were judged to be feeble-minded, insane or otherwise incompetent. This is perhaps most obvious in the eugenics movement that swept much of the United States and Europe in the first half of the twentieth century. Attempting to draw lines that exclude the incompetent from health care would therefore threaten the competent as well as the incompetent. In addition, children who are not yet competent need to be covered by universal health care because they will become competent if well cared for. Health care is also necessary for effective moral agency and participation at whatever level of competence is attainable by a person.

There are also reasons based on compassion and benevolence to care for those who are incompetent, and democratic equality does not undercut these reasons. In fact, democratic equality provides support for the fostering of such virtues because of the role they play in resisting oppression. In the context of democratic equality reasons based on compassion and reasons based on fairness are compatible and not competitive. It is not so easy, however, to supplement luck egalitarianism with such care-based reasons because action to mitigate harm upsets the equality on which luck egalitarianism is grounded, just as supplementing luck egalitarianism with a needs-based principle does.

Shlomi Segall notes three additional objections that might severely limit the scope of democratic equality. First, it appears that democratic equality would not justify an entitlement to treatment for medical conditions that neither curtail the ability to resist oppressive relationships nor restrict political or civil participation (Segall 2010, p. 41). Second democratic equality is open to the objection that democratic participation as equals is compatible with everyone's living a squalid life and having significant ill health (Segall 2010, p. 38). Third democratic equality would justify health entitlements only within the context of democracies (Segall 2010, p. 41).

These problems are not as severe as might appear, however. Consider first the worry about serious medical conditions that do not curtail democratic or civic participation. The counter-example gains its force from imaging, for example, a person who is suffering from a medical condition so severely that it ought to be covered by a health care plan even though the person can still participate in society as a free and equal citizen. The problem is that conditions that cause enough suffering to enliven the counter-example also limit such participation. Keep in mind that Anderson construes democratic participation broadly to cover participation in civil society generally, including participation in the economy (Anderson 1999, p. 317).

We also need to take account of practical considerations in moving from the basic principle of democratic equality, which guarantees health care access for health conditions that limit such participation, to an enforceable health care policy. In particular, types of illnesses, disabilities and disorders need to be covered that typically limit such participation even if there are some individual cases of those maladies that are mild enough not to limit civic participation. There is reason to cover conditions such as arthritis, chronic pain, and depression because of the frequency with which they limit civic participation, especially engagement in the economy, even though there are some cases of arthritis, for example, that are bothersome without affecting such participation. Although mild conditions that typically do not affect participation as free and equal citizens will not be covered as a practical matter, special provision can be made for those rare persons whose participation is in fact limited. In general, however, health conditions that are significant enough to warrant medical help also limit some sort of functioning in one's political or civil society broadly construed.

Democratic deliberation also has a role to play. Individual societies need to design a universal health care system on the basis of what is necessary for participation in their society and on the basis of which maladies typically limit participation.

Health care resources also need to be weighed against other requirements for effective participation in society as a free and equal citizen, and this is a matter for democratic deliberation. Democratic equality allows for democratic deliberation, but specifies that participation as free and equal persons is to be the guiding principle (Anderson 1999, p. 332). When resources are scarce, for instance, those conditions that are more likely to limit participation can be given a higher priority. Participation in society, after all, is necessary for the exercise of a broad array of rights from employment to education to political rights.

This argument can also be used to deal with the objection that democratic equality is compatible with everyone living a miserable or squalid life. Consider, for instance, a community in which schistosomiasis is so prevalent that virtually all adults suffer from it. According to the objection, in spite of the pain and flu-like symptoms those who suffer the illness experience they are still able to participate in a democracy and civil society as equals because they all suffer equally. In dealing with this objection it is important to keep in mind that democratic equality is concerned with resisting oppression and exploitation as well as participating in one's community as free and equal citizen. Countries with endemic health problems that are shared by nearly all members of society find it difficult to participate as equals in the global economy, and the people in such nations are rendered vulnerable to exploitation by more wealthy nations.

There is, however, an underlying issue that needs to be dealt with. How should health care resources be allocated when funds are meager and health care resources needed to deal with maladies shared by all compete with resources needed to combat maladies that affect only some in the community? The ability of people to thrive as free and equal citizens and to resist oppression is likely to be more relevant within the context of a particular nation than the rather tenuous global community. As a result, when resources are scarce in a particular society there is reason, other things being equal, to give priority to conditions that prevent some members from participation as a free and equal citizen within that society.

Anderson is concerned with participation as equals in democratic society, and Segall's third objection is that democratic equality applies only within the context of democracies. There are two respects, however, in which democratic equality applies to non-democratic societies. First, it is even more important that people have the capabilities to resist oppression in non-democratic societies, since the potential for oppression may be higher than in democratic societies. Second, as previously noted, democratic equality can be argued in terms of community participation generally and not just political participation. Even in non-democracies, people are of equal moral worth and should be treated as equal members of the community. They have a right to be treated as equal citizens, which they do not lose because they are presently living in an undemocratic nation that fails to respect their rights. The label "democratic equality" is unfortunate in this respect, because it misleadingly connotes that the theory is restricted to equality within democracies.

In summary, democratic equality provides a justification for access to health care and is thereby able to avoid the abandonment of the imprudent objection without the need to supplement democratic equality with competing principles of justice. Although democratic equality can be supplemented with reasons based on compassion and benevolence, these do not compete with democratic equality and are best not viewed as principles of justice in any case. While democratic equality provides reason to hold people who take unreasonable risks morally blameworthy for imposing burdens on others and to tax unreasonably dangerous products and activities, democratic equality would nonetheless hold it as a violation of their rights not to provide meaningful access to treatment. In short, defenders of democratic equality have reason to claim that democratic equality captures the central insight of luck egalitarianism regarding responsibility and fairness without the unpalatable consequences that require supplementation with competing principles of justice. In this way democratic equality justifies a duty on the part of society to care for its citizens in order to ensure the ability to participate in political and civic community life and a duty on the part of individuals to care for themselves to avoid becoming a burden on others.

8.5 Implications for End-of-Life Care

Democratic equality mandates that people be guaranteed certain capabilities, including some related to health, throughout their lives. This applies to the elderly, the very elderly and those who are terminally ill whether elderly or not. As previously noted, democratic equality is grounded in the belief that all persons are of equal moral worth. Elderly people and those who are terminally ill and receiving end-of-life care are still members of the community and of equal moral worth, according democratic equality. Moreover they can, unless disabled to the point of entirely lacking competence, continue to participate at some level in society as free and equal citizens and resist oppression. This has implications for a variety of issues, three of which I will consider: (1) rationing life-extending health care resources, (2) physician-assisted suicide, and (3) waiving the right to life-extending treatment.

8.5.1 Rationing Life-Extending Health Care

It is a sad fact that not all of the guaranteed capabilities needed to enable persons to function as free and equal democratic citizens can be fulfilled in all cases. Medical treatments that could extend life will sometimes be so costly that they undercut resources needed for other guaranteed capabilities or require transplantation of organs in short supply. The result is that some of those waiting for a scarce organ such as a heart or kidney die while still on the waiting list. If the government does not develop a rationing policy, the distribution of expensive or scarce health care resources will be allocated by some other means such as private insurance or ability to pay. One way or another, scarce and expensive resources are allocated, and this amounts to rationing, either explicit or implicit.

Democratic equality does not tell us precisely what rationing policy ought to be adopted, but it does provide useful background principles. The most important is that rationing policies need to treat people as having equal moral worth throughout the course of their lives. Democratic equality would not, for instance, countenance using criteria of social worth such as those used by the infamous Seattle Life or Death Committee set up in 1960s by the Seattle Artificial Kidney Center to determine who would have access to the newly invented dialysis machine (Alexander 1962). Democratic equality contrasts sharply with luck egalitarianism in such cases, since luck egalitarianism would require some mechanism to take into account the responsibility of the individual for his or her medical condition. One of Anderson's main objections to luck egalitarianism is the need for intrusive investigation to determine responsibility for the burdens one suffers (Anderson 1999, p. 310).

In addition, rationing decisions should be made democratically on the basis of enabling free and equal participation in community life. Democratic equality supports the view of those who argue that rationing decisions should be made at the policy level where they are open to public inputs rather than by individual doctors or health care providers even though they are the ones who apply the policy. This requires a move to explicit rationing, as opposed to the implicit rationing of the market. Democratic equality is compatible with the adoption of medical criteria for determining which treatments will be funded, as opposed to who will receive treatments. In particular, the use of quality-adjusted life years (QALYs) and cost-benefit analysis could be used as criteria. Treatments are evaluated on the basis of QALYs in terms of both how much improvement they would make for a particular sort of patient and how many additional years of life would be gained by the treatment. Treatments can then be assigned a cost per QALY for purposes of allocating resources and rationing.

Rationing on the basis of age is far more controversial, and democratic equality provides reasons for caution. In a society in which the elderly face discrimination in employment and live in a culture that is pervaded by the value of youth rationing medical care on the basis of age can exacerbate the discrimination the elderly already face. From the point of view of democratic equality, it is important to prevent age from becoming the basis of an oppressive hierarchy in which the elderly are treated as having less moral worth than the young.

Age, however, can be an indirect factor in rationing because of the way in which it might be relevant either in determining need or in calculating the likelihood of medical success. In the United States, for example, between 1997 and 2007 the 10-year patient survival rate for heart transplant recipients between the ages of 35 and 49 was 59%, while the survival rate for recipients at least 65 years old was 46.9% (U.S. Department of Health and Human Services Organ Procurement and Transportation Network 2009). In such cases age may be a factor in determining the likelihood of success of the operation, although there may be exceptions in the case of younger persons who have health problems that make success less likely. Of course, rationing sometimes favors the elderly. When flu vaccine is rare there is some reason to give preference to the elderly first who may be more likely to die from flu. Even here, however, it should be noted that younger people with chronic lung ailments might warrant priority on the list to receive flu vaccine. Using age as one factor to determine whether treatment is medically warranted on the basis of likelihood of success should be distinguished from using age itself as a criterion for rationing. The former is justified on democratic equality, but not the latter.

It might be objected that in a situation where there are far more people needing heart transplants than there are available organs, it is simply unreasonable to transplant a heart in a 70-year old patient when it means that a 40-year old patient will die. Ronald Dworkin, for example, states that it is reasonable on grounds of fairness to save the life of one young man rather than two older men because "they have already lived substantial lives and he has not" (Dworkin 2011, p. 282). This is reasonable if we see human dignity and equality in terms of having a life as a project that one creates since the elderly have had more of a chance to succeed at their life projects. It is not so reasonable, however, if moral equality is seen in terms of being a moral agent or a potential moral agent. Also, it will not do to say that age-based rationing is reasonable because giving the younger person the transplant purchases more years of useful life. That line of argument has the unfortunate consequence that the younger a person is the more justification there is for a transplant. But, it is far less plausible to say that we should prefer a 40-year-old person to a 45-year old for purposes of a heart transplant because of a slightly longer life expectancy.

Norman Daniels provides a more plausible justification for age-based rationing of scarce health resources (Daniels 1988, ch. 5 and Daniels 2008, ch. 6). Daniels argues that we need to consider birth cohorts, rather than age groups. Age groups are groups of people at various ages (30-year olds, 40-year olds, etc.). Birth cohorts are groups born at the same time. Birth cohorts move through all of the different age groupings together (Daniels 1988, pp. 12–14). Age-based rationing can be given a contractualist justification, according to Daniels, if we take account of birth cohorts (Daniels 1988, pp. 85–91). Daniels adopts what he calls the "prudential lifespan account" and asks what prudent deliberators would decide for distribution of medical resources over the course of their lives if they did not know their age or view of the good life (Daniels 1988, pp. 56–63). People who deliberate under these constraints have reason to prefer that scarce medical resources be given to the young so that they will increase their chance of living a normal lifespan (Daniels 1988, pp. 53 and 86). On Daniels's view, this is not unjust age discrimination because people who live a normal lifespan go through all of the stages of life as a cohort. As long as birth cohorts are treated equally from one generation to the next, rationing based on age need not be unjust (Daniels 1988, p. 98). This does not eliminate the charge that age-based rationing is unjust discrimination, however. It is true that it would be prudent for a person behind Daniels's version of the veil of ignorance to design health policies that maximize the potential for a normal lifespan including rationing of scarce health care resources based on age. It does not follow, however, that it is the best policy for an actual community dealing with issues of age discrimination. Justice is not to be grounded ultimately in prudence, according to democratic equality.

Since, on democratic equality, all persons have equal moral worth regardless of their age, they do not lose the right to needed medical care because they have become elderly. As a result, when organs are scarce they should be allocated on the basis of criteria related to medical diagnosis and prognosis. Moreover, they should not be allocated on the basis of criteria that exacerbate already existing patterns of discrimination. As previously noted, there may be medical reasons based on such factors as 5-year survival rates to give an organ to a person who is 45 rather than 70, but age itself is not to be appealed to as the deciding factor.

8.5.2 Physician-Assisted Suicide

A variety of reasons have been offered for prohibiting physician-assisted suicide. Those who oppose it offer a variety of reasons including the basis of the state's interest in life, the sacredness of life, and potential harm to the reputation of the medical profession. Those who argue in favor of assisted suicide often appeal to the value of ending suffering or to individual autonomy. Democratic equality offers further support for autonomy-based arguments in support of the right to assisted suicide. According to democratic equality, policies regulating assisted suicide should be evaluated in large part on the basis of what sort of legislation is necessary to enable individuals to resist oppression. Certainly it is a form of oppression to be coerced or manipulated into living or dying on the basis of values that one does not share. Thus, democratic equality provides a fairness-based reason to adopt standards that ensure that people will be able to freely choose whether to forgo life-extending treatment or even to seek assisted suicide. At the same time, however, democratic equality provides strong reason to adopt adequate safeguards to ensure that people are not forced into refusing medical care or opting for assisted suicide.

It is also important that democratic equality provides reason to supply those who are approaching the end of life with sufficient medical resources that they are not driven into refusing available life-extending treatment or, if legal, physician-assisted suicide to avoid treatable pain and suffering or becoming a burden. This includes providing access to a range of comfort care including effective analgesics and mental health therapy. It also includes providing access to life-extending medical treatment provided that it is not ruled out by the necessity of a justifiable rationing scheme. Over a third of those seeking lethal medication under Oregon's Death with Dignity Act cited the desire to avoid being a burden on friends and family as a reason for their request, and 3% citied the cost of medical treatment (Oregon Department of Health and Human Services 2006, p. 23). This is a serious problem, especially in the United States where severe illness can bankrupt a family. Family caregivers also experience significant stress and often suffer health-related problems. There are good reasons based on democratic equality for providing enough health care that those who care for family members approaching death will not be physically, financially and emotionally exhausted and will have sufficient capabilities for functioning as free and equal citizens. While democratic equality guarantees access to the sorts of medical resources that might reduce the motivation for physician-assisted death, it also provides strong reasons to adopt safeguards to ensure that people are not manipulated into choosing to die, whether by refusing treatment or assisted suicide.

This contrasts with some forms of luck egalitarianism. Those who are denied resources from society because their misfortune is the result of bad option luck may end up seeking assisted suicide when they otherwise would have continued to live. To avoid this problem luck egalitarianism needs to be supplemented with another principle such as meeting basic needs or democratic equality itself. But these additional principles tend to simply supplant or even undermine luck egalitarianism, as was previously argued.

8.5.3 Relinquishing the Right to Health Care

It might be argued that people should be able to permanently waive or relinquish their right to health care. Some might want to do this so that they can take unreasonable risks without having to pay a fee or becoming a burden to caregivers. Others might also be willing to forgo the right to health care in order to avoid having to pay taxes or insurance premiums. This is compatible with luck egalitarianism, but in the case of life-extending treatment and treatment necessary to prevent severe suffering it is not compatible with democratic equality. Shlomi Segall advocates a system of universal health care that one cannot opt out of or waive one's right to health care coverage. This is grounded in his supplementary principle of a duty to meet basic needs, however, not in luck egalitarianism (Segall 2010, ch. 5). According to Segall, coverage for basic needs including health care cannot be waived, but we should not force treatment on people (Segall 2010, p. 78). This reflects Joel Feinberg's distinction between waiving the exercise of a right on a particular occasion and permanently relinquishing the right (Feinberg 1978, pp. 120–123).

Anderson also holds that the access to basic health care cannot be permanently waived, although she offers a quite different argument. Put in terms of rights, democratic equality distinguishes permanently waiving or relinquishing the right to health care along with its corresponding duty from merely declining the health care that is offered. It holds, in short, that rights to capabilities needed to secure free and equal citizen, including the right to health care, are inalienable. Anderson briefly argues for this by saying that we cannot ignore those with severe health needs because they have moral worth that no one can disregard (Anderson 1999, p. 330). More needs to be said, however. It is certainly true that we cannot ignore the moral worth of people, but what does it mean to respect moral worth? It might be argued, given the centrality of moral agency to democratic equality, that this means that we need to respect their moral agency and hence their choices. We allow people to limit future liberty in a variety of contexts such as employment contracts and other long-term contracts, however. Why not also allow them to limit future health care guarantees by relinquishing the right to health care, especially when the risks are low and the treatment is expensive? If respecting a person's moral worth means respecting his or her choices, including the right to refuse needed health care, then it is arguable that this should also include respecting an autonomous decision to relinquish the right to health care. On the other hand, if respecting a person's autonomy means protecting the ability to make autonomous choices, then it is not clear that we should allow a person to refuse life-extending medical treatment that, after all, preserves autonomy. To avoid this dilemma and still defend democratic equality, we need a different argument.

There are certainly good reasons based on democratic equality to allow someone to refuse medical care on a particular occasion. To respect a person's moral worth is, in part, to respect the free and informed choices the person makes, and sometimes a person has very good reason to refuse life-extending medical treatment. Such treatment may, for instance, only prolong the dying process or lead to unbearable suffering. There are also reasons for limiting future medical care in some cases. Advance directives, for instance, can limit medical care in the event one becomes incompetent. The right to medical care is not permanently waived or relinquished in such cases, however, because it can be reasserted and life-extending care can later be demanded, and advance directives can be revised.

None of this justifies permitting permanent waiver of the right to life-extending treatment, according to the tenets of democratic equality. At the outset it needs to be noted that people change, often radically. As Derek Parfit points out, the youth who smokes may be virtually a different person from the older adult who gets cancer (Parfit 1984, section 106). Respect for moral agency requires respecting the choices that are made by the adult as well as the choices made earlier in life. In effect, the youth who permanently waives the right to medical care is not respecting his or her future self. This lack of respect should not be reinforced by society's refusal to offer care on the basis of the decisions of the youth.

It should also be noted that permanent waiver of the right to receive medical care necessary for avoiding severe suffering or death places a heavy burden on others, even if not a financial burden. Not offering help to those who are suffering or dying requires a degree of hardness that undercuts virtues such as compassion and benevolence, and it is in the interest of society to foster such virtues. The situation is different when someone refuses care that is made available and offered. In that case those offering care need to respect the choice of the potential recipient, and the fact that the offer remains open is compatible with benevolence and requires far less hardening on the part of others.

The duty of society to provide access to health care can also be defended by appealing directly to the tenets of democratic equality. Even if it is based on a person's prior choice, to permanently deny the person's requested access to care needed to participate in society as a free and equal citizen when it is not justified by rationing is to consign that person to second-class citizenship. Hence democratic equality justifies the claim that society ought to provide meaningful access to health care whether or not people are viewed as having a right to that health care. This differs from the person who renounces his or her citizenship altogether and is no longer a member of that society. Those who renounce their citizenship are not second-class citizens; they are not citizens at all in that society.

There is reason, then, to suppose that even if the right to life-saving health care could be relinquished society ought, nonetheless, to guarantee access to life-saving health care. It is just that it would not be based on a right to health care. If it assumed that the right to life-saving health care could be relinquished, what would be relinquished is the moral status of being able to demand performance on the duty to provide access to the needed health care. The duty remains, but the right-holder moves from being a person to whom the duty is owed to being merely a person who is the object of the duty. From the point of view of democratic equality, one would no longer have the status of moral equality with those who had not relinquished their right because one would no longer be in a position to demand a capability necessary to functioning as an equal citizen (Feinberg 1970, p. 252). So we are again faced with worries about second-class citizenship. It follows that the right to life-extending health care cannot be permanently waived or relinquished. The right to life-extending health care is inalienable, though not inviolable.

8.6 Conclusion

Democratic equality has much to recommend it. It is able to capture some of the intuitively appealing features of luck egalitarianism regarding responsibility and fairness while avoiding some of the problems such as abandoning the imprudent. It is a stronger theory than objections raised by luck egalitarians indicate. Moreover, democratic equality has important things to say about health care in general and end-of-life care in particular.

References

Alexander, S. 1962. They decide who lives, who dies. *Life* 53: 102–125.

Anderson, E. 1999. What is the point of equality? *Ethics* 109: 287–337.

Brown, A. 2005. Luck egalitarianism and democratic equality. *Ethical Perspectives* 12: 293–339.

Carter, I. 2011. Respect and the basis of equality. *Ethics* 121: 538–571.

Daniels, N. 1988. *Am I my parents' keeper? An essay on justice between the young and the old.* Oxford: Oxford University Press.

Daniels, N. 2008. *Just health: Meeting health needs fairly*. Cambridge: Cambridge University Press.

Dworkin, R. 2011. *Justice for hedgehogs*. Cambridge: Harvard University Press.

Feinberg, J. 1970. The nature and value of rights. *Journal of Value Inquiry* 4: 243–257.

Feinberg, J. 1978. Voluntary euthanasia and the inalienable right to life. *Philosophy & Public Affairs* 7: 93–123.

Nussbaum, M. 1997. Capabilities and human rights. *Fordham Law Review* 66: 273–300.

Nussbaum, M. 2000. *Women and development*. Cambridge: Cambridge University Press.

Nussbaum, M. 2011. *Creating capabilities: The human development approach*. Cambridge: Harvard University Press.

Oregon Department of Health and Human Services. 2006. *Eighth annual report on Oregon's death with dignity act*, p. 23. http://Public.Health.Oregon.Gov/Providerpartnerresources/Evaluationresearch/Deathwithdignityact/Documents/Year8.Pdf. Accessed 29 July 2011.

Parfit, D. 1984. *Reasons and persons*. Oxford: Oxford University Press.
Pollock, L. 2001. Moral equality. *Public Affairs Quarterly* 15: 241–260.
Rawls, J. 1971 (rev. ed. 1999). *A theory of justice.* Cambridge: Harvard University Press.
Segall, S. 2010. *Health, luck, and justice*. Princeton: Princeton University Press.
Sen, A. 1984. Well-being, agency and freedom: The Dewey lectures. *Journal of Philosophy* 82: 169–221.
Sen, A. 1992. *Inequality reexamined.* Cambridge, MA: Harvard University Press.
U.S. Department of Health and Human Services, Organ Procurement and Transportation Network. 2009. *Annual report of the U.S. Organ procurement and transplantation network and the scientific registry of transplant recipients: Transplant data 1999–2008*. http://Www.Ustransplant.Org/Annual_Reports/Current/1114_Agecat_Hr.Htm. Accessed 29 July 2011.
Voight, K. 2007. The harshness objection: Is luck egalitarianism too harsh on the victims of option luck? *Ethical Theory and Moral Practice* 10: 389–407.
Wilkinson, R., and K. Pickett. 2009. *The spirit level: Why greater equality makes societies stronger*. New York: Bloomsbury Press.

Chapter 9
Dignity-Enhancing Care for Persons with Dementia and Its Application to Advance Euthanasia Directives

Chris Gastmans

9.1 Introduction

The number of elderly people continues to increase worldwide. Over the past decades, the growth of the aged population has been particularly notable for the oldest-old individuals, those who are 85 years and older (Christensen et al. 2009). This group will continue to grow significantly over the next decades (United Nations 2004). Given that the elderly are especially prone to suffer from dementia (Corrada et al. 2010; Prince and Jackson 2009), many countries will be confronted with a rising number of people with dementia. It is estimated that the population suffering from dementia will double every 20 years to 42.3 million by 2020, 81.1 million by 2040, and 113 million by 2050 (Ferri et al. 2005; Prince and Jackson 2009).

This demographic evolution has prompted an important societal interest in dementia. This societal interest, together with the experience of many people of being confronted with aging parents with dementia, has increased clinical interest in early diagnosis of dementia and even presymptomatic testing to determine one's risk for developing dementia. These developments were accompanied by advances in genomics, biomarkers, neuroimaging, and refinements in neuropsychology (Draper et al. 2010; Brodaty et al. 2011). Early diagnosis of dementia has some benefits, especially with regard to the autonomy of patients. Patients with dementia recognize early on what is happening, and they can foresee what lies in the future. This offers people the possibility of writing an advance directive while they still have the necessary capacities to do so. In this way, orientations for future care in case of incompetence can be provided (de Boer et al. 2010a). But these opportunities also bring challenges to these affected people. They must adjust emotionally to

C. Gastmans (✉)
Centre for Biomedical Ethics and Law, Catholic University of Leuven,
Kapucijnenvoer 35, box 7001, 3000 Leuven, Belgium
e-mail: Chris.Gastmans@med.kuleuven.be

Y. Denier et al. (eds.), *Justice, Luck & Responsibility in Health Care*,
Library of Ethics and Applied Philosophy 30, DOI 10.1007/978-94-007-5335-8_9,

a condition that will result in loss of mental competence, and they must learn to deal with a complicated future perspective (Draper et al. 2010). Moreover, they have to deal with a lot of uncertainties. The time of onset of symptoms and decline to a dependent state are inexact. Perhaps the most difficult prediction involves whether quality of life will be compromised by the development of dementia, at least during the early and middle stages (Draper et al. 2010).

The demographic as well as clinical evolutions regarding the prevalence, diagnosis, and treatment of dementia result in important new responsibilities for elderly people, in general, and people with dementia, in particular. How do they deal with the risk of being affected by dementia? What do they think about the quality of their life with dementia and about their subsequent end of life? What are their opinions about vulnerability and dignity in case of dementia? What arrangements do they want to make with their family about the care they will need when they become more dependent? What do they consider to be 'good care' and 'good death' for persons with dementia? What do they consider to be their own responsibility in 'preparing for the future'? Do they want to write advance directives in order to plan their life and death after they become incompetent? What do they think about legal regulations regarding patients' rights, advance directives, euthanasia, and assisted suicide, and what do these legal frameworks mean for their own situation?

In this chapter, we will propose a comprehensive clinical-ethical framework that addresses the above-mentioned questions about end-of-life care for persons with dementia. First, we briefly outline the general philosophical-ethical background from which we developed our framework. Against this background, we identify three cornerstone concepts that must be observed in an ethical approach on end-of-life care for persons with dementia: vulnerability, care, and dignity. A central topic that is used in this chapter in order to make our ethical evaluation more concrete is that of advance euthanasia directives.

9.2 The Principles Approach

Medical ethics has undergone spectacular growth over the last few decades (Beauchamp and Childress 2009). Most work in medical ethics grew almost entirely from the field of acute care medicine and medical technology (Moody 1992). From the viewpoint of principlism, the dominant model in medical ethics, an ethical problem can be considered to be one of rights and duties. These rights and duties can be expressed at a theoretical level as conflicting principles, namely respect for autonomy, non-maleficence, beneficence, and justice (Beauchamp and Childress 2009). These theoretical principles form the basis for finding a solution to clinical-ethical problems and for determining what is or is not relevant from an ethical point of view. They can be used to develop possible standard procedures, which – when followed strictly – can result in a defendable solution for clinical-ethical problems. Principlism exhibits all the characteristics of an ethical spirit of abstraction that focuses on identifying, categorizing and solving problems, and the abstraction of concrete persons and contexts, etc. (Gastmans 2002).

As Moody (1992) pointed out that an important feature of the principle approach is its time-limited or action-focused quality. The central question is always: 'What is to be done?' That is, what act or decision is to be taken, under what intentions, and with what foreseeable consequences? The primary focus is a specific, delimited act or choice, not for example, a dynamic process of care or questions about someone's attitudes or character. According to Moody, what is missing in the principle approach is an appreciation of the more process-oriented, intuitive, and interpersonal ingredients of ethical decision making: the role of a person's character, the importance of lived experience, and the importance of interpretation and communication. 'Everyday ethical problems,' as they appear in elderly care, chronic care, and end-of-life care processes seem to be neglected by the principle approach, states Moody (1992). Hence, a broader and more comprehensive ethical approach is needed.

9.3 An Interpretative Dialogue Based on Lived Experience and Normativity

The scope of medical ethics has broadened from being a strictly medical field to including the entire healthcare sector such as nursing care, chronic care, elderly care, management, etc. This evolution has lead to 'healthcare ethics' as the generally accepted umbrella concept. This evolution of scope has urged for some substantive methodological changes (Abma et al. 2010). For instance, persons with dementia offer a particular challenge to the principle approach. Ethical considerations in dementia care go beyond the concepts of respect for autonomy, non-maleficence, and beneficence, because these concepts are mainly developed for competent persons who can reason through the steps of ethical decision making (Kamel and Hajjar 2004). Hence, an alternative framework is needed based less on cognitive competence and on autonomy as independence and more on respect for persons in their full concrete reality marked by vulnerability, care dependency, and dignity. The ethical dilemmas of dementia care cannot be contained within a few isolated decisions made by physicians or made in a single moment of time (Moody 1992). Persons with dementia go through a whole process of care, during which they, in close interactions with physicians, nurses, and members of their family, continually have to make minor and major decisions (Widdershoven 2000). It is the whole history of the care process, of the patient, and of the relationships between all involved in the care process, that is crucial. Also important is the concrete context wherein such a clinical-ethical decision-making process takes place.

For ethics in elderly care, and specifically for the ethical issues of dementia care, we need a wider ethical perspective characterized by three aspects: (1) the lived experience aspect, (2) the dialogical interpretative aspect, and (3) the normative aspect.

9.3.1 Lived Experience

The approach that we adopt is committed to the view that concrete *lived experiences* (e.g., of autonomy, caregiving, care receiving, vulnerability, dignity, etc.) rather than abstract constructions (e.g., principles of respect for autonomy, beneficence, etc.), should be the primary guide for developing an ethical framework for ethics in dementia care (Agich 2010). Instead of trying to improve the ethical quality of care practices on the basis of an external framework of normative principles to be applied to these practices, our approach is more firmly rooted in the practice of care itself (Abma et al. 2010). Valuations, intuitions, or subjective feelings and ideas about care experiences must indeed be clarified, as they have an illuminative character regarding the phenomenon of dementia care as it exists and is experienced in everyday life. Hence, central to our approach are the lived experiences of human persons. Giving priority to concrete care experiences, which of course are not only those being shared by physicians, but also by patients, nurses, and others belonging to the care process, reveals that the phenomenon of dementia care and the ethical problems associated with it are far more complex than is routinely captured in theoretical approaches. Promoting this view, we claim that ethics can benefit from a better understanding of care experiences as a whole and the rich context wherein they are situated, i.e., from empirical research in ethics.

Generally speaking, qualitative research methods can be considered to be the most appropriate for investigating lived experiences. As Dierckx de Casterlé et al. (2011) pointed out:

> Qualitative research about the lived experience investigates how people (e.g., patient, family members, caregivers) experience their life when characterized by the presence of a specific condition, such as vulnerability. Lived experience researchers study reality as it is seen and lived by the participants. They try to uncover the meaning that events and occurrences have for the participants and how they give meaning to their situation (Dierckx de Casterlé et al. 2011, p. 234).

These studies produce knowledge that can help us to better understand the perceptions of patients, their family, and caregivers concerning good care in specific circumstances.

9.3.2 Interpretative Dialogue

An important fact connected with care is the *dialogical context* in which care practices are situated. Several parties are always involved in caring for others. Besides the patient and the patient's family, there is the team of caregivers, usually of an interdisciplinary composition. It is necessary that all those involved in care processes are motivated to explore jointly the possible alternatives. The stories told by all people involved outline the rich narrative context in which concrete care processes take shape. Applied to dementia care, Moody (1992) argues that the main advantage of encouraging persons with dementia and their families to draw up advance directives may be that the very act of writing the advance directive provides an occasion for all concerned parties – patient, family members, healthcare professionals – to talk to one another about treatment decisions. Although ambivalence and confusion may remain, the process of communication and dialogue itself is worthwhile (Moody 1992).

If we are to consider seriously the dialogical aspect of clinical-ethical decision making, then it automatically follows that decision-making processes also have an *interpretative aspect*. The analysis of a problem from an interpretative perspective is characterized by the large amount of attention paid to interpreting the viewpoints of those involved with the ethical problem. One assumes that these viewpoints are never completely clear to those concerned. Even the person who voices a certain opinion is never totally aware of the complete contents, meanings, and consequences of his or her opinion. What a person exactly wants is never really clear, especially when confronted with life-threatening situations (Gastmans 2002). Hence, viewpoints expressed by those concerned need to be gradually developed and then interpreted. Applied to dementia care, this means, for instance, that advance directives can provide valuable information about a patient's wishes and viewpoints. But like all information, they are subject to interpretation, evaluation, and deliberation, as care circumstances and the patient's situation continuously change (Moody 1992).

9.3.3 Normativity

An ethical approach is always in some way linked to the issue of *normativity*. The question of *normativity* in healthcare refers to two intrinsically interwoven groups of questions (Gastmans et al. 2011): One on the obligatory character of care (Why do we feel as if we should care?) and one on what makes care ethically sound (What counts as good care? What exactly does it mean to do good? What character should I cultivate?). Both groups of normative questions that guide our approach invoke a certain view of mankind that underlies care, that is, a specific anthropological framework (Vanlaere and Gastmans 2011). Only when the objective normative basis of care is sufficiently clarified, care practices can be evaluated and optimized from an ethical point of view. To this end, the nature of the person performing care and the nature of the person receiving care should be sufficiently clear. Hence, in our approach we intend to deepen the normative value of dementia care by referring to its anthropological foundations.

9.4 Dementia Care Considered as Dignity-Enhancing Care

What do these three characteristics of our new ethical approach mean, if we apply them to dementia care? Persons with dementia who are in need of care are vulnerable human beings. Their vulnerable situation forms the starting point of the care relationship. This vulnerability colors the care process from the beginning and transforms it into an ethically laden phenomenon. In dementia care, it becomes clear that ethics is born out of the appeal to be susceptible to the vulnerability of the person with dementia. All people involved in care relationships take up their responsibility to lessen and to deal with the vulnerability of the care receiver. The attitudes of responsibility and competency translate themselves into the act of caregiving. Care is a means that is used to lessen the vulnerability of a fellow human being or to deal with it in an appropriate way. As vulnerability and responsibility are essential components of care processes, these care processes should always meet an ethical standard: Care should respect the dignity of the vulnerable patient. Good care is aimed at the enhancement of the dignity of the human person in all his or her dimensions and also succeeds to realize this intention in practice. Hence, good dementia care can be considered to be dignity-enhancing care.

Based on the above-mentioned characterization of dignity-enhancing care, the ethical essence of dementia care practices can be defined as providing *care* in response to the *vulnerability* of a human being in order to maintain, protect, and promote his or her *dignity* as much as possible. In the following sections, the meaning of vulnerability, care, and dignity – and thus of dignity-enhancing care – will be explained in the context of dementia care. It will become clear that vulnerability, care, and dignity fully correspond with the three aspects – the lived experience aspect, the dialogical interpretative aspect, and the normative aspect – of our ethical framework on dementia care. We mainly focus on responsibly dealing with advance euthanasia directives as a specific case in dementia care in order to make our ethical framework more concrete and applied.

9.4.1 Vulnerability

Vulnerability is closely connected to our lived experience as human beings, as vulnerability is an essential part of the human condition. Harm may come from many sources and we are never entirely free from the possibility of being harmed. But besides the ordinary human vulnerability we all share, there are people who are extraordinarily vulnerable (Sellman 2005). More particularly, the experience of dementia produces such an extraordinary vulnerability (Martin and Post 1992). The vulnerability that can be considered to be the point of departure of dementia care processes is irreversible. Moreover, this vulnerability is more overwhelming in the sense of being 'total.' The vulnerability of persons with dementia must be situated in all dimensions of their being. Persons with dementia are not only vulnerable with respect to their frail bodies, but also in regard to the psychological, relational, social, moral, and spiritual dimensions of their being human, regardless of whether they experience or are cognitively aware of their vulnerability (Tadd et al. 2010). Moreover, their vulnerability is so total that it affects the feelings of respect and human dignity of these persons (De Boer et al. 2007).

9.4.1.1 Physical Vulnerability

A person is more than just the sum of rational capacities. The fact that a person is a subject manifests itself in what is the most unique, but in a sense also the most vulnerable aspect of our being, that is to say our corporality. It is precisely in the vulnerability of our corporality can we find a common element: People can lose their mental and physical health (Vanlaere and Gastmans 2011). Applied to dementia, some of the physical ambiguities are linked to the diagnosis of the disease. The insidious onset of the disorder results in complicated questions. Deciding whether a given patient has a specific dementing illness is an example of such a difficult question (Moody 1992). Up to now, the diagnosis of dementia, irrespective of etiology, has been based on a complex spectrum of clinical inclusion and exclusion criteria and on neuropsychological and radiologic results. In this way, the reliability of dementia diagnoses ranges from 65 to 90% in specialized clinical settings (Dutch Association of Clinical Geriatrics 2005; Brodaty et al. 2011). However, very often, decline is apparent for years before the diagnosis is made, resulting in a lack of appropriate treatment and care for the person with dementia (Draper et al. 2010).

Closely related to diagnostic ambiguity is the question of whether we should think of dementia as a 'terminal' condition. Even though hospice services benefit persons with severe dementia, most persons with dementia do not receive these palliative services. Cees Hertogh pointed out that, for example, in the United Kingdom as well as in the United States of America, patients with dementia are much less likely to receive hospice care compared to cancer patients (Hertogh 2006). Barriers to hospice enrollment include problems with accurate prognostication, lack of recognition of dementia as a terminal condition, and poor accessibility of hospice services in nursing homes (Mitchell et al. 2007). In order to improve the care for patients with advanced dementia, Hertogh emphasized that it is necessary to investigate whether life-sustaining interventions, such as tube feedings, antibiotics, and a whole host of psychoactive drugs, can truly contribute to the quality of life of people with advanced dementia (Hertogh 2006). Subsequently, as pain often remains undertreated (Mitchell et al. 2004; Scherder et al. 2005), more research is needed in order to diagnose and treat pain in persons with dementia more adequately.

9.4.1.2 Psychological Vulnerability

Persons are fundamentally equal: All persons share in the same *condition humaine*. At the same time, each person is an original, a unique subject that, through interaction with his or her historical and sociocultural environment, develops his or her own viewpoints. This general insight is reflected in the specific way in which today's generation of older people perceives the prospect of progressing dementia. The mental suffering that one experiences as one faces one's progressing dementia is influenced by the fear of having to be dependent on others and the fear of losing one's dignity. Many healthy seniors take for granted their ability to arrange their lives according to their own desires and needs, with only minimal assistance from others. Autonomy as a social goal does not only mean that elderly people who lose the capacity to lead an autonomous life are perceived as a 'burden' rather than as human beings. It also entails that these people consider themselves to be 'less of a person' or as people 'who count as nothing,' resulting in psychological suffering (Agich 2003; De Boer et al. 2007).

The elderly often associate dignity with autonomy, independence, and preserving one's intellectual powers (Woolhead et al. 2004). Some especially believe that the fear of losing one's intellectual capacity and the risk of being handed over to the will of others when one becomes incompetent are notable reasons for wanting to be euthanized or to commit suicide in a timely way (Hardwig 1997, 2009). Although most research supported the view that the risk of suicidal behavior is low in persons with advanced dementia, this may not be the case in early dementia (Harris and Barraclough 1997; Margo and Finkel 1990; Lim et al. 2005). Especially the potentially lethal combination of insight into declining cognition and ability to perform the act of suicide may put people in the early stages of the disease at risk. However, Hertogh et al. suggested that this risk should not be exaggerated, as psychological coping strategies could prevent people in the early stage of dementia to commit suicide (Hertogh et al. 2007).

9.4.1.3 Relational Vulnerability

The human person is fundamentally related to and enters into relationships with other persons. A human being only becomes human through contact with other persons. However, in dementia care, attention to the relational dimension of being a person can reveal another aspect of vulnerability. Most people with dementia are cared for at home and are supported by informal caregivers (family members, friends, etc.). Central informal caregivers often assume their duties in good spirits and because of their commitment to the person suffering from dementia; however, sometimes the task of caregiving can become overwhelming (Goldsteen et al. 2007; Papastavrou et al. 2007). Informal caregivers face the physical burden of daily physical care and they also face mental stress. The latter derives from several sources: grief over the loss of the person who was once their partner, father, or mother; guilt for sometimes falling short in some aspect of caregiving; losing one's temper or relinquishing care to a nursing home; shame because of the behavior of the person suffering from dementia; and social isolation. Even doubt about the course and the unpredictable nature of dementia symptoms can be a real burden.

Given the above-mentioned care-oriented diagnostics in dementia care, for a growing number of seniors the fear of becoming a burden to their relatives is greater than their fear of death (Pearlman et al. 1993; Vanlaere et al. 2007). They mainly fear that their relatives will have to pay a high emotional price when caring for them (McPherson et al. 2007; Parsons-Suhl et al. 2008). These persons may face a self-perceived duty to die for the benefit of the family (Ott 1998).

9.4.1.4 Social Vulnerability

Just as a person is fundamentally related to other persons, each person is related to a group or community of persons as well. Persons with dementia are, as is every human being, part of broader social entities, like institutions, organizations, and societies. The phenomenon of dementia affects these societal frameworks, not only demographically but also financially and legally. In all these vital societal dimensions, vulnerability can be identified. As life expectancy rises, the number of persons with dementia will continue to increase drastically. At the same time, smaller nuclear families limit the availability of adult children for caregiving (Stuifbergen and Van Delden 2011). With societal debates on healthcare rationing and intergenerational justice, how much will our society be willing and able to spend on dementia care? Stephen Post wondered whether we could afford to create state-of-the-art nursing homes for all persons with dementia who need them (Post 1994). The question of what is a fair distribution of resources to apportion toward the care of people with dementia ought to be become even more pressing (Battin 1992).

The social vulnerability of persons with dementia can also be demonstrated from a totally different perspective. In some Western countries, assisted suicide and euthanasia are legally permitted. This brings us to the following problem: How much does the societal-legal environment affect a person's decision to draft an advance euthanasia directive or to commit assisted suicide in the early stages of the disease? Making it easy for people to develop an advance euthanasia directive could be considered to be an intervention that promotes euthanasia in persons with severe dementia as a 'normal' medical practice, or it can be experienced by people with dementia as a form of social pressure 'to take up your responsibility.' In case of extreme care dependency, taking one's responsibility can easily be understood as 'a duty to die' (Gastmans and Denier 2010).

9.4.1.5 Moral Vulnerability

The basis of each morality is the human being as a subject, as somebody who is capable of acting consciously and freely, and therefore is capable of acting responsibly. The characterizing quality of the human being is the self-conscious experience of freedom from which the question of responsibility arises. Freedom appears here as the ability to detach oneself from self-interested pursuits (or from instinctive behavior) and to choose for oneself as to how to direct one's pursuits. Inevitably, there is a direct correlation between freedom and responsibility. As subjects, persons are essentially moral subjects, namely, human beings that must justify their free actions to their conscience (Vanlaere and Gastmans 2011).

In order to respect the patient as a moral subject, it is the caregiver's duty to give the patient the opportunity to make decisions concerning his or her health-related condition and care based on sufficient information. However, due to the illness, the demented person's capacity to freely make decisions is often weakened or even totally lacking. Given the decline of mental capacities in dementia, in countries such as the Netherlands where euthanasia in persons with severe dementia is legal, a growing number of people are drawing up advance euthanasia directives in which they express the wish to terminate their lives if they develop dementia (Rurup et al. 2006). These advance euthanasia directives rely on the authority of the competent pre-dementia person to govern the welfare of the incompetent person with dementia (Draper et al. 2010). However, much discussion exists about the relationship between the 'then' self that existed prior to the onset of dementia and the 'now' self that lives almost entirely in the present without any connection to the past. This distinction definitely calls into question the concepts of respect for autonomy and responsibility of demented persons. After all, who exactly is the autonomous and responsible person following the onset of dementia? Proponents of the 'precedent autonomy or critical interest' approach underline the stewardship responsibility of the 'then' self for the journey into forgetfulness (Post 1995). As a consequence, post-dementia decisions should be based on historical lifetime values and beliefs. Proponents of the 'experiential interest approach' argue that

> there can be major changes in values and preferences between the time when persons complete their advance directive and when it comes into effect. This led them to propose that the predementia person and the same person with dementia are two different people, and that any advance directive made by the predementia person is effectively directed to someone else (Draper et al. 2010, p. 78).

Moreover, the actual experiences of persons with dementia are important, as dementia involves a slow process of diminishing competence. Even if persons with dementia might be incompetent, they still have the capacity to experience their life and the context wherein it is embedded (De Boer et al. 2010a). Hence, according to the experiential interest approach, contemporary preferences, needs, and desires, coupled with the present well-being of the person with dementia should be the main area for substituted decision making.

Furthermore, both competing notions are accompanied by bias risks. If the advance directive includes choosing a proxy, it is almost impossible for the substitute decision maker to take his or her values out of the decision-making process (Mahieu and Gastmans 2012). According to Draper et al. (2010), this can be quite problematic, because caregivers, especially when burdened by care, have a tendency to report lower scores on quality of life than the patients themselves. Hence, the values, choices, and dignity of the person with dementia are also vulnerable to harm or neglect.

9.4.1.6 Spiritual Vulnerability

The fundamental relatedness of the human person is not limited to its orientation to other persons and to social groups. At the same time, it is also characterized by openness toward a spiritual context. Human beings experience at the deepest level of their existence that they are supported by and oriented toward a meaningful 'life context.' The question of the meaningfulness of life mainly arises in times of pain, illness, and suffering, e.g., in the case of receiving the diagnosis of dementia. In such circumstances, these questions change from a dormant into a very intense presence, resulting in spiritual vulnerability.

9.4.2 Care

Vulnerable people are in need of care. Margaret Walker characterizes care as a practice of responsibility, in which the different persons involved take responsibility in a process of reacting to vulnerability (Walker 2003). It is the situation of vulnerability of the fellow human being that prompts us to care for the other. In this way, care starts from the appeal to be susceptible to the lot of other people in an actual, responsible, and concerned way. Furthermore, according to Vanlaere and Gastmans (2011), it is exactly with persons whose rational capacities and powers are minimal and whose physical or corporal vulnerability are the greatest – like persons with severe dementia – that care appears to be the way in which another person connects himself or herself to them as a person and treats them as a person. Dialogue and interpretation seems to be crucial aspects of these caring interactions.

9.4.2.1 Care as Dialogical and Interpretative Phenomenon

An important fact connected with care is the relational and dialogical context in which care practices must be situated. By providing care, and the attitudes and skills associated with this activity, we enter as a person into a relationship with a vulnerable fellow human being who is in need of care. Concern about the vulnerable state in which a fellow human being finds himself or herself is the point of departure of care. Tronto (1993) referred in this respect to the ethical attitude of attentiveness. Attentive people take up a receptive position with respect to the vulnerable fellow human being: They are challenged to step out of their own personal reference system in order to take up that of the vulnerable person, so that they can better understand his real-life situation. Without an attitude of attentiveness the request for care will not even be noticed.

However, it is not clear from the beginning what answer can be considered as the most adequate and appropriate answer to the care needs of a particular vulnerable person. Finding the right answer is not the result of a general and abstract balancing of principles or of logical deduction, it is reached through a shared dialogical process of communication, interpretation, and understanding that takes place within the care relationship (Widdershoven and Berghmans 2001). It is precisely in this relational context – through a process of choice and deliberation – that goals and appropriate means for providing care are set up. All people involved in care practices are searching for answers to the question concerning the degree to which the present caring practice can be improved in order to contribute to the vulnerable person's well-being and dignity. Care practices are characterized by the unique capacity to make choices in particular situations that bring about more dignity for vulnerable fellow human beings (Gastmans et al. 1998). Responsibility and competency are the two ethical attitudes that are needed to find a good answer to the vulnerability of fellow human beings (Tronto 1993).

Care, when viewed as a way in which people relate to each other, is the dialectic of giving and taking. Care consists of the needs and wants of one person and the responsibility and competency that another person adopts to meet those needs. However, the vulnerable person is not just a passive partner in the care process. Ethically sound care only exists when it is properly provided and properly received. Care demands feedback and the verification that caring needs are actually being met. Thus, reciprocity is an essential part of care (Lindemann 2003). According to Agich (2003), care recipients show respect to their caregivers by allowing themselves to be cared for and by responding appropriately to the care; for example, by expressing gratitude or by expressing displeasure. For this reason, Tronto (1993) considered 'care receiving' to be an essential dimension in the care process, linked to the attitude of responsiveness.

The dialogical and interpretative characteristics of care will now be applied to and illustrated by the use of advance euthanasia directives in the context of dementia care. An important question to be answered is whether these advance euthanasia directives can be considered to be care instruments that provide adequate and appropriate answers to the demented patients' vulnerability, as described in previous sections of this chapter.

9.4.2.2 Advance Euthanasia Directives as Care Instruments That Require and Facilitate Dialogue and Interpretation

Within the principles approach of medical ethics, advance directives provide the opportunity for people to have their autonomy respected, as they can write down their wishes concerning end-of-life care while they still have the capacities to do so. In this scenario, respect for a person's autonomy is extended into the future when competence is lost. This scenario is an example of the above-mentioned precedent autonomy approach (de Boer et al. 2010a). De Boer et al. clarifies:

> The former decisions of a person with dementia, laid down in an advance directive, remain in force because the person now lacks the necessary capacity to exercise autonomy, and because the critical interests of the formerly competent person (the 'then' self) prevail over the actual preferences or experiences of the person who is now in a state of dementia (the 'now' self). The experiences of the demented person are not part of the autonomous decision-making (de Boer et al. 2010a).

An important presupposition of this approach is that individuals are perfectly capable of determining their wishes concerning their end-of-life care individually and cognitively, and in such a way that advance directives unambiguously tell caregivers what to do. Persons are, in this approach, mainly considered as beings with thoughts, intelligence, reason, reflection, and consciousness (Hughes 2001). In order to facilitate the development of advance directives, decision aids are presented. These aids help people by providing neutral information about the dementia process, so that they can make an informed decision (Levi and Green 2010).

We would like to point out what we believe are some clusters of problems that are associated with the use of advance directives according to the above-mentioned principles approach. We will focus on the use of advance directives for requesting euthanasia (Gastmans and Denier 2010). The first group of problems is related to the interpretation of a patient's wishes. As many authors have already pointed out, clearly expressing one's wishes and thoughts can be difficult. But also interpreting the meaning of a patient's wishes is a difficult task for fellow human beings, such as family members, caregivers, etc. A patient's wishes cannot be considered to be a given, whose contents can easily be deduced from an advance directive and which clarifies for all those involved what must be done for the patient throughout the consecutive stages of his or her care. What a patient would have wanted under specific circumstances needs to be constructed through fairly elaborate interpretative processes, based on what we know of his or her life, previous pronouncements (e.g., advance directives), and the patient's actual reactions to concrete proposals (cf. the experiential interest approach) (Gastmans 2002; Agich 2003).

Even if, as in advance euthanasia directives, the medical decision to be performed – euthanasia – is very clear, communication and interpretation is still needed. The specific difficulty resides in having to determine the moment when euthanasia should be performed. Suppose, for instance, that a person with an early dementia diagnosis has been able to clearly state that he or she wants euthanasia from the moment that he or she no longer recognizes his or her child. This advance euthanasia directive is not self-executing. The physician has to determine whether this person's actual situation does indeed match the circumstances specified by him or her in the advance directive calling for euthanasia to be performed. This is very difficult, for even carefully formulated specifications about the chosen moment of death require interpretation (Widdershoven and Berghmans 2001; Hertogh et al. 2007). For instance, how should one determine the act of recognition? There are many ways of recognizing a person. Where should the line be draw? (Widdershoven and Berghmans 2001) The fact that it is almost impossible to determine the moment of death in such cases is especially due to the development stages of dementia itself. Patients suffering from severe dementia can still have good moments from time to time, no matter how diminished these may be (Gastmans and Denier 2010).

This brings us to the category of problems with future forecasting. They refer to the fact that a person's preferences and values can change; to the fact that people's ability to constructively adapt to even the most severe debilities; and to the fact that previously communicated wishes may not reflect a change of heart (De Boer et al. 2007; Hertogh 2009). The problem with a person suffering from dementia, however, is that it is impossible for that person to reconsider the decisions outlined in his or her advance euthanasia directive. The issue of irreversibility is much stronger in persons with dementia. It may be that the aforementioned person with an advance euthanasia directive offers resistance when the action is performed. How is such resistance to be interpreted? Hence the dilemma faced by physicians and proxies: how to balance the actual preferences and experiences of the person with dementia against the patient's earlier opinions laid down in a now-forgotten advance directive (Widdershoven and Berghmans 2001; Hertogh et al. 2007; Gastmans and Denier 2010; De Boer et al.

2010a). Following the 'experiential interest approach, the well-being and interests of the 'now' self are of moral significance, and the absolute primacy of precedent autonomy seems to be wrong (Post 1995). Goering clarifies:

> This does not mean that we should never make plans for our future-selves; rather, it means that we should take care to provide for flexibility in any advance directive, with the recognition that our values or priorities may change, and due to declining decisional capacities, those judgements may need to be made by others in conjunction with our future-selves, rather than solely and individually by our presently competent selves (Goering 2007, p. 63).

This brings us to another group of problems that is situated on the level of the patient's autonomy versus the patient being related to other people such as relatives, friends, and caregivers. It seems that, in the case of advance euthanasia directives, supporting the respect for autonomy principle is much more complicated. People's wishes and values are very often of a pre-reflexive and emotional kind. Without sufficient attention to emotions, feelings of grief, or even resistance, within an ongoing, interpersonal face-to-face dialogue between the patient and other people (e.g., relatives, friends, caregivers), one risks entering into a situation in which people can easily draft an advance euthanasia directive on their personal computer, while being in a state of panic or depression, or having little or unclear information about the course of dementia. In this case, advance euthanasia directives could even increase the vulnerability of the patient, as they do not reflect a well-informed wish of the patient (Gastmans and Denier 2010).

Finally, a patient's decision to write an advance euthanasia directive has important implications for all parties involved in the patient's care (Hertogh et al. 2007). The decision to perform euthanasia at a certain moment in time has to be made by someone other than the patient himself or herself. This can create dissensions between the parties involved. This clearly demonstrates the contradiction that is inherent to the autonomy approach when applied to advance euthanasia directives in persons with dementia: To what extent can our fellow man be given the responsibility to ensure that our right of self-determination is respected?

Given the above-mentioned difficulties that arise from advance euthanasia directives when conceptualized within a principles approach, we suggest a more dialogical-interpretative approach to deal with advance euthanasia directives. As Moody says: "The heart of the matter is not to be found in the legal instrument as much as in the process of communication and negotiation which leads up to the result" (Moody 1992, p. 92). In our approach, the search for what is best for the patient should not solely focus on the patient's wishes as an isolated individual, but should always start with listening to the concerns expressed by the patient, his or her close relatives, his or her caregivers, etc., because they outline the rich relational context in which the person's care has to take shape. Understanding persons implies an understanding of the relational stories in which they are embedded (Hughes 2001). Decision making is a process of sharing the decision between all people involved. There will never be a legal instrument or a simple paper process that provides an escape from this demanding process of communication and interpretation among parties to a decision. Therefore, we suggest that advance euthanasia directives have their uses, for example, to facilitate the ethical dialogue and the interpretation process among all people involved. However, such directives in fact cannot replace communication and interpretation (Widdershoven and Berghmans 2001; Tulsky 2005).

9.4.3 Dignity

The care that is provided to persons with dementia is expected to be 'good care' in the ethical meaning of the word. But what does good care mean? We assume, for instance, that good dementia care deals with all kinds of vulnerabilities persons with dementia are confronted with. This is care that, given the vulnerable status of the demented patient, supports the dignity of the human person as much as possible. We use the concept of 'dignity-enhancing care' to name this kind of care. By using the concept of 'dignity-enhancing care,' we are inspired by Harvey Max Chochinov (2007), who uses the concept of 'dignity-conserving care.' In order to clarify this concept from a normative perspective, we should start with the clarification of the inherent ethical meaning of dementia care considered as dignity-enhancing care. Thereafter, we answer the question of whether advance euthanasia directives can be considered as care instruments that enhance the dignity of the human person with dementia.

9.4.3.1 Dementia Care as Dignity-Enhancing Care

When we look at dementia care from an ethical perspective, noteworthy is the goal-oriented character of dementia care. Whatever caregivers do must always be related to the final goal that is set. Generally, the goal of dementia care is described as the promotion of the dignity of the patient by providing good care in the wider meaning of the word – i.e., on the physical as well as the psychological, relational, social, moral, and spiritual level. As dementia care is directed toward the realization of human goals – in this case, the promotion of the dignity of the patient by providing good care – the myth of the neutrality of the caring process is radically questioned. Dementia care can be considered to be a moral practice. The ethical concern for the demented person's well-being and dignity, which is mainly based on respect for the person in his or her totality, is fundamental to the moral demand that inspires dementia care. In each particular situation, the patient, together with caregivers and family members, searches for appropriate means to achieve as much good as possible. In every care situation, the demented person, caregivers, and family members have to make personal choices and decisions based on the good that dementia care sets as a goal. Hence, filling in the content of dignity-enhancing care is of essential importance for the ethical evaluation of dementia care.

It is difficult to formulate an acceptable description of a normative concept such as dignity-enhancing care. In dementia care, the bodily aspects often come first, because generally they are most easily translated into complaints for caregivers to address. However, a caregiver who intends to approach the person with dementia as a whole pays attention not only to the physical aspects, but also to the relational, social, psychological, ethical, and spiritual dimensions of being a person. The vulnerability that affects the demented person in all these dimensions results in the dignity of the person being threatened. This brings us to the premise that our ethical reflection on dementia care is closely related to the notion of personhood. The ethical reflection on care practices always starts from the assumption of a certain view on the human person. When this view on the human person is made explicit, what is understood by 'good care' or 'dignity-enhancing care' can be clarified (Vanlaere and Gastmans 2011). Elsewhere, we made our view on the human person more explicit by linking it to the anthropology of Louvain Personalism (Vanlaere and Gastmans 2011). In general, we can claim that the care for the demented person is most meaningful when the patient is respected as a human person in all his or her dimensions: namely being related to the whole of reality, being embodied, being related to others, being related to the material world, being related to one's own history, being a product of one's culture, and being a unique and autonomous subject. In other words, in order to determine whether a caring act or instrument is morally good, one must apply the criterion of dignity of the human person, considered in all his or her dimensions. Applied to the topic of this chapter, we should answer the question of whether advance euthanasia directives are ethically appropriate care instruments that enhance the dignity of the person with dementia in all his or her dimensions.

9.4.3.2 Can Advance Euthanasia Directives Be considered to Be Dignity-Enhancing Care?

In our ethical approach, the value of the dignity of the human person is the ultimate criterion used to assess human behavior. Human choices, acts, and instruments are ethically good if they respect and improve the dignity of the human person, who is considered as a whole with a multitude of dimensions and as related to others. In this respect, three fundamental critiques can be formulated toward the use of advance euthanasia directives in dementia care: the overemphasis of cognition, the overemphasis of individual autonomy, and the under-emphasis of dialogue and shared understanding.

The first critique concerns the overemphasis of the cognitive dimension of the human person. As Western society places a high value on cognition as an integral part of an individual's dignity, the loss of cognition that occurs in dementia may be equated with hopelessness and loss of dignity. For some people, this may in itself be a reason to opt for euthanasia via an advance euthanasia directive. This perception leads to what Post referred to as 'exclusionary ethics': The value that society places on rationality and memory excludes individuals with dementia from the sphere of human dignity and respect, and leaves them socially marginalized (Post 1995). Furthermore, this argument reduces human dignity to what Nordenfelt describes as 'dignity of identity.' This is the dignity that depends on whether one has or does not have certain capacities (e.g., intellectual capacities). However, the most fundamental notion of dignity – *Menschenwürde* – cannot be lost as long as persons exist, even in the case of extreme bodily and cognitive deterioration (Nordenfelt 2004). *Menschenwürde* refers to a kind of dignity that all humans have, just because they are humans. Those who have lost their cognitive abilities or have extreme pain, embarrassment, and anxiety have no less or no more dignity than the most fortunate. According to this interpretation, loss of fundamental human dignity cannot be used as an argument for completing an advance euthanasia directive in order to request euthanasia in persons with dementia.

Not only the motivation that leads to drafting advance euthanasia directives, but also the way how advance euthanasia directives are drafted, illustrates the overemphasis of the cognitive dimension of the human person. There is some kind of presupposition that people are perfectly capable of determining their wishes concerning end-of-life care in a purely cognitive way (Levi and Green 2010). Decision aids are developed to 'educate, explain, and help' individuals to 'identify, clarify, and prioritize' a 'coherent set of medical wishes' and a 'tailored advance directive' that 'represents the individual's views and wishes' (Levi and Green 2010). Surprisingly, drafting an advance euthanasia directive seems to be fully deprived of attention to the emotional aspects of becoming care dependent, and deprived of the fact that people's wishes and values are very often of a pre-reflexive and emotional kind (Gastmans and Denier 2010).

The second critique concerns the overemphasis of individual autonomy. It is mostly presupposed that the wishes of people with advance euthanasia directives can easily be respected. However, in case of advance euthanasia directives of patients with dementia, supporting respect for the autonomy principle is much more complicated and even ambiguous than it is suggested. For instance, in the previous sections of this chapter, we already mentioned the central dilemma faced by physicians and proxies: How does one balance the actual preferences of the person with dementia (the now self) against the patient's earlier opinions (the then self) laid down in a now-forgotten advance euthanasia directive? In other words: Whose autonomy should be respected?

Authors of advance euthanasia directives often find themselves in a very weak position when their advance euthanasia directives become applicable, because it is often unclear whether they had this particular situation in mind when writing it. One should always interpret the situation, but interpretation involves risks. Life-terminating behavior is irreversible and thus prompts us to be very careful. The most basic fact, however, is the patient's dignity; and endangered autonomy is just one of the many dimensions of this dignity. Autonomy cannot be the only concern in medical-ethical decision making, since it is linked with other fundamental values in human life. The human autonomy we are required to respect, therefore, cannot result in an absolute dominion of one's own life but has to be understood in a broader framework of fundamental ethical values, e.g., the value of human life and the value of interpersonal connectedness.

The 'relative' value of autonomy is also supported by our relational and interpretative approach to care and the human person: A person's autonomy should always be seen within the relational network of care practices. Within this relational context, the patient, his or her family, and his or her caregivers should clarify, through communication and interpretation, what decisions should be taken in order to respect the dignity of the person with dementia; this is, what decisions are most meaningful for the patient involved.

This brings us to the third critique that weakens the use of advance euthanasia directives: the lack of communication and shared understanding between the demented patient, on the one hand, and the caregivers, on the other hand. Margaret Battin confirms:

> To end the life of a patient, even if fully legal, is not an easy process for a physician. We can assume it would be even more difficult when it is no longer possible for the physician to discuss the issue rationally with the patient and to have the patient's wish explicitly confirmed, and especially difficult when there is no evidence of current suffering other than the fact of having dementia disease (Battin 2007, p. 59)

This observation is confirmed by studies from the Netherlands where, despite the legal recognition of advance euthanasia directives for persons with dementia, euthanasia occurs very rarely or even not at all in this patient group (de Boer et al. 2010b, 2011; Rurup et al. 2006). The Dutch researchers concluded that

> communication and interpretation are crucial in determining the circumstances as well as the exact moment of performing euthanasia and this cannot be captured in or replaced by advance euthanasia directives. This is precisely what seems to cause the fundamental problem of complying with advance euthanasia directives in cases of severe dementia (de Boer et al. 2010b, p. 261).

According to Cees Hertogh (2009), conducting euthanasia in a person with severe dementia on the basis of an advance euthanasia directive seems to be equivalent to attempting to operate in the dark. Hereby, he refers to a fundamental vulnerability physicians are confronted with if the dialogical and interpretative aspects of end-of-life care are no longer present, as it becomes clear when caring for severely ill demented patients who are unable to discuss their euthanasia requests as formulated in advance euthanasia directives. Hence, taking into account the dialogical and interpretative nature of ethical decision making should be a standard and indispensable element of dignity-enhancing care. It will also foster a sense of attentiveness, responsibility, competency, responsiveness, and trust. These are essential attitudes of all those involved in dementia care, in order to make dignity-enhancing care real in everyday dementia care.

On the basis of the three fundamental critiques for using advance euthanasia directives, we come to the general conclusion that advance euthanasia directives do not fulfill the ethical requirements linked to dignity-enhancing care.

9.5 Conclusion

Ensuring dignified care for persons with dementia is a subject that requires more and more attention from ethicists, caregivers, and society in general. This chapter presented a comprehensive clinical-ethical approach to dementia care, taking into account three essential dimensions: lived experience, interpretative dialogue, and normativity. This framework, linked to three core concepts in dementia care – vulnerability, care, and dignity – enabled us to conduct an ethical assessment of advance euthanasia directives. We concluded that advance euthanasia directives do not meet the essential criteria of dignified care. Nevertheless, further ethical analysis is needed, not the least because dementia is becoming more prevalent.

References

Abma, T., V. Baur, B. Molewijk, and G. Widdershoven. 2010. Inter-ethics: Towards an interactive and interdependent bioethics. *Bioethics* 24: 242–255.

Agich, G. 2003. *Dependency and autonomy in old age: An ethical framework for long-term care*. Cambridge: Cambridge University Press.

Agich, G. 2010. Why I wrote... dependence and autonomy in old age. *Clinical Ethics* 5: 108–110.

Battin, M. 1992. Euthanasia in Alzheimer's disease? In *Dementia and aging: Ethics, values, and policy choices*, ed. R. Binstock, S. Post, and P. Whitehouse. Baltimore: The Johns Hopkins University Press.

Battin, M. 2007. Right question, but not quite the right answer: Whether there is a third alternative in choices about euthanasia in Alzheimer's disease. *The American Journal of Bioethics* 7: 58–60.

Beauchamp, J., and J. Childress. 2009. *Principles of biomedical ethics*. Oxford: Oxford University Press.

Brodaty, H., M. Breteler, S. DeKosky, P. Dorenlot, L. Fratiglioni, C. Hock, P.-A. Kenigsberg, P. Scheltens, and B. De Strooper. 2011. The world of dementia beyond 2020. *Journal of the American Geriatrics Society* 59: 923–927.

Chochinov, H. 2007. Dignity and the essence of medicine: The A, B, C and D of dignity conserving care. *British Medical Journal* 335: 184–187.

Christensen, K., G. Doblhammer, R. Rau, and W. Vaupel. 2009. Ageing populations: The challenges ahead. *Lancet* 374: 1196–1208.

Corrada, M.M., R. Brookmeyer, A. Paganini-Hill, D. Berlau, and C.H. Kawas. 2010. Dementia incidence continues to increase with age in the oldest old: The 90+ study. *Annals of Neurology* 67: 114–121.

De Boer, M., C. Hertogh, R.-M. Dröes, I. Riphagen, C. Jonker, and J. Eefsting. 2007. Suffering from dementia – The patient's perspective: A review of the literature. *International Psychogeriatrics* 19: 1021–1039.

De Boer, M., C. Hertogh, R.-M. Dröes, C. Jonker, and J. Eefsting. 2010a. Advance directives in dementia: Issues of validity and effectiveness. *International Psychogeriatrics* 22: 201–208.

De Boer, M., R.-M. Droës, C. Jonker, J. Eefsting, and C. Hertogh. 2010b. Advance directives for euthanasia in dementia: Do law-based opportunities lead to more euthanasia? *Health Policy* 98: 256–262.

De Boer, M., R.-M. Droës, C. Jonker, J. Eefsting, and C. Hertogh. 2011. Advance directives for euthanasia in dementia: How do they affect resident care in Dutch nursing homes? Experiences of physicians and relatives. *Journal of the American Geriatrics Society* 59: 989–996.

Dierckx de Casterlé, B., S. Verhaeghe, M. Kars, A. Coolbrandt, M. Stevens, M. Stubbe, N. Deweirdt, J. Vincke, and M. Grypdonck. 2011. Researching lived experience in health care: Significance for care ethics. *Nursing Ethics* 18: 232–242.

Draper, B., C. Peisah, J. Snowdon, and H. Brodaty. 2010. Early dementia diagnosis and the risk of suicide and euthanasia. *Alzheimer's & Dementia* 6: 75–82.

Dutch Association of Clinical Geriatrics. 2005. *Diagnostiek en medicamenteuze behandeling van dementie*. Alphen aan de Rijn: Van Zuiden Communications.

Ferri, C.P., M. Prince, C. Brayne, H. Brodaty, L. Fratiglioni, M. Ganguli, K. Hall, K. Hasegawa, H. Hendrie, Y. Huang, A. Jorm, C. Mathers, P.R. Menezes, E. Rimmer, and M. Scazufca. 2005. Global prevalence of dementia: A Delphi consensus study. *Lancet* 366: 2112–2117.

Gastmans, C. 2002. Towards an integrated clinical ethics approach: Caring, clinical and organizational. In *Healthy thoughts: European perspectives on health care ethics*, ed. R. Lie, P. Schotsmans, T. Meulenbergs, and B. Hansen. Leuven: Peeters Publishers.

Gastmans, C., and Y. Denier. 2010. What if patients with dementia use decision aids to make an advance euthanasia request? *The American Journal of Bioethics* 10(4): 25–26.

Gastmans, C., B. Dierckx de Casterlé, and P. Schotsmans. 1998. Nursing considered as moral practice: A philosophical-ethical interpretation of nursing. *Kennedy Institute of Ethics Journal* 8: 43–69.

Gastmans, C., L. Mahieu, L. Vanlaere, and Y. Denier. 2011. Author response: What's wrong with a broad and particularistic perspective on normativity? *Nursing Ethics* 18: 264–265.

Goering, S. 2007. What makes suffering "unbearable and hopeless"? Advance directives, dementia and disability. *The American Journal of Bioethics* 7(4): 62–63.

Goldsteen, M., T. Abma, B. Oeseburg, M. Verkerk, F. Verhey, and G. Widdershoven. 2007. What is it to be a daughter? Identities under pressure in dementia care. *Bioethics* 21: 1–12.

Hardwig, J. 1997. Is there a duty to die? *The Hastings Center Report* 27(2): 34–42.

Hardwig, J. 2009. Going to meet death: The art of dying in the early part of the twenty-first century. *The Hastings Center Report* 39(4): 37–45.

Harris, E., and B. Barraclough. 1997. Suicide as an outcome for mental disorders. *British Journal of Psychology* 170: 205–228.

Hertogh, C. 2006. Advance care planning and the relevance of a palliative care approach in dementia. *Age and Ageing* 35: 553–555.

Hertogh, C. 2009. The role of advance euthanasia directives as an aid to communication and shared decision-making in dementia. *Journal of Medical Ethics* 35: 100–103.

Hertogh, C., M. de Boer, R.M. Droës, and J. Eefsting. 2007. Would we rather lose our life than lose our self? Lessons from the Dutch debate on euthanasia for patients with dementia. *The American Journal of Bioethics* 7(4): 48–56.

Hughes, J. 2001. Views of the person with dementia. *Journal of Medical Ethics* 27: 86–91.

Kamel, H., and R. Hajjar. 2004. Sexuality in the nursing home, part 2: Managing abnormal behavior – Legal and ethical issues. *Journal of the American Medical Directors Association* 5: S49–S52.

Levi, B., and M. Green. 2010. Too soon to give up: Re-examining the value of advance directives. *The American Journal of Bioethics* 10(4): 3–22.

Lim, W., E. Rubin, M. Coats, and J. Morris. 2005. Early-stage Alzheimer disease represents increased suicidal risk in relation to later stages. *Alzheimer Disease and Associated Disorders* 19: 214–219.

Lindemann, K. 2003. The ethics of receiving. *Theoretical Medicine and Bioethics* 24: 501–509.

Mahieu, L., and C. Gastmans. 2012. Sexuality in institutionalized elderly: A systematic review of argument-based literature. *International Psychogeriatrics* 24(3): 346–357.

Margo, G., and J. Finkel. 1990. Early dementia as a risk factor for suicide. *Hospital & Community Psychiatry* 41: 676–678.

Martin, R., and S. Post. 1992. Human dignity, dementia, and the moral basis of caregiving. In *Dementia and aging: Ethics, values, and policy choices*, ed. R. Binstock, S. Post, and P. Whitehouse. Baltimore: The Johns Hopkins University Press.

McPherson, C., K. Wilson, and M. Murray. 2007. Feeling like a burden to others: A systematic review focusing on the end of life. *Palliative Medicine* 21: 115–128.

Mitchell, S., D. Kiely, and M. Hamel. 2004. Dying with advanced dementia in the nursing home. *Archives of Internal Medicine* 64: 321–326.

Mitchell, S., D. Kiely, S. Miller, S. Connor, C. Spence, and J. Teno. 2007. Hospice care for patients with dementia. *Journal of Pain and Symptom Management* 34: 7–16.

Moody, H. 1992. *Ethics in an aging society*. Baltimore: The Johns Hopkins University Press.

Nordenfelt, L. 2004. The varieties of dignity. *Health Care Analysis* 12: 69–81.

Ott, B. 1998. Physician-assisted suicide and older patients' perceived duty to die. *Advanced Practice Nursing Quarterly* 4: 65–70.

Papastavrou, E., A. Kalokerinou, S. Papacostas, H. Tsangari, and P. Sourtzi. 2007. Caring for a relative with dementia: Family caregiver burden. *Journal of Advanced Nursing* 58: 1–12.

Parsons-Suhl, K., M. Johnson, J. McCann, and S. Solberg. 2008. Losing one's memory in early Alzheimer's disease. *Qualitative Health Research* 18: 31–42.

Pearlman, R., K. Cain, D. Patrick, M. Appelbaum-Maizel, H. Starks, N. Jecker, and R. Uhlmann. 1993. Insights pertaining to patient assessments of states worse than death. *Clinical Ethics* 4: 33–41.

Post, S. 1994. Alzheimer's disease: Ethics and the progression of dementia. *Clinics in Geriatric Medicine* 10: 379–394.

Post, S. 1995. Alzheimer disease and the 'then' self. *Kennedy Institute of Ethics Journal* 4: 307–321.

Prince, M., and J. Jackson (eds.). 2009. *World Alzheimer report*. London: Alzheimer Disease International.

Rurup, M., B. Onwuteaka-Philipsen, A. Van der Heide, G. Van der Wal, and D. Deeg. 2006. Frequency and determinants of advance directives concerning end-of-life care in the Netherlands. *Social Science & Medicine* 62: 1552–1563.

Scherder, E., J. Oosterman, D. Swaab, K.A. Herr, M. Ooms, M. Ribbe, J. Sergeant, G. Pickering, and F. Benedetti. 2005. Recent developments in pain in dementia. *British Medical Journal* 330: 461–464.

Sellman, D. 2005. Towards an understanding of nursing as a response to human vulnerability. *Nursing Philosophy* 6: 2–10.

Stuifbergen, M., and J. Van Delden. 2011. Filial obligations to elderly parents: A duty to care? *Medicine, Healthcare and Philosophy* 14: 63–71.

Tadd, W., L. Vanlaere, and C. Gastmans. 2010. Clarifying the concept of human dignity in the care of the elderly: A dialogue between empirical and philosophical approaches. *Ethical Perspectives* 17: 253–281.

Tronto, J. 1993. *Moral boundaries: A political argument for an ethic of care*. New York: Routledge.

Tulsky, J. 2005. Beyond advance directives: Importance of communication skills at the end of life. *Journal of the American Medical Association* 294: 359–365.

United Nations Department of Economic and Social Affairs. 2004. *World population to 2300*. http://www.un.org/esa/population/publications/longrange2/WorldPop2300final.pdf. Accessed 29 Oct 2010.

Vanlaere, L., and C. Gastmans. 2011. A personalist approach to care ethics. *Nursing Ethics* 18: 161–173.

Vanlaere, L., F. Bouckaert, and C. Gastmans. 2007. Care for suicidal older people: Current clinical-ethical considerations. *Journal of Medical Ethics* 33: 376–381.

Walker, M. 2003. *Moral understandings. A feminist study in ethics*. New York: Routledge.

Widdershoven, G. 2000. *Ethiek in de kliniek: Hedendaagse benaderingen in de gezondheidsethiek*. Amsterdam: Boom.

Widdershoven, G., and R. Berghmans. 2001. Advance directives in dementia care: From instructions to instruments. *Patient Education and Counseling* 44: 179–186.

Woolhead, G., M. Calnan, P. Dieppe, and W. Tadd. 2004. Dignity in old age: What do older people in the United Kingdom think? *Age and Ageing* 33: 165–170.

Chapter 10
The Authority of Advance Directives

Govert den Hartogh

10.1 The Problem

In my wallet I always keep my membership card of a road service company, my organ donor card, a blood group card, and a ragged piece of paper stating my living will.

> It is my will to live no longer and die in a humane way in the event of my entering into a mental or physical condition that offers no or hardly any prospect of returning to a state of life that I consider acceptable and dignified.
>
> 1. If this condition should occur I hereby refuse my permission for any life-sustaining treatment.
> 2. If I should be unable to die shortly in a humane manner as a result of abstention from (further) medical treatment I hereby urgently request the doctor attending me to fulfil my wish to die by administering to me the medication that will ensure a humane death.

And by this condition I mean, among other things: "the permanent and (almost) entire loss of my ability to perform mental activity or to communicate or to live an independent life". What I have in mind is of course an advanced stage of Alzheimer or another form of dementia.

But do I honestly think that both these stipulations, the negative as well as the positive advance directive, will be honoured when the moment arrives? I do believe there is a real chance that the negative stipulation (refusal of treatment) will indeed be observed when it applies.[1] Although intensive care specialists still routinely

[1] All states in the USA have legislation governing advance directives, as do most of the Canadian provinces, a number of Australian states, New Zealand, and a number of European countries, including Denmark, the UK, the Netherlands, Belgium, France, Spain, Austria, Hungary, Serbia, Georgia and recently Germany. The Netherlands is the only country which gives some legal status to positive advance directives.

G. den Hartogh (✉)
Department of Philosophy, University of Amsterdam,
Oude Turfmarkt 141, 1012 GC Amsterdam, The Netherlands
e-mail: G.A.denHartogh@uva.nl

Y. Denier et al. (eds.), *Justice, Luck & Responsibility in Health Care*,
Library of Ethics and Applied Philosophy 30, DOI 10.1007/978-94-007-5335-8_10,

brush aside such clauses when they have to decide about re-animation after an accident or stroke (Kleijer 2005, pp. 100ff),[2] nursing home doctors appear to take them somewhat more seriously, perhaps out of a more intense personal involvement (Vezzoni 2005, ch. 7; The et al. 2002; van Delden et al. 2011, pp. 151ff).[3] My confidence is greatly increased, because my living will also identifies legal representatives whom I can trust to know my interests well and to be active in promoting them. As regards the positive provision (request for termination of life), however, I have hardly any illusions. Although the Dutch euthanasia law makes it possible to determine, on the basis of the living will, that a 'voluntary and well-considered request' has been submitted, the rest of the requirements of due care still need to be met. And until now it has been the general view of the medical community, confirmed by three authoritative documents, that the suffering which results from dementia cannot by itself be considered unbearable, as the law requires (KNMG 1997; NVVA 1997; Gezondheidsraad 2002). According to these documents any severe suffering demented patients may experience results from symptoms caused by other disorders. Not surprisingly, then, so far no cases of euthanasia on patients in an advanced state of Alzheimer have been reported to any of the euthanasia review committees, although in recent years the number of cases concerning patients in a early stage, who are still able to express their requests, has been rising, to 25 in 2010 (Regionale Toetsingscommissies 2011).[4]

So why have I put that clause in my advance directive? What am I so afraid of, do I have exaggerated ideas of the suffering that awaits an Alzheimer's patient? One of the most common criticisms of the authority of advance documents is that the people who sign them do not, perhaps even cannot really know from the inside what it means to be in an advanced state of dementia, and hence act on unfounded fears (Dresser and Robertson 1989; Buchanan and Brock 1990, p. 153; Hope 1992; Dresser 1995, p. 34, 1984, 2003,; Fagerlin and Schneider 2004; Fried et al. 2007; and other authors referred to by Levi and Green 2010).[5] However, when I first took such a document with me, somewhere in the early 1980s, the thought of future suffering was hardly on my mind at all. In the meantime, it is true, I have begun to appreciate that it is indeed a horrible thing to become aware, or merely dimly suspect, that you have entered upon an irreversible process that will end in a complete

[2] Family doctors have similar attitudes (Vezzoni 2005, ch. 8).

[3] It may be that the availability of a negative advance directive doesn't make much of a difference in this case because nursing home doctors are inclined to act as they request anyway, even without being requested (Teno et al. 1994). But according to van Delden et al. (2011, pp. 151 ff), Dutch doctors tend to take the directive into account in identifying the relevant values of the patient, and hence his 'best interests', even if most of them don't know that it is (*pro tanto*) legally binding and, even if they know, don't recognize its authority.

[4] Only recently for the first time an appeal to the living will has been made in such a case, because the consultant and the review committee considered the patient incompetent at the time of his actual request. In all other cases the actual request has been assessed to be well-considered. Only 20% of Dutch doctors know that the law does not require this to be the case (Van Delden et al. 2011, p. 165).

[5] Berghmans (1998) calls epistemic failure inevitable.

loss of your mental faculties and hence of your independence and perhaps to become a burden on others. By now I also believe that the permanent confusion and disorientation to which you will probably fall prey in the subsequent stages of that process, your inability to put on your shoes, the fear and paranoia, constitute very severe suffering. I well remember my mother-in-law being restless all the time, for hours on end looking for her coat and the front door since she wanted to go 'home', meaning her parents' home. Hence I believe that the view that a demented person cannot be considered to be suffering unbearably, at least not as a result of the dementia, needs reconsideration (see Sect. 10.4 below). But the fear of suffering is still not my main motive for carrying an advance directive. My dread of losing decorum is certainly relevant as well. But even if I would do nothing *then* of which I would *now* feel ashamed, I still would not like that final stage of my life to be a part of *my* biography. What scares me is the peeling away of my self, the gradual loss of everything that was important in my life. I would not want my grandchildren to remember me in the way in which my own children remember my mother-in-law. Both to be in that state and to be perceived to be in it would, I believe, taint my life (Cf. Nys 2012 in this collection).

The usual reaction to these motives is that my attitude may be understandable in a professor who thinks that life has no value if he is no longer capable of writing big books that nobody reads. But what typifies the whole process of becoming subject to dementia is precisely the fact that this peculiar system of values will irretrievably disappear and this self-conception be completely effaced. Even when I first have to go through a stage of suffering, that stage will pass. A moment will come when I will sit in the sunshine and doze off and not even remember what a book is.

In a column in a medical journal Frans Meulenberg tells the story of Iris Murdoch watching Teletubbies, and a number of similar dramatic tales of loss. He comments: becoming older is attended by much loneliness and sorrow, but the shrinking of the brain prevents us from experiencing it all. No process of de-humanization, then, rather a protective mechanism to secure our happiness:

> Horrible? Grotesque? Tragic? Degrading? It depends on how you look at it. The Teletubbies, after all, doubtless bring joy to the demented. What's wrong with that? Man is just a happiness-seeking animal (Meulenberg 2006).

Why should we treat people according to the conceptions of their past self? We would then accept that this earlier self tyrannizes the later self.[6] An advance directive would have the effect of tying oneself to the mast like Ulysses. But why should we regard the sweet call of life in the case of the elderly suffering from Alzheimer's as a Siren's song?

This is how the problem of the authority of advance directives has been posed in the literature: as the question of who has the final say on the matter, the earlier or the later self. Although some of the authors who thus formulate the problem make courageous attempts to save the authority of the advance directive, I fear they are waging a losing battle. After all, the person doctors are confronted with and

[6] Dresser (1984) calls this 'self-paternalism'; cf. Davis (2004).

probably the only one they have ever known is the Alzheimer patient, and it seems unthinkable to disregard his actual will and his actual interests on the authority of a piece of paper representing a will and interests he no longer shares. My main argument in this paper will be, however, that the problem is wrongly posed in this way. With one important exception (Sect. 10.5), there is no conflict of will or interests between different stages of the self.[7]

I have given the problem I want to discuss a first-person formulation. My aim was not so much to alert my readers to my personal interest in the matter, although I think it is only fair that they know. I have mainly done so to neutralize from the start a standard objection against recognizing the authority of a living will in such cases: that this reveals a depreciation of the life of the mentally less gifted.[8] I'm not talking about the value of other people's lives (the value it holds to themselves) but about the value, to myself, of a possible stage in my own life. Such personal interests cannot be determined independently of a person's own priorities. My priorities are different from Meulenberg's. For me the prospect of being happy with the Teletubbies would not detract from the horror; it would rather be its culmination.

But could I not be mistaken in my priorities? Or, for that matter, could Meulenberg not be mistaken in his? I do not deny that, even if personal interests are to a large extent dependent on personal values, personal values can be criticizable themselves. But even in that case, I will argue, both Meulenberg and I have the right to be treated in accordance with our own mistaken views.

10.2 The Structure of My Argument

The discussion about this subject has been dominated during the past 15 years by an impressive chapter that Ronald Dworkin dedicated to it in his book *Life's Dominion* (1993).[9] Dworkin makes a distinction there between critical interests and experiential interests. Experiential interests are interests you have in the quality of your experience, from moment to moment. Do you on the whole feel well or badly? Critical interests are interests that are based on a value judgement about your life as a whole. My advance directive, says Dworkin, must be regarded as an authoritative representation of my critical interests. What I value is ending my life in a way which

[7] When Davis (1999) advocates pre-emptive suicide for people who expect their advance directive to be disregarded, Gedge (2004) even interprets this as an act of aggression of the former against the later self, as do Hertogh et al. (2008), in their reply to critics. That of course presupposes that the later self has the will to live or at least an overriding interest in survival. Davis' worry, however, concerns people who are prepared to overrule *her* authority because *they* have such beliefs as regards later selves.

[8] Such views do not take into account the fundamental difference between the personal value of life, that is, the value life has for the one living it, and a possible impersonal value (Cf. Sect. 10.7 below).

[9] An important predecessor is Rhoden (1990).

is consonant with the character of my life as a whole, just as one might want a play to end with a scene that fits the play as a whole, or a poem with a stanza that brings the work to an appropriate climax. On the other side of the balance we only find the frail happiness of some pleasant moments the Alzheimer patient may still experience. Critical interests, however, carry more weight than experiential interests, and therefore my advance directive has authority.

Dworkin's argument has been countered in two ways.[10] The first option is to deny that experiential interests must always give way to critical interests. The second one is to argue that the patient suffering from Alzheimer's still *has* critical interests of his own. Meulenberg's comment on Iris Murdoch enjoying the Teletubbies presupposes her to be a mere passive recipient of fragmentary and fleeting pleasant and unpleasant experiences who has lost every sense of self. But until a late stage[11] that patient is still interested in issues outside him, including other people, and acts on the basis of that interest, often in ways which can be recognized as simplified variants of her earlier patterns of behaviour, and therefore as an expression of a personality that still exists.

On closer consideration these strategies do not really exclude each other because they seem roughly to apply to succeeding stages of the disease. The remnants of the self are gradually broken down until the patient really only has experiential interests. We have therefore to consider the authority of advance directives in both stages. I will do this in Sects. 10.3 and 10.4 respectively. In addition I will discuss (Sect. 10.5) the objection that, even if my living will is not opposed by my present interests as an Alzheimer patient, it may be opposed by my present will. It is at this point that I will be prepared to accept an exception to my general thesis.

People like me who want to uphold the authority of advance directives, at least to a significant extent, are often accused of an inflated respect for personal autonomy, as the one and only relevant value in this area (Dresser and Whitehouse 1994; Widdershoven and Berghmans 2001; Dawson and Wrigley 2010). In my argument the appeal to that principle, however, will have no central role to play. Basically that argument will be that, given the values to which my life as a whole has been oriented, it will be in my interest to have my living will executed. That interest should not be conceived of as merely the interest of a past self standing opposed to the interests of a present self. It is only to those who protest that I am mistaken in my view of my own interests that I will reply (Sect. 10.6) that in the end that doesn't matter. It is at that point, and only at that point, that, properly speaking, I will argue for the *authority* of my advance directive. For by allowing someone to have authority you recognize that his decision stands, even if it is mistaken.

It is important to distinguish between these two possible roles of living wills. They provide evidence concerning the relevant personal values in terms of which

---

[10] A third is to argue that the critical interest is only the interest of the former person, which now has been replaced by the interests, critical or only experiential, of the present individual. I consider that argument in the first paragraphs of Sect. 10.6.

[11] Perhaps to be identified with scale 7 on the Functional Assessment Staging Scale (Mitchell 2007).

we have to understand a person's best interests. And they claim to be a binding representation of those interests, whether or not they represent them correctly. In regard to the first role it is standardly said that they allow us to act on the substituted judgment of the person, but that notion actually confuses the two roles. You can only act on someone's authority when that authority has been exercised, and a person's commitment to certain values is not an exercise of authority.[12]

Even if my living will should be seen as an authoritative representation of my interests, and if this applies to the positive clause as much as to the negative one, it doesn't follow that doctors are morally required, or even permitted to comply with it. Other relevant values may be at stake. I discuss this possibility in my final section (Sect. 10.7).

As announced I will argue that on the whole it is a mistake to believe that in deciding whether or not to comply with a living will we have to take sides in a conflict between two stages of the self. But I will put aside one radical way to deny that there may be such a conflict: by denying that there is one self. Relatives of patients in an advanced stage of Alzheimer's sometimes say: "That is no longer my husband, my mother". They mean to say this metaphorically, but couldn't they be right literally? Isn't there a point in the demolition of the self at which the connection between the present individual and the former person has become too thin to hold that they are stages of the same being? In that event the advance directive would have no authority whatsoever (Dresser and Robertson 1989; Wrigley 2007). It seems preposterous to claim the final say about someone else's life.[13]

When do "I" start to exist, when do "I" cease to exist? What constitutes my numerical identity? That is a fascinating topic, but it deserves a separate treatment. In this paper I will just assume that I am the same person, or at least the same being, as the future Alzheimer patient carrying my name, that my relatives will make no mistake in celebrating my anniversary and not starting to apportion my estate, and that my concern about getting into that stage is entirely warranted.[14]

---

[12] On content-independence as the essence of authority see den Hartogh (2002, ch. 7) with references.

[13] Buchanan and Brock (1990, ch. 3) and Kuhse (1999), however, suggest that a person may have authority about the fate of his post-person successor, his "living remains", just like he has authority about what happens to his estate and his mortal remains. But we do not normally consider even radically incompetent people to be at the disposal of others in this way; they have interests of their own and therefore moral status, whether they are persons or non-persons.

[14] I will also put aside some pragmatic objections commonly made. The most common objection probably is that advance directives do not enable a doctor to identify a unique decision because they always require interpretation (E.g. Widdershoven and Berghmans 2001; Gastmans and Denier 2010). It is worth observing about such doubts that they invariably only reflect a worry of possibly being too early, never of being too late. Of course I do not dispute that advance directives may be so inadequately formulated that they are of no use at all, see for an interesting example Crippen (2000), and commentary by Truog. However, every law requires interpretation, but only legal realists think that this implies that judicial decisions are not constrained by law. According to research by Rurup et al. (2005) doctors generally are able to recognize the conditions for which the living will has been made. Their claim to the contrary as registered by other researchers may mainly reflect a reluctance to comply with it. Because of this common reluctance, it is essential to give the durable power of attorney to a trusted friend or relative, and extensively discuss future decisions with that person.

10.3 The Experiential Interest in Survival

When I drew up that advance directive, I thought, as I told you, of the implications which a period of increasing dementia at the end of my life would have for my life as a whole: a gradual disintegration of my person leaving me a mere ruin of my former self. One could look at it as a way of slowly dying. But once I arrive in an advanced phase of Alzheimer's, I will not be able to think in that way anymore. When that happens, at a certain moment only the quality of my experiences from day to day will count for me: the days will be bad when I suffer and relatively good when I feel well.

Suppose I am on the whole pleasantly demented. Should my supposed critical interests still take precedence as a matter of general principle? Should I always be treated in accordance with the values which I have subscribed to during my life as they could be discovered by 'reading' the story of that life?

Maartje Schermer discusses the not uncommon case of a woman who has always, throughout her life, put great value on good appearances, but who in the nursing home opposes all attempts to make her look a bit decent (Schermer 2003).[15] For Schermer it is of major importance that the attempts to force her into the system of her own previous values not only withhold something good from her, but positively cause anguish. It also seems relevant that the reason why it is important to you to look good is that you derive some self-respect or self-confidence from that. But that is no longer possible if you can no longer see yourself through the eyes of others.

I agree that in general critical interests do not necessarily prevail over experiential interests. For that reason we should probably disregard an advance directive instructing us not to provide palliative care to a severely suffering Alzheimer patient, even if we could understand the directive as deriving from the fundamental values she has subscribed to during his life. However, the question now is about the interests one can have in *continuing* one's life. If an Alzheimer patient still has a positive hedonic balance from day to day, is this sufficient to conclude that for the time being she has an interest in survival?

This question could be rephrased in terms of the famous Epicurean challenge. Let me quote Epicurus himself from his letter to Menoeceus:

> Death is nothing to us. For all good and bad consists in sense-experience, and death is the privation of sense-experience. That knowledge makes the mortality of life a matter for contentment, not by adding a limitless time to life but by removing the longing for immortality. For there is nothing fearful in life for one who has grasped that there is nothing fearful in the absence of life.... So death is nothing to us; since when we exist, death is not yet present, and when death is present, then we do not exist. Therefore, it is relevant neither to the living nor to the dead, since it does not affect the former, and the latter do not exist.

According to Epicurus the fear of death is irrational, and in this brief passage he gives various reasons for thinking so. One reason is: what you do not experience as

[15] But cf. Post's example of Mrs. S who agrees to cohabit with Mr. R falsely believing him to be her husband of 40 years marriage (Post 1995).

good or bad cannot be good or bad for you. But once you are dead, you do not experience anything anymore, so it cannot be good or bad for you to be dead. A second reason is as follows: *for whom* would it be an evil to be dead? It cannot be an evil for you while you live, and once you are dead you do not exist any longer, so then it does not bother you either. Therefore, there is never a subject that actually has the bad luck.

On first sight these are strong points, but the conclusion cannot be true. If it were true, you would not harm anyone by killing them, as long as you do so unexpectedly and without causing pain. *Of course* death is an evil for almost everybody. But Epicurus does force us to wonder *why* exactly this is the case.

As early as Antiquity the following objection has been raised against Epicurus. He is right when he says that death is not a positive evil, it is not a terrible situation to be in, because it is not a situation in which you can be at all. But that does not mean that death may not be a negative evil, an evil that consists of what you are deprived of. This *pure deprivation account*, by now the standard refutation of the Epicurean argument,[16] claims to be correct irrespective of the notion that one has of the value of life, so even if one grants Epicurus (or rather modern Epicureans) that that value consists of the sum total of the positive and negative experiences one gradually gathers.[17]

But Epicurus could still ask: who is really *affected* by that deprivation? Suppose you compare two possible lives: a shorter life which leads to death in 2020 and a longer life which ends in 2050. In that case, it is only a bookkeeping truth that the longer life until 2050 will probably consist of a greater sum total of positive rather than negative experiences than the shorter life until 2020. There is no moment in time, if the shorter life is yours, that this can make any difference to you. Both lives are completely identical until 2020, hence up to 2020 the deficit cannot make any difference to the value of your life. But after 2020 there are no longer two lives to compare with each other. You cannot be worse for no longer existing, as you cannot be worse for never existing.

How can the evil of death be explained then? Let me give two examples of people who really are deprived of something when they die. The first example, a variant on a story told by David Velleman, concerns a woman who is seriously ill during her youth, and long after that is still affected by it (Velleman 1991). Moreover, she grows up in a situation of social-economic deprivation. Furthermore, during her study she has to take care of a disabled parent, even while not completely cured herself yet, and she has to accept a boring job to provide for her cost of living. She succeeds in finishing medical school only with the help of enormous will power and extraordinary talent, but the day before she will receive her master's

[16] Apparently also subscribed to by Dworkin (1993, pp. 229–231).

[17] McMahan (2002, pp. 496ff) accepts the deprivation account and therefore agrees that the Alzheimer patient has experiential interests in survival. That patient may also, as testified by his living will, still have critical interests in non-survival, but because the psychological continuity between his last and his present self is extremely reduced, on McMahan's view of prudential concern, these interests should be radically discounted. See footnote 34.

degree in medicine she dies as the result of a traffic accident. The second example is about a relationship in which both partners are continuously in conflict with each other so that every month they are about to break off the relationship while nevertheless staying together because they mean so much to each other. Some dramatic experiences bring them closer together and finally they feel not only a strong attachment but also an increasing harmony between them. Exactly at that point one of the two dies. That is, I would say, just as awful for both of them, not only for the surviving partner. In both cases there is a stage with a lot of sadness which seems to usher in a period that is happy and successful. That this development is interrupted is a loss as such, but it moreover deprives that first stage of its positive meaning, retrospectively: this preparatory stage has then been leading to nothing.

From an Epicurean point of view the value of each moment of life is independent of the value of each other moment, and the value of life as a whole is the sum of those discrete units. That is why it does not really matter that you are deprived of some experiences when you are no longer there to experience them. In my examples it is the other way around: the value of each moment depends on the value of a whole life or of a certain stage of that life, and that value is based on the structure or pattern that is being realized in that life. That structure may take on the shape of the execution of a plan, as in my first example: the meaning of each step is then based on the attainment of the final result. When the building collapses, its construction has made no sense. But the structure of life may also be more like a plot than a plan, as in my second example.[18]

A plan presupposes someone who makes a plan, and that must necessarily be someone who can place his present actions into a continuous line of actions and events from yesterday to tomorrow. A plot presupposes a main character who can put today's experiences into a continuum of experiences from yesterday to tomorrow. We must therefore object as follows to Epicurus' first argument: good and bad not only consist of single experiences, but also of the achievement of a certain life structure, of which death may be a radical interruption. We must answer the question which he formulates in his second objection as follows: the subject of the evil, the one suffering the evil, is the main character of the life story which has thus been interrupted.[19]

This latter answer could be objected to by saying that it seems to imply a form of backward causation which is usually held to be impossible. The key to a clear understanding here lies in the theory of action. Actions have a teleological structure, an

[18] It is worth noting that Epicurus himself basically understood the value of a life in a structural way, as a quest for *ataraxia*. For that reason he could found a school and even leave a will, actions for which Cicero already accused him of inconsistency.

[19] As will become clear in Sect. 10.4, I do not wish to make very strong claims as regards these 'structural elements', as narrativists sometimes are tempted to do. I certainly do not presuppose "a self that is steadfastly committed to a stable set of identity-defining values and convictions, a self that expresses continuity over time, a self that is separate from all other selves and that essentially decides alone", as Koppelman (2002) describes the view she opposes. For discussion see also Delaere (2010, ch.2).

action is designed to bring about a situation which only obtains as a result of and therefore after the action. Therefore the success of that action can only be judged afterwards. No reverse causality is involved: the facts themselves are not determined retroactively, only the meaning and the value of those facts. An action may of course be valuable as such, even if it is not successful. But it is also possible that only useless expenses have been incurred when it fails to achieve its object.

But Alzheimer's patients in the penultimate stage no longer carry out any plans and do not live a life story any more. They can no longer align their present actions and experiences with those of the previous and next years, not even with yesterday's and tomorrow's actions and experiences. Because of that they can no longer deliberate about their actions, and because they have lost their sense of agency, not even really act anymore. They cannot engage in meaningful relations with others, because these presuppose a sense of reciprocity (Harvey 2006). They can only have pleasant and unpleasant experiences which do not add up in any meaningful way (McMahan 2002, p. 503). So the point Epicurus made *does* apply to such patients. For them death is no longer an evil. Only suffering is.

I have carried that advance directive with me half my life, and everyone who knows me can witness that my feelings about it never have changed. It is of vital interest to me that I need not go through that last stage, that I do not have to live on like that in the memories of my grandchildren. That is not the interest of my earlier self, my self in 1980 or in 2011, it is the interest of myself as such, as the main character of my life story from the beginning to the end, whether or not I am still aware of it. And during that last stage I will not have a conflicting different interest.

Suppose that during that last stage the unrest and confusion are gone and I just doze off in the sunshine and watch the Teletubbies. Is it, then, not in my interest to have a few more of those peaceful days? Following Bernard Williams we can make a distinction between conditional and categorical interests (Williams 1973). If I do get some extra days, then I would prefer them to be calm and pleasant: that is a conditional interest. It is no reason for wanting more extra days. In both my examples the main characters have an interest in the success of their enterprise or the development of their relationship, and that interest can only be realized if they are given time to live on. These are categorical interests. The personal value or disvalue of the life of the Alzheimer patient has to be decided in terms of his categorical interests, and these can only be determined from the views about his life as a whole which he had when he was still capable of having them.[20]

If we reject the pure deprivation account of the value of survival, we must conclude that you cannot have a purely experiential interest in survival. If it can be concluded from your living will that it is your critical interest to avoid that final stage of decay and devastation, that critical interest is therefore unopposed.

---

[20] "…to affirm that severely demented patients retain an interest in experiencing simple pleasures while alive is quite different from saying that these patients retain an interest in being kept alive, so as to experience whatever pleasures are available to them" (Brock 1988, p. 90). Kuhse (1999) makes the same point. But most of the literature simply presupposes that it is a matter of showing compassion to the pleasantly demented to allow her to live, see e.g. Kadish (1992).

10.4 The Threatened Self

But this conclusion only applies to a late stage in the development of Alzheimer. Before that stage has been reached, the patient still has traces of critical interests on which he presently acts. He may be involved in some elementary project which he is able at least intermittently to recognize as such. Or he may interact with other people in ways which justify us to conclude that he cares for those people and to some extent responds to their responses, and therefore to ascribe to him an ongoing relationship with them. In such cases, it seems that he has a categorical interest in survival, because it is a precondition for going on with his project or his relationships.

Until that very last stage Alzheimer's patients still have a sense of self and concerns for that self. But you can only have a sense of self if you have some conception of the permanency of that self as existing through time. That is even shown when the patient like my mother-in-law wants to return to her familial home: she still identifies herself as the child of her parents. It is also shown when patients express their resentment for being treated in a way they feel to be humiliating, that very basic human concern for being properly respected (Sabat and Harré 1992; Sabat 1998; Jaworska 1999, 2007; Shiffrin 2004).

Hence it is still true of her that the value of each moment of her life depends on some rudimentary structure exhibited by that life through time. She may have lost the grasp on her life as a whole, or perhaps even on any significant stretch of it which includes the present. But she still has a conception of herself, and that may be enough to ascribe to her some interest in survival. Relatives may, for example, be touched by some characteristic way of responding to circumstances, a trace of humor, an act of gentleness. One structural element which binds the stages of our life together, in addition to our projects and ongoing intimate relations, is our characteristic way of coping with the vicissitudes of life, and it could therefore be suggested that it adds to the value of her life if that character is still expressed in some recognizable form under such adverse conditions.

In recent years laudable efforts have been made to get access to the inner life and in particular the remaining sense of self and agency of demented patients (Post 1995, 2000; Kitwood 1997; Sabat 1998; Cheston and Bender 1999; Nolan et al. 2002; MacQuarrie 2005; Hertogh et al. 2007). But what this new psychology of dementia has revealed to us, is fairly alarming.[21] Yes, there is a remaining sense of self, but it is not an intact sense of an intact self, and it is precisely for that reason that the descent into the abyss normally involves severe suffering. Being to some extent aware of the progressive loss of one's powers -a source of never-ending grief-, not being able to take care of oneself, feeling frightened because of events one cannot

[21] For example, MacQuarrie (2005, p. 434), lists "annoyance, anger, hurt, shock, sadness, and exasperation" as the common emotional responses of Alzheimer patients to their situation; cf. the list in Kitwood (1997, p. 78). Because these emotions to some extent are adequate responses, they should not simply be considered symptoms to be treated, e.g. by anti-depressants.

understand, judging social situations incorrectly and then interpreting, sometimes correctly, other people's responses as disrespectful, panicking about events which don't happen, embarrassment, sadness and paranoia, all these states of consciousness reflect a sense of self, indeed, but a sense of a progressively threatened and disintegrating self. The increasing losses of cognitive ability leave a self which is confused and disoriented in the world, unable to execute any effective control, and to the extent that it is aware of its condition, feeling uprooted and insecure, lacking basic trust. Hence it is a mistake to suggest that an advance directive expresses an overrating of rationality and other cognitive performances at the expense of the affective dimensions of human life, which are sufficient to make it worthwhile. Basic cognitive abilities are our primary instruments of coping with the normal tasks of life, and therefore losing them can hardly fail to be experienced with extreme distress and alarm, even if it happens with only some dim awareness of the fact. It is also a mistake that the condition of dementia by itself doesn't cause extreme suffering. The physical symptoms may be relatively mild (although physicians often fail to recognize them because of communication problems). But, as Eric Cassell has taught us, pain, cramps, contractures, and other such symptoms only constitute suffering because of the attack on the self which they imply (Cassell 1991). To the extent that the demented patient has a sense of self which is still in some contact with reality, that self is and only can be a self under attack. Contrary to received opinion,[22] agitation, confusion, delusion and anxiety are therefore to be understood as essentially resulting from the dementia itself, and not from concomitant disorders (Post 1995).

It is therefore true that the demented self has still (contemporaneous) critical interests at a later time than Dworkin may have presupposed, but to the extent that the person can still assess her condition, this will only deepen her sense of loss.

It is only to be expected that the self defends itself by destroying its contact with reality, even beyond the extent to which this is already been done by its cognitive losses. Cees Hertogh has stated this well: the patient

> has to find a way of shutting out what happens to him, even if this means losing contact with reality, or he has to face the changes which occur, but this amounts to an apprehension, probably too painful to bear, that one is on the brink of losing oneself. (Quoted from Hertogh 2006; cf. Hertogh et al. 2007, p. 53)[23]

But then Hertogh cannot be right when he also holds that advance directives lose their authority because Alzheimer patients, like patients suffering from other fatal illnesses like cancer, adapt their preferences to their conditions. When they arrive in the state they abhorred, they find it not so bad as they feared. They are pushing back their frontiers (Hertogh 2008; Hertogh et al. 2007; cf. Dresser 2003). This analogy fails for two reasons. On the one hand Alzheimer patients do not, like cancer patients,

---

[22] As represented by the three Dutch documents referred to in Sect. 10.2. Research by Rurup et al. (2005, cf. Rurup et al. 2010), however, shows that according to most nursing home doctors the suffering of demented patients can be unbearable, even in the absence of a concomitant illness.

[23] For a more general analysis of denial, including so-called anosognosia, as a coping strategy see MacQuarrie (2005).

arrive at a new assessment, taking into account new experiences, they progressively lose their capacity to assess. At the time at which their new condition would most likely lead them to change their mind, they may not have enough mind left to call it 'changed'. But, secondly, whatever assessment they still make may itself be an expression of a fear too large to be faced, in particular with the coping resources still at their disposal. The only possible way of coping left is denial.[24]

But shouldn't we even take them seriously in this state of denial? A critical interest, as Dworkin rightly stresses, is an interest in things happening, not only in experiencing them to happen. Your critical interests are not fulfilled when you are only given the impression of being respected or of being praised for doing something worthwhile.[25] Any interests satisfied in that case are only experiential ones. Similar your 'critical interest' in safely returning to the home of your parents cannot be fulfilled when they have been dead for many years. To the extent that the demented person has a wish to continue living, this cannot itself be seen as an expression of her critical interests, because it results from losing contact with reality.

As long as the demented patient still has a sense of self, and therefore a life which possibly might be sufficiently structured to sustain an interest in survival, that self will tend to be threatened to such an extent that his life will be characterised by continuous severe suffering. If the patient succeeds in avoiding this suffering, he can only do so by retreating into Meulenberg's world of unreflected pains and pleasures.[26] Only in the first case he may still have categorical critical interests, but on balance these can hardly be interests in survival.

10.5 The Possibility of Conflicting Wills

In the last two sections I have discussed the possibility of a conflict between the earlier and later self, considering this conflict as a conflict of interests. However, it could also be a conflict of wills. The authors who use the conflict model often assume without any further analysis that patients suffering from Alzheimer's normally choose life and resist death, as requested in their advance directive, when their disease has made considerable progress. The ambiguous terminology

---

[24] The analysis is also inconsistent with the view that the suffering of Alzheimer patients is largely the result of 'malignant social psychology' (Kitwood 1990). For example, the restrictions on their freedom which Alzheimer patients understandably resent, are often necessary in order to prevent unacceptable risks to others. To the (considerable) extent that this view really *is* true, moreover, it only highlights the frailty of agency which to that extent is dependent on the good will of others.

[25] I do not deny that the beliefs and emotions of an Alzheimer patient may still match reality. But if they do, this will largely be a matter of accident. Sabat gives his professor to some extent a deserved sense of self-respect by including him in his research on the inner life of Alzheimer patients (Sabat 1998). But the professor would have the same feelings if no such research was actually going on.

[26] As a result either of the psychological mechanism, described by Hertogh, or simply of the progressive loss of his mental faculties.

is sometimes used that "they no longer want to die". The phrase suggests that something is present: the will not to die, though it only asserts that something is absent: the will to die.

A recent paper deduces the will not to die from the fact that patients accept the care offered to them (Hertogh et al. 2007). But if patients have the conditional wish to be well taken care of while they live, it does not follow that they also have the categorical wish to continue to live. Only if the care offered to them is solely aimed at prolonging life, one could in principle decide, on the basis of the acceptance of the offer, that patients have a wish to stay alive. However, that presupposes a correct understanding of the meaning of the offer. It is doubtful whether Alzheimer patients understand that meaning, even when they are given explicit information about it.

During the development of Alzheimer's there is a moment when the patient can apparently still experience something – he reacts to pain stimuli, for example – but no longer want something. An act can only be said to be willed if the acting person understands that the act contributes to a result that she desires.[27] That presupposes the ability to have preferences for possible situations and an elementary understanding of cause and effect. Of course we do all sorts of things without thinking about causality and it is not even necessary for us to be able to explain causal relations in language. However, if these are the only 'acts' we perform, at a certain moment it becomes likely that the acts are only mechanical reactions to stimuli. That we still want something only appears from non-standard situations, when we think of a relatively new way to satisfy a wish. People who care for demented patients often and understandably tend to give an 'anthropomorphic' interpretation to completely automatic behaviour. They thus sometimes deduce a 'rejection of food' from a negative reaction to food being offered or from pulling out a tube.

If a will no longer exists, neither does a will to live on, so much is clear. However, the opposite is not true. It is quite possible that the patient suffering from Alzheimer's still wants all sorts of things, and may even *say* that he does not want to die, while not really knowing what it is that he says he wants. It has to my knowledge not been studied to what extent Alzheimer's patients still have a grasp on the concept of death, but it has been studied in the case of children (Carey 1985). It turns out that children until the age of three cannot distinguish between living and non-living objects. Until the age of about five they see death as a sort of sleep from which you can wake up at any moment. Only after that do they understand that death is final, but not yet that this is associated with the termination of vital functions. It is therefore a cognitively complicated task to understand that something that exists may cease to exist, that this also goes for living beings, human beings, and even yourself.

[27] It is therefore mistaken to think that we do not and cannot know whether a patient in an advanced state of Alzheimer's still sticks to her request (Dresser 1995; Harvey 2006; Gastmans and De Lepeleire 2010). If the counterfactual question is asked: what would the person have chosen if he had still been able to choose anything, we should observe that the answer is irrelevant, because in that case she would not be in the condition for which her living will has been made.

When someone is capable of willing something, that does not mean that he is competent to determine his will. The ability to evaluate and the ability to deliberate are crucial to this ability. These two abilities are interrelated: an evaluation is distinguished from mere preference, or even from a characteristic pattern of preference, because it is a judgement with a pretension to truth, a judgement which may be the object of reflection and discussion. Hence someone can only be competent if he has a minimal insight into the alternatives among which he can choose and into the consequences of his choices for the realization of his values. There is a time during the development of Alzheimer's when the patient may still be able to want something, but is not able to evaluate, to deliberate and to communicate about her values and choices.

Prior to this, there is a phase in which those general capabilities are not fully absent but when we nevertheless cannot regard the patient as competent to make a decision about life and death, because she cannot assess the particular alternatives from which she must choose and their consequences. Let us assume that the patient at this stage still has a sufficiently adequate concept of death. Then, and only then, a conflict may arise between the advance directive and the actual will of the later patient.

Authors who defend the authority of the living will, such as Ronald Dworkin, have a ready solution to that conflict: an incompetent decision does not count. In response various authors have tried to extend the concept of competence in such a way that it can still be attributed to patients suffering from Alzheimer's in rather advanced stages of the disease (Jaworska 1999; Shiffrin 2004).[28] This fits in with a general trend in the literature about our interaction with people having serious cognitive defects. It is clearly the result of the special prominence that the principle of respect for autonomy has received in medical ethics: in order to be able to take into account the will of people with serious cognitive defects we must first attribute competence to them.

I have problems with both positions. If, as Hertogh's observation suggested, the rejection of the living will's provisions results from a denial of the truth because it is too horrible to be faced, this rejection cannot be understood as being made competently, whatever the general abilities of the patient. On the other hand, the starting point that Dworkin and (most of) his critics share – that decisions do not count at all, if they are made incompetently – seems also false to me. To begin with, I don't think that there is a very clear borderline on the scale of the relevant abilities between the competent and the incompetent, which can justify treating them in completely different ways (Arneson 2005). But moreover, we should not simply disregard the will of clearly incompetent people, for example young children. Not only competent people value taking charge of their own lives and feel slighted by paternalism.[29] We should

[28] It is interesting that Jaworska (2007) does not analogously claim that the capacity for caring which she ascribes to patients in an advanced stage of Alzheimer amounts to a capacity for autonomy. But she does argue that such cares, as those of small children, should be taken into consideration.

[29] Shiffrin (2004, pp. 203ff) and Jaworska (2007) are fully aware of this, as is Kadish (1992, p. 874).

certainly do so as long as meeting that will does not impose unreasonable demands on others, and does not conflict with the interests of the person in question. The question whether someone is competent is only asked in practice when the latter is the case. Even when there is a conflict between will and interest, it may sometimes be justified to decide in favour of the will of the incompetent person. This may be a matter of respect, but it may also be instigated by the wish to maintain a good relationship with her.

I have no general view about the solution of this conflict in the case of a negative living will. Much depends on a sympathetic understanding of the extent of the patient's suffering. Because doctors are liable to err at the side of rejecting the directive, it may be all to the good that the law provides a counterbalance to this, in particular when the courts do not blindly enforce the law.[30] As for a positive request for euthanasia, it seems unthinkable to me to actively put an end to the life of a patient who knowingly resists, even though the situation is so dramatic that we would be prepared to consider it in a patient who can no longer express his will and even though the patient has completely erroneous ideas about his circumstances and prospects.

10.6 What Should the Doctor Do with My Negative Will?

When the person is still trying to adjust to her new condition, this is normally an extremely painful process which fully warrants a precedent wish to avoid it. The objection made to the view that an Alzheimer patient only has experiential interests is that his life story goes on, and this is true, but it is normally a tragedy. The authors who have so much contributed to our new understanding of the Alzheimer patient as a person, have also, mostly contrary to their own intentions, deepened our appreciation of the possible appropriateness of the living will. Precisely the appeal to take the patient's perspective seriously should make us sensitive to the extent to which the deteriorating condition of the Alzheimer patient involves unbearable suffering.[31]

It is a blessing when eventually "all the confusion, embarrassment and agony of self-observation are forfeited in favour of grateful amnesia" (Post 1995). To that

[30] Maclean (2008) shows that British courts tend to countenance a physician's rejection of a living will when the physician appeals to the best interests of the patient. On his view this tendency undermines the Mental Capacity Act 2005, because he interprets that law as exclusively aiming at promoting respect for autonomy. Dutch law explicitly permits the doctor to depart from the directive for "well-founded reasons", but this should not be taken to mean that the doctor can simply act on his own judgement of the patient's best interests. Perhaps the British law should be interpreted in a similar way, as giving the living will a limited authority.

[31] Goering (2007). Hertogh et al. (2008) concede in their reply that "he has a point", but then go on to ask whether it is not too much to ask of a doctor to kill such a patient. Perhaps it is, but the reason cannot then be provided by the interests of the patient, see Sect. 10.7.

extent Meulenberg's comment on Iris Murdoch which I quoted in my introduction was to the point. But it is by itself a fully understandable wish to avoid that stage as well, and that wish is again unopposed by any interest of the demented individual in survival.

So do I think that the doctor who treats me must simply carry out my advance directive when the time is there? Certainly the first stipulation, on abstention from treatment. Of course, people change their view of life, sometimes dramatically, while they live and it would be ridiculous to put claims on Paul's life deriving from the value system of Saul. That would indeed be a form of "self-paternalism", of domination of the earlier over the later self.[32] Saul's values are no longer valid for determining Paul's interests, because they have been *revoked*. But the development of dementia is not a process of conversion. If I find myself in the situation that I describe in my advance directive, I have not revoked the values expressed in that directive, they have only disappeared beyond the horizon. That is why those values are still in place for the evaluation of what my life means to me, even though I can no longer perform that evaluation myself. Otherwise you could have no reason either to honour after my death my wishes concerning my estate, my body, my sperm or my organs.[33] The interests expressed in my living will are my categorical critical interests, and will be so at the last stage of dementia as much as they have ever been.[34]

Even if I have subscribed to those values all my life, couldn't I be mistaken about them? That is possible but irrelevant. If my doctor, or even my family, disagrees with me, either about my values or about my beliefs, for example my rejection of the pure deprivation account of the evil of death, why should my fate depend on their views?[35] If, on the other hand, Frans Meulenberg draws up an advance

[32] My view is that the interests of a past self do not only count for less than the interests of the present self, as Jaworska (2007) proposes. Rather, as such they count for nothing. In Parfit's famous example of the Russian count the dilemma for the count's wife is only created by her promise to disregard his present preferences, not by his former preferences as such. Similarly, if we frustrate a child's present desires in order to protect his future flourishing, we do not solve a conflict of interests between stages of the self in favour of the future self either, because the child already has an interest in his future condition. The concept of 'interest' is backwards transitive. I therefore agree with Dworkin (2004, p. 367), when he comments that both Shiffrin and Jaworska do not really accept that the child, the adult and the Alzheimer patient are one and the same person.

[33] The denial of the possibility of posthumous interests often rests on the mistaken idea that they would involve some kind of reverse causality, see Sect. 10.3.

[34] McMahan (2002) denies this, see footnote 17. But he then goes on to claim that the value of the coherent character of my life as a whole should still override these interests. But if that value is not a personal value to me, as I will be at that time, it can only be either an impersonal value, or a personal value to my irrevocably past self. On neither interpretation this seems sufficient to justify killing someone.

[35] Blustein (1999), Koppelman (2002) and Nys (2012, this collection) advocate leaving the decision to arbitrate between the former and the later self to surrogates, significant others who have co-authored and therefore are still able to continue authoring the story of my life. Perhaps that is wise counsel, but, as Nys recognizes, that doesn't mean that these surrogates have any *authority* to decide unless I have given it to them.

directives requiring all life-prolonging measures in the case he is pleasantly demented, why should it be relevant that his doctor or his family agrees with Epicurus and me? Both his and my advance directive is not only a document which informs you about our point of view as regards our life and its stages, and thus enables you to form your own idea about our categorical interests. It is also a public act by which we authoritatively determine the normative position of any doctor who considers treating me. That the determination is authoritative means that it's validity does not depend on an assessment of its content.[36] I would claim that this content-independence even covers the philosophical issues I have discussed. Even if I am mistaken in my view that one cannot have a merely experiential interest in survival, that doesn't justify a doctor to put my living will aside in order to give me some additional happy days. Doctors are only on the scene because of their medical expertise, not because they have any special competence in determining people's basic interests as regards life and death. That is one reason not to entrust them with the authority to determine those interests. Note that this reason does not derive from the value of autonomy.[37]

The only possible exception to the authority of a negative living will is the situation in which the person involved, although incompetent, expressly states that she does not want to die, while also understanding to some significant extent what it is she does not want. In this single case there is a conflict of wills between an earlier and a later self. And in that case, I have suggested, there may sometimes be some reason for doubt about the binding nature of the directive. For in this case it is in some sense correct that the earlier self imposes itself on the later self. It is true: not from aggression but from justified compassion evoked by the present self,[38] hence not as a tyrant, but still in a paternalistic fashion. And in this particular case such 'self-paternalism' is not absolutely justified by the fact of incompetence.

10.7 What Should the Doctor Do with My Positive Will?

But what about the second stipulation, about the active ending of my life? That is a more complex question. For there is something inherently problematic about ending life, even about putting an end to the life of a person who wants to die and has a fundamental interest in dying.

Almost all doctors feel that way, even when euthanasia is requested by a patient who is beyond doubt suffering unbearably. As a result they don't consider

[36] As observed in footnote 3 most Dutch physicians only accept the living will as a source of relevant information, not as a binding document.

[37] Authors who believe that recognizing the authority of advance directives amounts to overrating this value (see Sect. 10.2) fail to properly distinguish between the value of and the right to autonomy, cf. Feinberg (1986, ch. 18). The right may protect the value, but it can also be founded on many other considerations (den Hartogh 2000).

[38] Cf. footnote 7 (Kadish 1992, p. 871; Koppelman 2002, p. 75).

the situation as providing a 'medical exception' to the prohibition on killing, but rather as a conflict of duties, even though the duty to prevent further suffering may ultimately tip the balance.[39] They are conscious of a duty not to kill which is not a duty which is owed to the patient. That compassion sometimes prevails may only be possible because severe suffering evokes that emotion directly and urgently, and even in that case only when they can share responsibility for acting on it with the living person herself, not only with a piece of paper.[40] But to sneak up with a deadly needle on that Govert den Hartogh who is dozing off in the sunshine is a different matter altogether. Even if you agree about his interest, it is a fairly abstract interest. And he might just as soon develop a pneumonia.

It is an important question for ethics whether the psychological obstacles to killing which doctors experience are just that, an atavistic remainder of an old taboo, or have moral meaning, and if so, why.[41] Let me only observe for now that it is just as well, particularly in a country where euthanasia is allowed (on strict conditions), that it is psychologically difficult for doctors to go about ending people's lives. I should be lucky if at the appropriate time I could find a doctor (you keep your hopes up) willing to honour my positive advance directive, but, speaking amongst ourselves, I would not entirely trust that same doctor in other circumstances.

So I do understand that I cannot simply expect doctors to fulfil my wish; in particular I understand that it is difficult for them to do so without my continuing cooperation. But they should not say that they refuse to do so because of *me,* in my interest, out of respect and consideration for the person that I am or have become. According to Cees Hertogh even in the most severe cases of suffering "what holds us back is the defenceless power of human need and vulnerability."[42] (Hertogh et al. 2006) That is extremely paradoxical: is it my very vulnerability to extreme suffering which prevents you from showing mercy?

If doctors say that they hold back because they care for me, they are both deceiving themselves and disrespecting me. That is what I would like to instill in them. And that is why I go on carrying that living will with me.

---

[39] It may be no more than an accident of history that the Dutch euthanasia law is basically founded on this idea of a conflict of duties, but this foundation at least reflects doctors' feelings, and may well be the appropriate moral framework for evaluating physician-assisted death.

[40] Most of the family doctors interviewed by Rurup could imagine executing the positive request of the living will, but only if these two conditions had been fulfilled (Rurup et al. 2010; cf. van Delden et al. 2011, pp. 157–159).

[41] The question requires a more extensive discussion which until now I have only provided in Dutch (den Hartogh 2009).

[42] Cf. footnote 31. He also states that such extreme suffering is not "unbearable" in the sense of the Dutch euthanasia law because this notion requires doctor and patient to agree about the unbearableness (Cf. van Delden 2004). Both van Delden and he note that on this interpretation the law is incoherent, because the request of a living will which the law recognizes as authoritative, can then never be granted. To me that rather seems a decisive reason to reject this interpretation of the law.

References

Arneson, R. 2005. Joel Feinberg and the justification of hard paternalism. *Legal Theory* 11: 259–284.

Berghmans, R.L.P. 1998. Advance directives for non-therapeutic dementia research: Some ethical and policy considerations. *Journal of Medical Ethics* 24: 32–37.

Blustein, J. 1999. Choosing for others as continuing a life story: The problem of personal identity revisited. *The Journal of Law, Medicine & Ethics* 27: 20–31.

Brock, D. 1988. Justice and the severely demented elderly. *The Journal of Medicine and Philosophy* 13: 73–99.

Buchanan, A., and D. Brock. 1990. *Deciding for others: The ethics of surrogate decision making*. New York: Cambridge University Press.

Carey, S. 1985. *Conceptual change in childhood.* Cambridge: MIT Press.

Cassell, E. 1991. *The nature of suffering*. New York: Oxford University Press.

Cheston, R., and M.P. Bender. 1999. *Understanding dementia.* London: Jessica Kingsley Publishers.

Crippen, D., M. Levy, R. Truog, L. Whetstine, and J. Luce. 2000. Debate: What constitutes 'terminality' and how does it relate to a living will? *Critical Care* 4: 333–338.

Davis, D.S. 1999. Rational suicide and predictive genetic testing. *The Journal of Clinical Ethics* 10: 316–323.

Davis, J. 2004. Precedent autonomy and subsequent consent. *Ethical Theory and Moral Practice* 7: 267–291.

Dawson, A., and A. Wrigley. 2010. A dead proposal: Levi and Green on advance directives. *The American Journal of Bioethics* 10(4): 23–24.

Delaere, P.J.J. 2010. Practical identity: An essay on personhood, autonomy, and pathology. Dissertation, Erasmus University, Rotterdam.

Den Hartogh, G.A. 2000. Introduction. In *The good life as a public good*, ed. G.A. den Hartogh, 1–28. Dordrecht: Kluwer.

Den Hartogh, G.A. 2002. *Mutual expectations: A conventionalist theory of law*. The Hague: Kluwer.

Den Hartogh, G.A. 2009. Gij zult niet doodslaan. *Algemeen Nederlands Tijdschrift voor Wijsbegeerte* 101: 164–195.

Dresser, R.S. 1984. Bound to treatment: The Ulysses contract. *The Hastings Center Report* 14(3): 13–16.

Dresser, R.S. 1995. Dworkin on dementia-elegant theory, questionable policy. *The Hastings Center Report* 25(6): 32–38.

Dresser, R.S. 2003. Precommitment: A misguided strategy for securing death with dignity. *Texas Law Review* 81: 1823–1848.

Dresser, R.S., and J.A. Robertson. 1989. Quality of life and non-treatment decisions for incompetent patients: A critique of the orthodox approach. *Law, Medicine & Health Care* 17: 23–44.

Dresser, R.S., and P.J. Whitehouse. 1994. The incompetent patient on the slippery slope. *The Hastings Center Report* 24(4): 6–12.

Dworkin, R. 1993. *Life's dominion: An argument about abortion and euthanasia*. London: Harper Collins.

Dworkin, R. 2004. Replies to critics. In *Dworkin and his critics, with replies by Dworkin*, ed. J. Burley. Oxford: Blackwell.

Fagerlin, A., and C.E. Schneider. 2004. Enough. The failure of the living will. *The Hastings Center Report* 34(2): 30–42.

Feinberg, J. 1986. *Harm to self.* Oxford: Oxford University Press.

Fried, T.R., J. O'Leary, P. Van Ness, and L. Fraenkel. 2007. Inconsistency over time in the preferences of older persons with advanced illness for life-sustaining treatment. *Journal of the American Geriatrics Society* 55(7): 1007–1014.

Gastmans, C., and J. De Lepeleire. 2010. Living to the bitter end? A personalist approach to euthanasia in persons with severe dementia. *Bioethics* 24: 78–86.

Gastmans, C., and Y. Denier. 2010. What if patients with dementia use decision aids to make an advance euthanasia request? *The American Journal of Bioethics* 10(4): 25–26.
Gedge, E.B. 2004. Collective moral imagination: Making decision for persons with dementia. *The Journal of Medicine and Philosophy* 29: 435–450.
Gezondheidsraad. 2002. *Dementie*. Den Haag: Gezondheidsraad.
Goering, S. 2007. What makes suffering "unbearable and hopeless"? Advance directives, dementia and disability. *The American Journal of Bioethics* 7: 62–63.
Harvey, M. 2006. Advance directives and the severely demented. *The Journal of Medicine and Philosophy* 31: 47–64.
Hertogh, C.M.P.M. 2006. Advance care planning and the relevance of a palliative care approach in dementia. *Age & Ageing* 35: 553–555.
Hertogh, C.M.P.M. 2008. The role of advance euthanasia directives as an aid to communication and shared decision-making in dementia. *Journal of Medical Ethics* 35: 100–103.
Hertogh, C.M.P.M., R.M. Dröes, and M.E. De Boer. 2006. Dementie sluit praten over euthanasie niet uit. *Medisch Contact* 61: 15–17.
Hertogh, C.M.P.M., M.E. de Boer, R.M. Dröes, and J.A. Eefsting. 2007. Would we rather lose our life than lose our self? Lessons from the Dutch debate on euthanasia for patients with dementia. *The American Journal of Bioethics* 7(4): 48–56.
Hertogh, C.M.P.M., M.E. de Boer, R.M. Dröes, and J.A. Eefsting. 2008. Beyond a Dworkinian view of autonomy and advance directives in dementia. Response to open peer commentaries. *The American Journal of Bioethics* 8(4): 4–6.
Hope, T. 1992. Advance directives about medical treatment. *British Medical Journal* 304: 398.
Jaworska, A. 1999. Respecting the margins of agency: Alzheimer's patients and the capacity to value. *Philosophy and Public Affairs* 28: 105–138.
Jaworska, A. 2007. Caring and full moral standing. *Ethics* 117: 460–497.
Kadish, S.H. 1992. Letting patients die: Legal and moral reflections. *California Law Review* 80: 857–888.
Kitwood, T. 1990. The dialects of dementia with particular reference to Alzheimer's disease. *Ageing Society* 10: 177–196.
Kitwood, T. 1997. *Dementia reconsidered: The person comes first*. Philadelphia: Open University Press.
Kleijer D.J. 2005. "Het wordt geregeld…", Een onderzoek naar (zelf)regulering bij het staken of onthouden van een levensverlengende behandeling op Intensive Cares in Nederland. Dissertation, RUG, Groningen.
Koninklijke Nederlandsche Maatschappij tot bevordering der Geneeskunst (Commissie Aanvaardbaarheid Levensbeëindigend handelen). 1997. *Medisch handelen rond het levenseinde bij wilsonbekwame patiënten*. Houten: Bohn Stafleu Van Loghum.
Koppelman, E. 2002. Dementia and dignity: Towards a new method of surrogate decisionmaking. *The Journal of Medicine and Philosophy* 27: 65–85.
Kuhse, H. 1999. Some reflections on the problem of advance directives, personhood, and personal identity. *Kennedy Institute of Ethics Journal* 9: 347–364.
Levi, B.H., and M.J. Green. 2010. Too soon to give up: Re-examining the value of advance directives. *The American Journal of Bioethics* 10(4): 3–22.
MacLean, A. 2008. Advance directives and the rocky waters of anticipatory decision-making. *Medical Law Review* 16: 1–22.
MacQuarrie, C.R. 2005. Experiences in early stage Alzheimer's disease: Understanding the paradox of acceptance and denial. *Aging & Mental Health* 9: 430–441.
McMahan, J. 2002. *The ethics of killing*. Oxford: Oxford University Press.
Meulenberg, F. 2006. 'Column'. *Medisch Contact* 6(13) 31 maart.
Mitchell, S. 2007. A 93-year-old man with advanced dementia and eating problems. *Journal of the American Medical Association* 298: 2527–2536.
Nederlandse Vereniging van Verpleeghuisartsen. 1997. *Medische zorg met beleid. Handreiking voor de besluitvorming over verpleeghuisgeneeskundig handelen bij dementerende patiënten.* Utrecht: NVVA.

Nolan, M., T. Ryan, P. Enderby, and D. Reid. 2002. Towards a more inclusive vision of dementia care practice and research. *Dementia* 1: 193–212.

Nys, T.R.V. 2012. The wreckage of our flesh: Dementia, autonomy, and personhood. In *Justice, luck and responsibility in health care: Philosophical background and ethical implications for end-of-life care*, ed. Y. Denier et al. Dordrecht: Springer.

Post, S. 1995. Alzheimer disease and the "then" self. *Kennedy Institute of Ethics Journal* 5: 307–321.

Post, S. 2000. Key issues in the ethics of dementia care. *Neurologic Clinics* 18: 1011–1022.

Regionale toetsingscommissies euthanasie. 2011. *Jaarverslag 2010*. Den Haag: Regionale toetsingscommissies euthanasie.

Rhoden, N.K. 1990. The limits of legal objectivity. *North Carolina Law Review* 68: 845–865.

Rurup, M.L., B.D. Onwuteaka-Philipsen, A. Van der Heide, G. Van der Wal, and P.J. Van der Maas. 2005. Physicians' experiences with demented patients with advance euthanasia directives in the Netherlands. *Journal of the American Geriatrics Society* 53: 1138–1144.

Rurup, M.L., H.R.W. Pasman, and B.D. Onwuteaka-Philipsen. 2010. Euthanasieverklaringen bij Dementie. *Nederlands Tijdschrift voor Geneeskunde* 154: A 1273.

Sabat, S.R. 1998. Voices of Alzheimer's disease sufferers: A call for treatment based on personhood. *The Journal of Clinical Ethics* 9: 38–51.

Sabat, S.R., and R. Harré. 1992. The construction and deconstruction of the self in Alzheimer's disease. *Ageing and Society* 12: 443–461.

Schermer, M. 2003. In search of the "good life" for the demented elderly. *Medicine, Healthcare and Philosophy* 6: 35–44.

Shiffrin, S.V. 2004. Autonomy, beneficence, and the permanently demented. In *Dworkin and his critics, with replies by Dworkin*, ed. J. Burley. Oxford: Blackwell.

Teno, J.M., J. Lynn, R.S. Phillips, D. Murphy, S.J. Youngner, P. Bellamy, A.F. Connors Jr., N.A. Desbiens, W. Fulkerson, and W.A. Knaus. 1994. Do formal advance directives affect resuscitation decisions and the use of resources for seriously ill patients? *The Journal of Clinical Ethics* 5: 23–30.

The, A.M., R. Pasman, B. Onwuteaka-Philipsen, M. Ribbe, and G. Van der Wal. 2002. Withholding the artificial administration of fluids and food from elderly patients with dementia: Ethnographic study. *British Medical Journal* 325: 1–5.

Van Delden, J.J.M. 2004. The unfeasibility of requests for euthanasia in advance directives. *Journal of Medical Ethics* 30: 447–451.

Van Delden, J.J.M., A. Van der Heide, S. Van de Vathorst, H. Weyers, and D.G. Van Tol. 2011. *Kennis en opvattingen van publiek en professionals over medische besluitvorming en behandeling rond het einde van het leven*. Den Haag: ZonMw.

Velleman, J.D. 1991. Well-being and time. *Pacific Philosophical Quarterly* 72: 48–77.

Vezzoni, C. 2005. The legal status and social practice of treatment directives in the Netherlands. Dissertation, RUG, Groningen.

Widdershoven, G.A.M., and R.L.P. Berghmans. 2001. Advance directives in dementia care: From instructions to instruments. *Patient Education and Counseling* 44: 179–186.

Williams, B. 1973. The Makropoulos case: Reflections on the tedium of immortality. In Id., *Problems of the self. Philosophical papers*, Cambridge: Cambridge University Press.

Wrigley, A. 2007. Personal identity, autonomy and advance statements. *Journal of Applied Philosophy* 24(4): 381–396.

Chapter 11
The Wreckage of Our Flesh: Dementia, Autonomy and Personhood

Thomas R.V. Nys

11.1 Introduction

Could the principle of respect for autonomy – a principle that is considered so essential nowadays – still be relevant in guiding our conduct with regard to people who suffer from severe dementia? This seems particularly questionable because, as a severely disruptive and debilitating disease, dementia erodes the necessary level of competence that is required for people to ground respect for their decisions, that is, they lack the *capacity* for autonomy as a necessary condition in order to enjoy the *right* to autonomy.

So-called advance directives seem to offer a way out of this conundrum as pro-active individuals could foresee the dangers of an impending state of disability and non-autonomy and take the required measures to assure that they would never have to live "that way." However, this road to rescue seems to turn into the proverbial *cul-de-sac* because dementia is precisely unique in the fact that it is *so* debilitating that the individual might have changed her mind. Whether this is cashed out in strong, metaphysical terms (about her being a different person), or just by emphasizing that she has different interests than before, the point is that advance directives do not seem to have a hold – i.e., they do not have the required authority – to guide our conduct vis-à-vis these individuals with dementia.

Recently, attempts have been made to underscore that the principle of respect for autonomy is still very relevant even in people with dementia but that this would *limit* the normative authority of advance directives. The occurrent, contemporaneous autonomy of the patient diagnosed with dementia would render previous 'living wills' null and void. Although these attempts are on to something, I will argue that the social nature of 'selfhood' as well as autonomy requires a different perspective.

T.R.V. Nys (✉)
Department of Philosophy, University of Amsterdam, Oude Turfmarkt 141, 1012 GC Amsterdam, The Netherlands
e-mail: T.R.V.Nys@uva.nl

Y. Denier et al. (eds.), *Justice, Luck & Responsibility in Health Care*, Library of Ethics and Applied Philosophy 30, DOI 10.1007/978-94-007-5335-8_11,

I will claim that this is the perspective of certain significant others, a perspective that is generally ignored, or underestimated or deemed suspect. Proxy decision-making, however, can be an extension of autonomy and a way to preserve one's personhood. Insofar as some people are worried about these matters, the best solution *for them* (and only them) would be to assign proxies; both because these proxies are in a privileged position to assess the continuity and compatibility of these different life stages, but also because their evaluative judgment *as such* matters to these individuals. On the one hand, this relies on the presence of consent with regard to the assignment of proxies. On the other hand, this 'living will' is more open-ended than it is normally construed as the individual leaves it to the discretion of the proxy as to determine her best interests.

11.2 Two Extremes: Dworkin and Dresser

Ronald Dworkin has famously argued in favor of the authority of advance directives when it comes to morally and legally vindicating the possibility of euthanasia in cases of dementia (Dworkin 1993, 2006). Actually, he offers *two* arguments: one based on the value of autonomy and the other on that of a person's wellbeing. The first sounds rather straightforward. A person has a right to determine her own way of life,[1] and decisions about life and death are indeed life-determining in the most profound way. Dworkin claims – rightfully, as I will hope to argue later on – that an episode of severe dementia can run counter to the way one perceives one's life as meaningful. The state should be neutral with regard to such fundamental choices, that is, it should neither promote nor prohibit their effectuation. Dworkin has used this argument in favor of abortion and procreative choice, but whereas these cases seem far more troublesome, due to the fact that there is a third party involved, the possibility to decide over one's own life seems more convincing.

Now, in order to lead a life of one's own, one has to have a 'coherent sense of self', a relatively stable 'character', and this is what people in a state of severe dementia lack. In *that* particular sense, they lack indeed the necessary competence for the right to autonomy (Dworkin 2006, p. 361). However, the individual with dementia retains the right to beneficence, that is, "the right that decisions are made in [her] best interests…But [she] no longer has the right, as competent people do, to decide contrary to those interests."

Dworkin, however, in a second move, also claims that a concern for the individual's wellbeing would point in the same direction. In this regard, he uses the distinction between experiential and critical interests. These latter interests determine whether my life goes well or not, whereas the first are just about the quality of experience. Now, in the normal case – i.e., healthy individuals – these critical interests

[1] "…a right to make important decisions defining their own lives for themselves" (Dworkin 2006, p. 359).

often take, and *should* take, precedence over experiential ones: we value a meaningful life over a mere happy, or pleasant existence. We often endure unpleasant episodes or experiences in our lives in order to achieve some meaningful end, and even if we are sometimes mistaken and we make 'bad' decisions, we still value the integrity that comes with being an autonomous decision-maker over a state in which we are safely kept out of harm's way. Now, from the perspective of critical interests, living in a state of severe dementia – even though happy and contented – could indeed make my life *worse*. In order to serve my best interests then, one should attend to my critical interests when I was still competent.

Rebecca Dresser (2006), in her reply to Dworkin, observes that this might be an elegant theory but that it results in a questionable policy. What it ignores, says Dresser, is the current fate of the person with dementia. We are persuaded to see things from the perspective of the rational person anticipating the onset of dementia and thereby forget that there is a living individual who *does not share* that perspective. In fact, Dresser mentions that the peculiar thing about dementia is that it might radically transform the 'old' person, even to the extent that it turns her into another one. She refers to Derek Parfit's seminal work on personal identity in support of this suggestion (Parfit 1984). If what makes individual X, at t^1, numerically the same individual as Y on t^2, is relationship R that shows sufficient continuity over time, then it seems reasonable – due to the devastating impact of dementia on human memory – that the continuity relationship is indeed severely impaired to the extent that justifies speaking about 'different persons'.

What should we make of this claim? Are there indeed different persons involved? Apart from theoretical problems like, "When does this new person come into existence?", or, "When was it born?", I think this is a case in which, in our quest for reflective equilibrium between theory and intuition, the scales refuse to tip in favor of an elegant theory.[2] If indeed we would change so dramatically as to become an entirely different person, or no person at all, why would we worry so much? Take the case of Margo, the demented individual who is seemingly happy in her condition, reading randomly in her detective stories and enjoying her peanut-butter-and-jelly sandwiches. To argue, as Dresser does, that these insights from theories about personal identity warrant us to take heed of the occurrent demented person's experiential interests, seems to imply that, in the end, we do not take care of *her* wellbeing at all. But her point is that it would be appropriate to Margo, not someone else. So Dresser should be careful in using such radical tools in order to support her conclusions.

Let us therefore put this radical assumption aside and look at what remains of her argument against Dworkin. In general, there are two strands in her argument: one focusing on the limited authority of advance directives, and the other on the limited importance of critical interests. Within this first strand, she develops three counter-arguments. First, many people do not issue such directives and this might indicate that 'such freedom' is not a 'major priority' for them. I do not see how

[2] For a discussion of these various problems, see Degrazia (1999).

this argument could provide any force against Dworkin's theory as it was meant to apply only to those who *do* issue such directives.[3] Second, people are often irrational when drawing up these directives (by way of including contradictory clauses, for example). But this is not a solid argument either, because we could again stipulate that the authority of advance directives only holds for those that are consistent. Finally, Dresser says that people are generally ill-informed about the prospects of dementia, even in the fundamental sense that cannot know not know what it will be like for *them* to be demented. This problem, which I will call the Problem of Uncertainty, has some force, but *only* to the extent that people are indeed concerned about the experiential side of the disease. I will argue later on that this is particularly doubtful.

The second strand in her argument leaves out the element of autonomy by assuming, for argument's sake, that there are no advance directives. What should we do then? Dresser claims that when others have to determine a person's best interests, they should not privilege her alleged, former critical interests over her occurrent experiential ones. Here it is clear that Dresser does not need any strong metaphysical claim about there being two different persons in order to get her point across. The fact remains that the person – and this could very well be the same person – at *this* time seems to have different interests than the ones she had before, whether or not they are stipulated in an advance directive. She then raises two important concerns: first, other people are quite bad in tracking our critical interests, so they are bound to get it wrong on Dworkinian terms. Let us call this the Problem of Interpretation. Secondly, and this is her central criticism: Dworkin is unwarranted (a) in drawing a sharp distinction between critical and experiential interests, and (b) in giving absolute priority to the first.

So let us take stock. Whereas Dresser does not refute Dworkin's argument for autonomy in case of advance directives, she does mention some important problems, namely the Problem of Interpretation and the Problem of Uncertainty. Most importantly, however, she raises the question of why former critical interests should invariably take precedence over an individual's present, experiential ones. In general, she redirects our attention to the person with dementia. For sure, the more elaborate faculties of these people may have waned, but what remains is a living being capable of pain and pleasure and we should take care of them, alleviating the burdens of suffering and enabling them to live as comfortable as possible.

These two theoretical positions then capture – and indeed *try* to capture – two conflicting intuitions: one about the worries that some people have in anticipating a disease such as Alzheimer's (as it threatens the very concept of a meaningful life) and the other about the fate of the person with dementia, the individual that we face (and have to face) here and now, with particular interests – though perhaps less complex – that we, from a moral perspective, still need to attend to.

[3] Dworkin, of course, does not argue for involuntary euthanasia (which would be an oxymoron). I will come back to this point as my own proposal concerning proxy decision-making also has this limited scope. It only holds for people who *agree* to such a policy.

11.3 Autonomy on Part of the Person with Dementia

The weakness of Dresser's account is that mere experiential interests on the side of the individual with dementia are insufficient to rebut Dworkin's theory. This is because she does not provide any argument for *why* these experiential contemporaneous interests are suddenly morally authoritative, whereas Dworkin has provided an argument of showing why they are generally less important. In order to address this shortcoming various other authors have tried to emphasize that the principle of respect for autonomy – and not merely a concern for wellbeing – applies to the person with dementia. This would again, and in a stronger sense, limit the authority of advance directives.

Agniezka Jaworska, for example, has argued that people with dementia retain a fundamental capacity to care and therefore enjoy, what she calls, 'full moral standing' (Jaworska 2007, 1999). Such 'full moral standing' implies that we cannot (that is, should not) interfere with her interests dictated by her caring about certain things. Human beings develop this capacity when they are about 2 years old and they maintain it even in the more serious stages of dementia. Jaworska connects this capacity and the entailing moral status to the notion of autonomy. On her account, what a person cares about constitutes the 'elemental building blocks' of her autonomy.[4] This capacity to care is what gives us full moral standing and therefore, any violation of this status – by not respecting what we care about – is a serious moral wrong. In fact, Jaworska seems to imply that the notion of 'full moral standing' is intended to denote a person's inviolability. This means that the demented person who has such full moral standing, due to her capacity to care, should not be delivered to the mercy of advance directives which go against her interests as a caring individual.

However, Jaworska also allows for a peculiar asymmetry: although paternalistic interference is unwarranted in case of individuals with dementia, we are allowed to override the full moral standing of young children in order to safeguard, protect, or promote their future wellbeing. The asymmetry is justified by the obvious observation that young children still have a future wellbeing to care about, while people with dementia are only left with this basic capacity to care. This makes sense but it shoots a hole in Jaworska's conceptual framework. The proverbial 'heavy lifting' is not performed by the fundamental capacity to care and the countervailing notion of 'full moral standing', but by this simple asymmetry. In case of dementia, the decay is irreversible; there is no hope of recovery, just a slow decline. Therefore, we have to deal with what is left, not with what supposedly lies around the corner, a mature, competent, rational, fully developed, full-blown individual. If so, however, the individual's mere capacity to care does nothing to invalidate Dworkin's point. Jaworska has merely raised the stakes on the side of the occurrent individual (from experiential

[4] This has an obvious Frankfurtian ring to it. In order to be autonomous, the individual's will – her effective desires – should conform with her system of cares. This system is the individual's evaluative horizon, so to speak, by virtue of which she is able to lead a life 'of her own'; this because she is fundamentally identified with what she cares about.

interests, to caring), but she has not dealt with the thorny issue of how previous 'cares' relate to these present ones. I will come back to this point later on.

Sheanna Shiffrin is another author who has emphasized that the principle of respect for autonomy still applies to the person with dementia (Shiffrin 2004). Like Jaworska, she wants to focus on a capacity that goes below the radar if we employ the ordinary standards for autonomy assessment. On her view, autonomy basically means that one has the ability to "control one's experience" and this is something that people with dementia retain for a fairly long time.

Shiffrin also draws an analogy with young children, but whereas Jaworska wants to rescue our intuition that children's interests can legitimately be overruled out of a concern for their future self, Shiffrin reminds us that we often do honor their 'immature' wishes simply because we care about their ability to control their own experience (Shiffrin 2004, p. 205). Indeed, we sometimes allow them to be in control, for example, by letting them choose between different sorts of candy. Now, once again, this basic yet fundamental capacity is all that people with dementia have left. Therefore it becomes even more important as there is no longer any need to compensate for the recklessness of youth in order to safeguard a 'healthy' future self. Respect for autonomy means that we grant them this capacity for control.

With Shiffrin, however, the problem is that she puts the bar too low. If autonomy is basically about controlling one's experiences, then animals would qualify as autonomous as well and therefore command our respect. Perhaps the analogy holds (I unleash my dog in the woods because I grant him/it the pleasure of being in control), but it still taxes our imagination. A more serious problem, however, is that Shiffrin's analogy between young children and people with dementia crumbles as soon as we realize that these latter individuals *were* in fact once fully competent and were perhaps very worried about their future selves. The prospect of a life in which such simple control is all there is left may be a source of deep distress. The same goes for Jaworska. What remains in terms of autonomy, be it the capacity for care or for control, may precisely reveal the nub of the problem: such a life may strike (some of) us as a life not worth living. In my view, by emphasizing a remaining capacity for autonomy on the side of people with dementia, Jaworska and Shiffrin seem to overprivilege *this* side. In my view, they make the same mistake as Dworkin, only in the opposite direction: they think that one can provide theoretical grounds for privileging either one of two possible candidates for respect – the former, competent person vs. the occurrent, incompetent one. I think this is a mistake and that we need to bring out a different perspective that seeks to reconcile these candidates.

11.4 To Care About Something

Let me first come back to Jaworska's contention that the ability to care on the side of the demented person should warrant respect for her current care-informed desires. I do not think that the mere ability to care – or better: the mere fact that one happens to care about something – is enough to warrant something like 'full moral standing' in the strong sense of inviolability on part of the demented person. Apart from the aforementioned asymmetry (which, as I have indicated does a lot of work in her account) I also believe that Jaworska overstates the *continuity in caring* when it comes to people with dementia. The problem is that, with the onset of the disease, we *stop* caring about a lot of things that used to be very important to us, and we develop new objects of care that would have left us indifferent before. Jaworska, however, seems to employ a Russian Doll model, in which our system of cares, although less complex, would retain the same general features as before. Although this could be true for a large number of dementia patients, it does not account for the possibility that the doll inside, could very well be a *different* doll; one radically at odds with the first.

Jaworska herself observes that caring about something is different from desiring it in the sense that caring somehow extends into the future: caring about something means committing oneself to *keep* caring about that object (Jaworska 2007). In Frankfurt's terms, by caring we seek to maintain some coherence and continuity of ourselves. However, this feature of caring, this link with our 'sense of self', strengthens the Dworkinian perspective, namely that a radical change in our system of cares could be interpreted as a 'loss of self'.

And such changes do seem to be part and parcel of dementia. The most striking example is perhaps that people in the advanced stages of dementia no longer recognize, and therefore no longer care about their husbands, wives, family members, close friends and relatives. And, as an example of a 'new' object of care that emerged with the onset of the disease, we could refer to the famous case of Iris Murdoch who suddenly took a great interest in watching the TeleTubbies.

This criticism also gains strength if we look beyond the Frankfurtian paradigm and acknowledge that we deeply care about – not merely about coherence and continuity – but also about *what* we care about, that is, about the *quality* of our cares. As Susan Wolf points out, we indeed want our children to care about something so that their lives will be imbued with importance, but it is not that we advise them to just "care about what they can" (Wolf 2002). Young children counting blades of grass, or torturing small animals, is generally considered as 'sad' or 'disturbing' rather than worthwhile or valuable. If so, then this extends to our future self as a demented person: we do not want to be engaged in or 'captivated by' such meaningless activities. In short, the focus on the capacity to care can easily be turned against Jaworska's project.

11.5 A Look Ahead

Even though I believe that the arguments of Jaworska and Shiffrin fail, I do think that we should attend to the identity and autonomy of the individual with dementia. In fact, this is what close friends and relatives often do. But they do so, not just by focusing on the 'here and now' (although they do, of course), but by relating the present state of the person with dementia – her current cares, desires and wishes – to the way they remember the person, that is, to the way she was *before* the disease kicked in.

I will try to provide a normative underpinning for this practice in the next section, but for now, I just want to anticipate this idea of what it means to respect the autonomy and identity of a person with dementia.

For example, many authors point out that good care for the demented person involves the preservation of personhood (Buron 2008; Murray and Boyd 2009) and the support of autonomy (McCormack 2002). McCormack, for example, emphasizes the above-mentioned 'Russian doll model' of autonomy, but he shows how this is not a matter of continuous cares (by which the occurent cares are remnants of the old ones) but that caretakers actively need to 'chip away' beyond the person's overt behavior and look for hidden emotions and beliefs. Respect for autonomy (or, as he calls it, authenticity) requires such chipping away: it requires effort and interpretation in order to discern those remaining elements. Also, such interpretation demands sensitivity to the person's life narrative.

He gives the example of Susan, who was once "an independent woman, a professional who was always in control of her own decisions and choices" but who is now in the mid-stages of dementia. Her story is now in need of interpretation. As such, it may not be a 'rational narrative' but it contains:

> …a *cachet of truth*, i.e. […] elements of the person's past life, their biography and autobiography and those of others around [her]. Susan's narrative is consistent with her previous roles in life, as a professional woman, a wife and a person whose family and friends knew to be dedicated to independence in all aspects of her life (McCormack 2002, p. 118).

On the other hand, John McMillan gives the example of Mr. D, a former classics teacher, who, over time became less affectionate to his wife due to his condition of dementia.[5] His wife, Mrs. D says "He's not the man I married – that man has been dead for at least two years." The question is whether Mrs. D is indeed correct: does it make sense to say that the old Mr. D is gone? McMillan claims that it does. He draws on the work of Charles Taylor and concludes that "our webs of interlocution are the foundation upon which our sense of self or qualitative identity is formed and that a typical instance of self-articulation involves developing a first-person narrative about our web of interlocution" (McMillan 2006). But Mr. D is no longer capable of telling such a first-person narrative. Yet, McMillan observes:

> Given his past dedication to family and marriage, his wife's views about his change are crucially important. She has been married to him for most of their lives and knows, possibly almost as well as the pre-dementia Mr. D would have known, what his webs of interlocution or frameworks of value were. So she is in a good position to give a narrative account of his agency and how dementia has damaged it (McMillan 2006, p. 69).

Even if the person herself no longer has access to her narrative or is unable to communicate it, there are certain 'significant others' around her that can make valuable assessments as to how a life with dementia relates to this general life story. The question, of course, is what role such significant others could or should play in deciding for the person with dementia. What these authors have stressed is the

[5] The case was originally described by Tony Hope (1994).

importance of restoring or protecting personhood in taking care of people with dementia. If we are concerned – as we should be – about their quality of life, then this focus on personhood is very important (Murray and Boyd 2009).

11.6 Socializing Autonomy

What I said in the previous section makes clear that respecting the autonomy and personhood of people with dementia is a matter of assistance and interpretation. Jaworska and Shiffrin may be right that the embers of autonomy are still glowing but we should add that it takes effort to get the fire burning again. Moreover, it is a matter of interpretation in light of the person's individual history and not a mere case of respecting occurrent cares. More precisely, to find out what a person cares about right now, is to interpret what she *seemingly* cares about in light of her life story, that is, taking into account "who she used to be".[6] Now perhaps Jaworska meant just that or, at least, she presumably does not want to exclude such interpretative assistance (although she may be afraid of such translation being distortive of the occurrent, salient 'cares' of the person with dementia). Nevertheless, I also believe that one might discover that the 'cares' of the old and the new self, as in the case of Mr. D, have radically come apart, and that it is impossible to reconcile these two stories without having to admit that the story of the present, demented self is fundamentally at odds with the way one envisioned one's entire life. I have therefore briefly indicated how others – caretakers, friends and family members – try to preserve the personhood and autonomy of the individual with dementia.

In this section, however, I want to return to the point of view of the individual herself and how this perspective is influenced (and even constituted) by social elements. There are many ways in which the notion of autonomy has been 'socialized'. A fairly straightforward way to bring out the social aspect is to say that autonomy requires some form of critical reflection and that this ability itself requires a social embedding, or environment, for being developed in the first place. Without some minimal level of education, for example, no-one would have the tools for critically assessing one's own desires or beliefs. This is something we learn, and we learn it from others (most notably, our parents). Crudely put: children 'raised' by wolves would not develop such a capacity. Also, the way we are, or "who we are", our personality – if you like – is the upshot of various social forces. In fact, it has been questioned whether there still is a self, or philosophically speaking, a 'subject', once we acknowledge the interplay and influence of such forces beyond our control. Anyhow, it is clear that we do not create ourselves *ex nihilo* and that critical reflection

[6] Bert Keizer, a famous Dutch physician and philosopher, once, during a workshop, gave the example of a woman with dementia who was unable to communicate her wants without the assistance, that is, interpretation and translation, of her husband. He had to help her in communicating her preferences to her caretakers. I believe this is a clear example of 'assisted autonomy'.

takes as a starting point or background, something which is given rather than created. Therefore, if autonomy essentially means self-determination, then the social nature of the self implicates a socialization of the notion of autonomy. A third way to 'socialize' autonomy is by pointing out its *relational* aspect. Although 'relational autonomy' is an umbrella concept that is used by a variety of authors, it signifies that the individual's autonomy is a matter of the right social relationships between different individuals (Mackenzie and Stoljar 2000). As I mentioned above: the capacity for critical reflection could only develop by virtue of a social environment that indeed fostered or inculcated this capability. In this case, however, the required social relationships are only causally necessary for autonomy. But they could also be *constitutive* of that capacity: for example Axel Honneth and Catriona Mackenzie stress that the required relationship-to-self can only hold if one stands in the appropriate relationship-to-others (Honneth 1995). In order to be autonomous and have normative authority, one has to possess the required self-trust, self-respect and self-esteem and this is impossible without the social recognition of others.

Although these accounts are very interesting, I want to draw attention to a slightly different way of 'socializing autonomy'. It ties in to the Hegelian theme of recognition in the sense that the manner in which the individual perceives of herself is dependent upon due recognition by others. The projects, values, and commitments I endorse – the ones that I identify with, and that identify me – are only valuable to the extent that they are vindicated by others. We do not *create* such value simply by virtue of the act of endorsement. This requires a horizon of significance – to use Taylor's famous phrase – that lies beyond the individual's direct control. Now, both Hegelians – that is, Honneth as well as Taylor – take their cue from Herbert Mead's seminal work on the role of so-called significant others and they develop it (or at least fit it) into an encompassing philosophical framework about social recognition.

For the purposes of this paper, however, I want to stick to this – if you may call it – psycho-philosophical point about the role of significant others. The central mechanism is that we, as individuals, interiorize the perspective of these significant others. We evaluate ourselves in light of their perspective. This is obviously related to the point I made earlier: I can only hold my projects, values and commitments to be valuable if and only if others validate that significance. It is also related to the remark that our 'self' is social in nature, though not because it is entirely swamped by social or natural structures or forces, but because in our own 'private' evaluation we take up the roles of others. The struggle for recognition, then, is a struggle for *their* recognition as constitutive of *our* own identity. The essential point is that for me to exercise my autonomy, to lead the life I want to live, to be committed to projects that I deem valuable, to which I subscribe and which I endorse, I am crucially dependent upon this inter-subjective interplay.

Consequently, as this has repercussions for the way we think of our 'selves', this has ramifications for autonomy as well. We want to be determined by 'what we care about', but this 'what' is not justified by our mere caring about it, we want it to be *worth* caring about and this requires the recognition of others. As I mentioned before, a person could dread the moment when she would no longer care about her family because it is constitutive of who she is. To lose this care is to lose herself. The cares that are left in this future scenario – watching endless episodes of TeleTubbies, dozing in the sunshine, eating peanut-butter-and-jelly sandwiches – do not make up for that terrible loss. In fact, we do not want to care about such worthless things. What I have added to this account now, is that this value judgment is tied in to this social dynamic, in which significant others play a crucial role.

Normally, during a lifetime, the individual retains a dialogical relationship with these significant others. She does not merely interiorize or absorb the others' evaluative perspective. One does not seek recognition through sheer conformity, but the dynamic takes the form of a genuine struggle, that is, an attempt to persuade others of the worth of one's desires, values and commitments. When severely demented (i.e., while incompetent) this dialogical character dissipates in the sense that one is no longer actively engaged in this struggle. In fact, I believe this is a major source of concern for some of us, and I will come back to this point later on. What remains, however, is this social background, the evaluative *milieu* that provided a web of interlocution (and that was indeed McMillan's point in the previous section). Therefore, I agree with both Jaworska and Shiffrin that we should deal with 'what is left', but we should not only look at the remaining capacities on the side of the individual, but also take into account this social fabric that was (and *is*) constitutive of one's identity.

The problem is that we, in cases of *severe* dementia, no longer seem to care about what is worthwhile or not. We just happen to care about certain things, and that's it. On my account, it is not just this bare capacity to care that really matters, but the capacity to care *about* these cares. To the extent that this dimension of evaluative reflections has disappeared, the Dworkinian perspective again gets the upper hand. The problem, however, with Dworkin's account was that it did not pay sufficient concern to the perspective of the person with dementia. So we need a vantage point that relates these two 'selves'.

However, the problem of a 'divide' between the two standpoints is particularly clear in what I called the Problem of Uncertainty. People who draw up advance directives make clear that they do not want to live 'that way'. Critics like Dresser, however, will point out that they do not know what it will be like to live 'that way'. They might think it is dreadful *now*, but it might turn out to be not that bad after all. In fact, in some cases it seems indeed that a life with dementia can be without pain and distress and be characterized as 'relatively comfortable'. Now, several remarks are in place. First, advance directives normally take the form of 'if-then' clauses. A person could therefore stipulate that, in case of such a 'happy' development, her desire for death should have no authority. Secondly, and more importantly, the phrase 'I do not want to live that way!' is confusing, because the quality of life 'on the other side' is seldom the issue. One does not fear being in pain, or being unhappy, but being somehow 'out of touch'. Let me elaborate on this phenomenon.

11.7 The Wreckage of Our Flesh

Why do people dread the prospect of severe dementia? This question is impossible to answer in any conclusive statement. Some people may not dread it at all. They may accept it as a natural part of life. Perhaps they would prefer to be spared of the disease, but if so, 'que sera, sera'. If there is any strength to the liberal-Dworkinian outlook, it is that it provides room for different conceptions of the good, and that it does not require people to share the perspective that a life with dementia is somehow unworthy or demeaning.

Of those who indeed dread the prospect, there could be people who want to avoid the pain,[7] or the confusion and bewilderment, or the general state of anxiety to which some persons with dementia are prone. In short, they may indeed shiver at the prospect of 'living that way', defined in experiential terms. It seems terrible to them to be afraid all the time, to see strange faces, and feeling haunted and wanting to escape. I do not believe that these fears are totally misdirected, and to the extent that they are not, this provides us with a third additional reason to withstand the Problem of Uncertainty. Although interesting from a theoretical point of view, we should not exaggerate this problem in practice. Thomas Nagel may have rightfully questioned our ability to answer the question 'What is it like to be a bat?', but the prospect of dementia is not that opaque. We do know that dementia can sometimes be a horrible state of mind.

Even so, I think Dworkin is correct in saying that we are not so much worried about the way it would *feel* to be demented, the way that we would *experience* the state of dementia. It is not so much that we are worried about what goes on inside, so to speak. We are worried about the fact that we have somehow lost touch with the things we deemed essential of ourselves, that we have lost touch with reality, with a world of meaning and importance. Just being demented – no matter how pleasant it could be – indicates a loss of self. It is the fear of us somehow living on as not-us.

People with dementia are sometimes described as 'living dead' (Buchanan 2001). What this hyperbole is meant to convey is the idea of a mere existence, not quite on a par with a 'life'. As my dramatic title suggests, the image that some of us might fear in dementia is that of the wreckage of our flesh just drifting about aimlessly, with no point or purpose, while we have lost all control over the way in which this driftwood may collide with the things we held so dear in life. But, of course, we don't know if and to what extent such a collision will take place. And this is where others enter the picture. For some people then, proxy decision-making is highly appropriate (and not just second-best).

Let me distinguish three ways in which the perspective of others can be crucially important to us when we are diagnosed with dementia. First, we sometimes care about what these others care about in the most obvious sense, namely that we would not like to be a burden to them. This is so because we care about them. Also, if we could still bring some joy to their lives, death would not be necessary; our life would still be worthwhile. Notice, however, that such joy is never sufficient: even if there is evidence that these others would be quite alright with us being in a state of dementia, this does not imply that – because of this – we should be kept alive at all costs. My point is merely that the evaluative standpoint of others is often relevant in deciding what should happen to us in a state of severe incompetence.

---

[7] There does seem to be reason to be worried about pain management for people with dementia (Malloy and Hadjistavropoulos 2004).

Secondly, we also value their perspective because they are the best available judges of our lives' continuity. This is, in fact, what we expect these proxies to do: that is, to assess whether some decision or option is in line with our character and personality. As they are familiar with 'who we were' and 'who we wanted to be', as well as with who we are *now*, they are in a privileged position to judge whether some course of action is either in line or 'out of synch' with our way of life. They are indeed the safe keepers of our personality, as the examples I mentioned above were meant to indicate. They alone are able to bridge the gap that separates the old competent self from the now-incompetent one. They were there when we were fully competent, and they are still there when these critical capacities have waned.

However, their incompetence in these matters has often been emphasized. It turns out, as Dresser notes, that many of these surrogates would take *different* decisions than the ones we would take ourselves. This was the Problem of Interpretation. Apparently others are not that good at articulating what are supposed to be our wishes. One way to respond to these accusations is pointing out that this imperfection is made good, is compensated, by their privileged position 'on the other side' of the competence divide. They may not be capable of perfectly tracking our point of view, but they do know something that we do not: they are there to compare the condition of us as a demented person with the one that was still unaffected by the disease. However, it could be further questioned, if such 'perfect tracking' is indeed what they are supposed to do. Those who choose to rely on proxies, I guess, value the perspective of others, as mere evaluative beings. And this would be a third way in which proxies are important. We appreciate the way *they* would evaluate our condition, and not just how they would think *we* would assess it. This ties in with the earlier remarks about our identity and the need for recognition. It matters to us if they would deem our life undignified or horrible, for example. Notice that this has nothing to do with the way that our existence as a highly dependent being affects their lives (that is the question of it being a burden or a joy to others), but about a value judgment that is independent of such other-regarding concerns. It is the mere perception of our life being somehow worth living or not, that matters to us.

So, it is not about the experiential side of the disease, nor do we want to make sure that they would decide as we would have done (again, we would have drawn up an advance directive, but how should we know all the relevant details?), but about the way others – some important others – perceive of the value of our life. This because already while fully competent, 'alive and kicking', we construct and shape our lives in a perpetual, ongoing dialogue with these significant others.

Let us take our inspiration from horror movies, one more time (the living dead, remember). The effect of dementia, of the disease slowly destroying our memory, is akin to the experience of walls closing in on us. Now, whereas in these movies part of the horror consists in the victim being a powerless witness to her own gradual, excruciating demise, in case of dementia, we are sometimes (yet, not always) spared from the cruelty of spectatorship. We do not have to be aware of us gradually losing all sorts of abilities. However, what remains is the uncomfortable fact that *others* will indeed be spectators to our decline.

Now, if there is any truth in this description of the concerns that some people have regarding dementia, then this indicates a standpoint that is able to surmount the standoff between Dresser and Dworkin for *it fundamentally shows the importance of others in the decision-making process in case of dementia.* As such, it solves the Problems of Uncertainty (because the experiential question is irrelevant) and the Problem of Interpretation. The latter because interpretation is not a threat to our supposedly 'true wishes' – i.e., others being unable to track them, contaminating them with their own views on things – but an integral part of what we want them to do. Dresser's remark that not many people draw up advance directives but instead rely on friends and relatives indicates perhaps not that they rely on some second-best standard, but that they do not expect them to approximate or mimic their former self. Notice that many of these surrogate decision-makers will do just that, and try and pay justice to the individual's own conception of the good, but the fact that they incorporate their own views is not a matter of unfortunate contamination. We do not expect them to shed their evaluative skin. It matters to us how they perceive our situation, whether they can still retain our self under these new conditions. This account then does not privilege either the former competent individual's perspective or the one of the present individual with dementia. What matters is how these different episodes interact, or make sense, in the eyes of these significant others.

11.8 Replies to Some Possible Objections

To conclude, let me briefly respond to some anticipated objections. To some it may seem as if I give too much power to others in deciding what should happen to people with dementia. Notice, however, that I do not claim that all individuals have these worries that I describe. Like Dworkin, I want to provide a normative underpinning to those who have such concerns. I do not in any way want to promote this approach to those who do not. Unlike Dworkin, however, my proposal does not rely on any hierarchy between critical and experiential interests, nor do I want to maintain any strict distinction between them. Yet, I do agree with him that to show respect for autonomy, these surrogates or proxies should somehow be appointed. And this may solve a second worry, namely "*Who* would have to take these decisions?" The answer is: those that we deem fit for the job. We may be mistaken, of course, about their capacities and intentions, but since people diagnosed with severe dementia are highly dependent upon assistance, I fail to see how we could eliminate such 'defective help' altogether. When I say that proxies should be assigned and therefore that this assignment is a matter of respecting one's autonomy while fully competent, I nevertheless wonder whether such assigning should require an explicit act of authorization or whether there can also be some kind of default option (e.g., one's children as default proxies) with the possibility, of course, to opt-out. Such a default would be justified, presumably, because we generally have a good idea of who these 'significant others' are (and who will be around when at the time of need). This is an empirical question. Finally, I must admit that my approach is not in any way new or groundbreaking.

Family members, for example, already have a say in the treatment of their relatives with dementia. What I intended to do is to provide some theoretical grounds for that authority and to question the common suspicion that befalls such proxies, whether as a poor substitutes for indicating the individual's own wishes, or as self-interested, and therefore not-to-be-trusted parties in the debate.

References

Buchanan, A. 2001. Advance directives and the personal identity problem. In *Bioethics*, ed. J. Harris, 131–156. Oxford: Oxford University Press.

Buron, B. 2008. Levels of personhood: A model for dementia care. *Geriatric Nursing* 29: 324–332.

Degrazia, D. 1999. Advance directives, dementia, and 'the someone else problem'. *Bioethics* 13: 373–391.

Dresser, R. 2006. Dworkin on dementia: Elegant theory, questionable policy. In *Bioethics: An anthology*, ed. H. Kuhse and P. Singer, 365–373. Malden: Blackwell Publishing.

Dworkin, R. 1993. *Life's dominion: An argument about abortion, euthanasia, and individual freedom*. New York: Alfred A Knopf.

Dworkin, R. 2006. Life past reason. In *Bioethics: An anthology*, ed. H. Kuhse and P. Singer, 357–364. Malden: Blackwell Publishing.

Honneth, A. 1995. *The struggle for recognition: The moral grammar of social conflicts*. Cambridge, MA: MIT Press.

Hope, T. 1994. Personal identity and psychiatric illness. In *Philosophy, psychology and psychiatry*, ed. A.P. Griffiths, 131–143. Cambridge: Cambridge University Press.

Jaworska, A. 1999. Respecting the margins of agency: Alzheimer's patients and the capacity to value. *Philosophy and Public Affairs* 28: 105–138.

Jaworska, A. 2007. Caring and full moral standing. *Ethics* 117: 460–497.

Mackenzie, C., and N. Stoljar (eds.). 2000. *Relational autonomy: Feminist perspectives on autonomy, agency, and the social self*. New York: Oxford University Press.

Malloy, D.C., and T. Hadjistavropoulos. 2004. The problem of pain management among persons with dementia, and the ontology of relationships. *Nursing Philosophy* 5: 147–159.

McCormack, B. 2002. The person of the voice: Narrative identities in informed consent. *Nursing Philosophy* 3: 114–119.

McMillan, J. 2006. Identity, self, and dementia. In *Dementia: Mind, meaning, and the person*, ed. J.C. Hughes, S.J. Louw, and R. Sabat, 63–70. Oxford: Oxford University Press.

Murray, L.M., and S. Boyd. 2009. Protecting personhood and achieving quality of life for older adults with dementia in the U.S. Health care system. *Journal of Aging and Health* 21: 350–373.

Parfit, D. 1984. *Reasons and persons*. Oxford: Oxford University Press.

Shiffrin, S.V. 2004. Autonomy, beneficence, and the permanently demented. In *Dworkin and his critics*, ed. J. Burley, 195–217. Malden: Blackwell Publishing.

Wolf, S. 2002. The true, the good, and the lovable: Frankfurt's avoidance of objectivity. In *Contours of agency: Essays on themes from Harry Frankfurt*, ed. S. Buss and L. Overton, 227–244. Cambridge, MA: MIT Press.

Chapter 12
On the Sacred Character of Human Life and Death: General Discussion and Conclusion of Part II

Herman De Dijn

12.1 Introduction

It is my task to briefly look back on the discussions and reflections in this book concerning the topic of justice, luck and responsibility in health care, and in particular on the second part with end-of-life care issues such as our individual and social duties regarding end-of-life care for the elderly, especially for people suffering from dementia. It was not difficult to discover two different methodological approaches to the topic.

In the first approach, the theoretical endeavour is predominant, particularly the attempt to justify existing, real-life practices and the ethical intuitions involved. Some theories seem able to do this better than others. Of course, theorization is here a dialectical process: practices and intuitions may require changes in the theory, or the adoption of a better theory; but theorization seems to imply the possibility and even the necessity to change practices and/or intuitions.

The second approach starts from very concrete and particular situations, involving sometimes difficult, tragic and complex problems that occur in everyday health care. In such cases, we have to provide answers to these situations, or to the problem at hand.

I will very briefly discuss these two approaches as they appear in the various contributions to this volume and formulate some questions that seem to deserve additional attention if we want to reflect on the relationship between justice, luck and responsibility in health care, in particular on matters related to the ethics of end-of-life-care.

H. De Dijn (✉)
Institute of Philosophy, Catholic University of Leuven,
Kardinaal Mercierplein 2, box 3200, 3000 Leuven, Belgium
e-mail: Herman.DeDijn@hiw.kuleuven.be

Y. Denier et al. (eds.), *Justice, Luck & Responsibility in Health Care*,
Library of Ethics and Applied Philosophy 30, DOI 10.1007/978-94-007-5335-8_12,

12.2 Starting from Concrete Situations

Other authors proceed quite differently. Instead of constructing or further developing a theory capable of providing certain answers to particular problems, they start from concrete difficulties, intuitions and pre-reflexive understandings encountered in the context of end-of-life care itself.

When looking at the contributions of John Hardwig, Govert den Hartogh and Thomas Nys, we see that they all start from everyday questions like: Do I have a right or a duty to die? What should we think about assisted suicide? Should our children care for us indefinitely? What should the doctor, or our family members, do with the advance directive in our wallet? And what exactly do we fear when we are afraid of Alzheimer's disease? In these contributions, common sense reflections and understandings, human experiences and worries occupy central stage.

In the course of reflection on these concrete issues, certain notions or distinctions (like the right to die) and certain ethical principles (like respect for autonomy) are being appealed to or developed. The question here seems to be: are they sufficient or adequate to solve the problem or difficulty; and, even more fundamentally, do we really understand these notions and distinctions well? Do we really know what we mean by 'justice' and 'autonomy', by 'the self', by the distinction made between the 'then self' and the 'now self', etc.? These are very important questions, since a major objective of this book supposedly is the clarification of fundamental concepts like justice, luck and responsibility.

One could add that this clarification should include many more notions, especially concepts which belong to what Elisabeth Anscombe called 'philosophical psychology'. According to Anscombe in her famous paper entitled 'Modern Moral Philosophy' (Anscombe 1958), we should refrain from doing moral philosophy until we have an adequate philosophy of (moral) psychology. I agree with Anscombe that, in addition to the fundamental reflections presented in this book, more inquiry is needed on elementary notions we may take to be unproblematic, but which we perhaps do not understand properly, especially not when we are doing philosophy, and which therefore may steer our discussion in directions that are misleading.

In any case, the discussions and reflections in this book demonstrated to me the need for additional and deeper reflection on certain fundamental concepts and questions, more or less related to moral psychology. Let me give some illustrations.

12.3 What Is a Human Life?

Many of the discussions in the second part of this book involve the question: What is a truly human life? What gives it its worth or value? Does it consist in having had a certain amount of life-years of a certain quality? Is a good life about having had a certain number of experiences of a certain kind? Or is a truly human life better to be judged holistically, in accordance with the fulfilment of overarching ends or purposes? If so, doesn't this mean that its value can only be determined in the context of recognition by others? And what do we mean exactly when we are saying that human beings are relational beings? Judging a human life's worth in terms of the number of QALY's (quality adjusted life years), as is being suggested in some lines of reasoning, may be evident in one perspective (e.g. in consequentialist reasoning), but utter nonsense in another (e.g. in a holistic consideration of the significance and value of a human life). Both perspectives cannot be right at the same time?

Involved in this discussion are the even more fundamental questions of the relation between life and time, self and other. These relationships (for example between *Dasein* and *Zeit,* between *Dasein* and *Mitsein*) have been the subject of deep thought in continental philosophy. Insights related to the notion of *life world* (*Lebenswelt*), have already been taken up also in analytic philosophy (cf. the work of authors like Peter Strawson, Bernard Williams, Stuart Hampshire, Richard Rorty, and many others) and could be made use of to refine our discussions. One can look upon people as atomistic individuals standing in purely contractual relationships with each other, for whom time is a succession of more or less agreeable or painful experiences, and on life as a space for self-management. Philosophers of the *life world* have put forward a completely different view of human beings, of their relation towards other human beings and towards themselves, of the way they experience and 'live' time while aiming at a human life, which is not directed at the fulfilment of needs, but rather at the pursuit of desires with respect to overarching values.

12.4 Theory as Central Preoccupation

Some contributors are interested in developing the consequences of theories of justice or equality with respect to end-of-life care issues, and vice versa. In the first part of the book, this is particularly the case with the contributions of Daniel Hausman and others. Hausman discusses the comparative merits of certain theories with respect to the justification of equality in health care or of the acceptability of specific inequalities; Shlomi Segall focuses on the merits of luck egalitarianism in relation to affirmative action in health; and Yvonne Denier inquires into the consequences of luck egalitarianism with regard to people's decisions in matters of reproduction.

From the second part of the book, we learn that a theoretical discussion can be helpful in providing answers to specific and concrete questions, like whether or not there is such a thing as 'a duty to die', or at least a responsibility not to extend 'futile' care. From Martin Gunderson's analysis, we learn that there might indeed be good reasons for not wanting to extend one's life indefinitely, but that individual freedom to decide what should be done at the end of one's life prevails over the duty to die. In his analysis, Elisabeth Anderson's theory of democratic equality serves as a corner stone. Another theory we meet in the second part of the book is the one defended in the contribution of Chris Gastmans, *viz.* the ethical theory of Louvain Personalism, which is based on the notion of respect for the dignity of the human person in his or her various dimensions. This theory is used in the discussion of the need for dignity-enhancing care for people with dementia.

In general, one can ask several questions as to the necessity of theorization in ethics. For instance, do we have to have a *theoretical* justification for ethical *practice*? And is that even possible? Furthermore, there also seems to be a problem with respect to the relationship between theory and fundamental ethical concepts. Are the concepts first? Or is their meaning ultimately determined by the theory? These are fundamental issues with respect to our ethical reflection. As is evident from these proceedings, the discussion between theories will continue; and it seems unlikely we will easily reach final conclusions in this domain.

12.5 What Is Autonomy in Relation to My Life?

Another problematic notion, explicitly or implicitly present in discussions in the second part of the book, is that of autonomy as related to my life as a whole. Sometimes autonomy is understood as the autonomy of a pure subject standing in a relation of ownership vis-à-vis its own body, a subject which through its own pure will can mould its own character and acquire competences in function of its self-chosen ends. The life of such a subject is considered as a kind of investment area to be filled with as many 'worthwhile' experiences as possible through self-management.

This is the ideology behind a lot of talk about autonomy today. Can real autonomy, as being lived in the *life world* ever mean anything like this? When I judge my life, can I do this objectively (as if it were the life of someone else)? Or is it the case that I am always already attached to it in an attachment, which precedes any conscious identification in such a way that even when I have a particular wish (even when I want to end my life, for instance), it is on the very basis of this ineradicable attachment ("*I* cannot go on like *this*".)?

In a discussion on genetic enhancement, Michael Sandel used Hannah Arendt's notion of *natality* (which reminds one of Heidegger's *Geworfenheit*) (Sandel 2007) in order to express the fact that human beings are born, not made (certainly not by themselves). Life is a (sometimes terrible) gift. It is only in the context of giftedness, as Sandel stresses, that a notion like autonomy can and must be given its proper meaning.

12.6 What Is the Relation of a Person to Another?

We have responsibilities toward other people, and *special* responsibilities toward particular others, like friends and family members. Again, with respect to these responsibilities, what looks perhaps straightforward at first, is less straightforward when thinking things through.

For instance, when we care about a family member, what exactly is it that we care about? When I care about my child, I care not simply because of its present or future interesting qualities or dimensions. Or put in stronger terms: when a pregnant parent cares for her unborn baby, she cares for it even before she knows what interesting qualities it has or will have. She cares for it because of its singularity and the singularity of the (family) relationship: because it is *her* child. What is behind this care is the appeal on us of the *symbolic* meaning attached to family relationships. The term 'symbolic' does not refer to that which is 'merely' symbolic, as opposed to *the real thing*. Blood relationship is symbolic in the sense that the material or causal tie is over-determined by culturally established meanings and values, whereby the tie is not the justification, but only the 'incarnation' of these meanings and values. This also means that the vicissitudes of the material tie have implications for these meanings and values; e. g. the death of a child means an *irreparable* loss. The importance of the symbolic tie linking one person to another person, one human body to another has been discussed by some of my colleagues here in Leuven (Breeur and Burms 2008; Burms 2001, 2008).

In all human societies blood relationship automatically has symbolic meaning, with special ethical consequences related to it. Some human relationships are of course a matter of choice. But even then, as for instance in marriage or adoption, they are symbolically over-determined which is noticeable from the symbols and rituals attached to their inauguration (adoption often or usually requires obtaining a new (family) name, making the child into *our* child, even though not in the sense related to biological offspring). The symbolic nature of family relationships implies that what interests us in the other person transcends all interesting qualities, the combination of which could also be found in someone else. The essence of family relationship is that it points to the importance for me of *this* person and *this* body as my next of kin, in whatever state he or she may be, whether handicapped, or old or depressed. Even dead, the person remains of extreme importance to the family. That is why we treat the deceased with care, and approach them in a respectful, even hallowed way. We do not want the dead body to be mishandled; even though the dead cannot possibly be the subject of harm (except symbolic harm).

It seems then that we cannot deny the fact that the relationship between human beings cannot be solely understood in terms of the useful or interesting qualities they have for each other. Indeed, not only family relationship is deeply symbolic, the same is true of our relationship with human beings in general. And again, this relationship has to do with the 'incarnation' of human beings in their body. The distress and horror people feel with respect to the violation of the human body, especially the female body or the body of children, and with respect to the desecration of dead bodies and graves, is not an irrational remnant of taboo mentality, but something central to human relationships as essentially mediated by the human body. Instead of an anomaly, it is something, which should be at the centre of our understanding of ethical behaviour vis-à-vis human beings. Again, this topic is not completely absent from analytic philosophy (see Diamond 1995). The conception of the 'sacredness' of the human body and of the human person is not the prerogative of religious thought. It is and should be a central topic in secular ethical thinking as well. Not only continental thinkers like Martin Heidegger, Hannah Arendt or Simone Weil, but also some analytic authors; some of whom, like David Wiggins (2009) or Stuart Hampshire (1983), have explicitly used this notion of sacredness in their reflections on ethics. 'Sacred' here means that which is *'hors commerce'*, which cannot be merchandised, which has no price. It is also that, which is set apart and cannot be violated. It is a concept, which has meaning also outside the strictly religious context.

12.7 Sacrifice and Piety

The symbolic union of family relationship can sometimes (rightly or wrongly) be the origin of great sacrifice. A well-known version of extreme sacrifice in the context of family relationships is to be found in Greek Thought where Antigone, the subject of Sophocles' tragedy, attempts to secure a respectable burial for her brother Polynices, even though he was a traitor to Thebes and the law forbade mourning for him, on pain of death. Antigone wants to bury her brother, because he is her brother, and because it is the will of the gods. For doing this, she willingly and knowingly risks and sacrifices her life.

In this book, we have learned from John Hardwig that voluntary family care for an elderly family member can be extremely demanding, even self-sacrificing. From Yvonne Denier's contribution, we have learned that pregnant couples can decide to continue the pregnancy of a seriously handicapped baby in the full knowledge that their lives will be very complicated and demanding. However, it is not only in such extreme cases, that we discover the sacrifices that come with family relationships. We also notice them in our daily lives. Having a family, being a family member, being a husband or a wife, a brother or a sister, having children or being a child oneself, bring with them all sorts of duty and obligation, and small or great sacrifices. Fortunately, the symbolic order in which we live, normally helps us to deal with the 'cost' of living in such relationships, like for instance the rites of burial or cremation help us to mourn the loss and to resume the ordinary course of life. We also should not forget that everyday family life is replete with its well-known, fixed moments of small rites, like having breakfast or dinner together, reading a bed-time story, the traditional Sunday-morning family walk, or afternoon-tea with the grandparents. It would be wrong to divorce all this completely from ethics.

Taking into account the symbolic context of human life and particularly of family life, it seems very odd to understand the quality of family relationships in terms of their usefulness, or on their output determined by a careful cost-benefit-analysis in terms of quality-adjusted life years (QALY's). To conceive of responsibility in family relationships in terms of measurement of QALY's seems to equate them with business-like relationship. To me, this seems to demonstrate a complete alienation from the perspective of *piety*, which is very closely related to the symbolic character of family relationships. George Santayana defined piety as follows: "Piety is the spirit's acknowledgment of its incarnation" (Santayana 1905, p. 184). In view of this definition, and in view of the nature of family relationships, it is not surprising that piety is so deeply involved in the incarnational ties between family members.

If this is the truth behind family relationships, how could I – as some lines of reasoning in the second part of this book seem to suggest – enter into a discussion with my mother or father, weighing the comparative weight of a little less QALY's for them vis-à-vis extensive financial benefits for me? What can more QALY's for me mean in comparison to the incredible lack of loyalty and piety betrayed by the very thought of such a discussion? The problem in real family relations is not about justice with respect to benefits and burdens measured in terms of QALY's, the problem is primarily about piety, love, guilt, shame, disgrace, atonement, etc. It is not surprising then – by the way – that ethics and ethical reflection are deeply narrative in nature. Movies like Wim Wenders' *Paris, Texas* (1984), or novels like J.M. Coetzee's *Disgrace* (1999), or Ian McEwan's *Atonement* (McEwan 2001) can show us a great deal of what it means to be part of a family and what it means to be ethical in this context. When this narrative background is not taken into account, ethics becomes an abstraction or, worse, an insensitive meddling with human affairs of great importance.

By pointing at all this, I do not wish to deny that there can be conflicts between the demands of filial piety and the financial survival of the family. However, these conflicts cannot be solved in a way which completely disregards the symbolic nature of family relationships. What is certainly needed here, are common institutions and common rituals telling us how to proceed. The need for institutions and rituals is, for instance, expressed in a dramatic way in the Japanese movie *The Ballad of Narayama* (1983). The movie is set in a small rural village in Northern Japan in the nineteenth century and pictures the tradition of a tribe living in very harsh conditions. To guarantee survival of the family, old people who have reached the age of 70 are carried to the top of the mountain Narayama at the beginning of winter, to leave them there to die, a practice known as *ubasute*. By custom, this task is assigned to the oldest son. What makes the movie so interesting, is that it demonstrates that it is only possible for the son to carry out this terrible task because it is a practice, which is steeped in tradition and rite.

It is not premeditated and orchestrated death per se which is ethically abominable; it is a death which is not part of meaningful human relationships determined by symbols and expressed in some form of ritual.

12.8 Notion of Personal Identity – The Sacredness of Each and Every Human Being

One last example of crucial notions and related questions to be much more thoroughly investigated in the context of our discussion of justice, luck and responsibility in end-of-life care is the notion of Self and the problem of personal identity. Certain notions of the Self make it impossible to understand the fear of disintegration of one's self, or of losing everything which has been important in one's life. Compare the opposition between the 'critical' self caring about disintegration and the purely experiential self, as has been discussed in the contributions of Chris Gastmans, Govert den Hartogh and Thomas Nys.

What exactly is the relationship between personal identity as referring to "a living organism of the human species in which houses *up to a point* a subject of experience", and a personal Self which in its constitution and self-awareness "is conditioned by its being-for-others"? As Hume has already demonstrated, it is impossible to find the ground for personal identity in the individual's self-awareness. But it seems equally unsatisfactory to let personal identity depend simply on the (re)cognition of others? Perhaps the identity of the body is what is the real basis of personal identity (which is not to say that inter-subjectivity plays no role at all)? (Breeur and Burms 2008).

Understanding the nature of care equally seems to suppose a close link between Self, Body, and Other. Suppose one is a living organism of the human species *without* a controlling subject (having a will, and long term projects). *Why* should this organism still be an object of care and piety, perhaps even overriding the advance directives of the 'earlier' subject? That this living organism no longer has normal physical, psychological, let alone relational or moral capacities (it no longer cares about anything), does this matter at all for care? If it doesn't, if simply *being a human body* (born from a woman) is sufficient for entitlement to care, what then is the basis of this entitlement? What is the basis for the special dignity of the human body?

It cannot be the special status of the human body from a neutral point of view, because from this perspective, it is only gradually different from other (complex) bodies (like those of animals). Again it must be the symbolic meaning and value attached to something material: *human* bodies (as in the case of the basis of care for family members, which is the symbolic meaning and value linked to family relationship). This time, special meaning and value is bestowed upon *any body* that stands in a certain causal-symbolic relationship with other human bodies. Belonging to the same (biological) species is given special moral significance here, not because of the objective difference with other bodies, but because *we see them as* 'untouchable' within our attitude of piety towards persons and the bodies they are incarnated in (De Dijn 1999). The attitude is not based on the objective difference. The objective difference is given special meaning, is symbolically over-determined in and by the attitude.

As such, and contrary to the thesis of George Kateb (2011), I defend the idea that there is no *external* justification for the idea of the special dignity of the human person or the human body. Human dignity has to do with the special meaning or significance with which each and every human body spontaneously appears to us (Wiggins 2009). The justification for our care can only be *internal*; it can only be grasped by someone who is seeing human bodies *as* persons. So if we want to ask *why* we should treat severely demented patients with respect (for instance why we cannot simply lock them out of our lives, or why we still have to respect their privacy when they are being washed, even when they are no longer aware of what we are doing), then the answer is simple. It is because they are human in this fundamental symbolic sense, which we express with terms like 'human dignity', 'sacredness', etc.

12.9 Concluding Reflection

If we want to reach our objective, which is the clarification of central notions like justice, equality, luck and responsibility, and their application to ethical discussions in end-of-life care issues, it seems unavoidable also to reflect on other, related, fundamental notions. It therefore seems to me insufficient to concentrate simply on the relative merits of certain theories presupposing an already adequate insight into our fundamental notions. On the contrary, more preliminary work in the field of 'moral anthropology' is indispensable, as well as more reflection on what we are doing in real life (the life of the *life world*) and on the expressions of this in narratives of all kind. If this means that streamlined philosophical management of ethical discussions is (indefinitely) postponed, perhaps it is not so unwelcome a result for people's ethical behaviour after all?

References

Anscombe, E. 1958. Modern moral philosophy. *Philosophy* 33(124): 1–16.
Breeur, R., and A. Burms. 2008. Persons and relics. *Ratio* 21(2): 134–146.
Burms, A. 2001. Wetenschap, ethiek en symbolische betekenis. In *Moeten, mogen, kunnen. Ethiek en wetenschap*, ed. B. Raymaekers, A. Van de Putte, and G. Van Riel. Leuven: Universitaire Pers.
Burms, A. 2008. Natuur en symbool. In *De sacraliteit van leven en dood. Voor een brede bio-ethiek*, ed. A. Burms and H. De Dijn. Kalmthout: Pelckmans.
Coetzee, J.M. 1999. *Disgrace*. London: Secker & Warburg.
De Dijn, H. 1999. Values and incarnation. In *Incarnation*, ed. M.M. Olivetti. Padova: CEDAM.
Diamond, C. 1995. Eating meat and eating people. In *The realistic spirit*, ed. C. Diamond. Cambridge, MA: MIT Press.
Hampshire, S. 1983. Morality and pessimism. In *Morality and conflict*, ed. S. Hampshire. Oxford: Blackwell.
Imamura, S. (dir.) 1983. *The Ballad of Nayarama*, Toei Company.
Kateb, G. 2011. *Human dignity*. Cambridge: The Belknap Press of Harvard University Press.
McEwan, I. 2001. *Atonement*. London: Cape.
Sandel, M. 2007. *The case against perfection. Ethics in the age of genetic engineering*. Cambridge: The Belknap Press of Harvard University Press.
Santayana, G. 1905. *The life of reason*. London: Constable.
Wenders, W. (dir.) 1984. *Paris, Texas*, Road Movies Filmproduktion.
Wiggins, D. 2009. Solidarity and the root of the ethical. *Tijdschrift voor Filosofie* 71(2): 239–269.

Epilogue: How to Move Forward?

Paul Schotsmans

In a recent publication on *Health and Social Justice*, Jennifer Prah Ruger puts the following question: "Can the world become a far healthier place?" She reacts without reservation: "Unquestionably", but therefore it is "time to move forward" (Prah Ruger 2010, pp. 235–236).

Indeed, democratically organized equality provides powerful reasons for individuals to take responsibility for their own health and at the same time for society to provide access to a minimal level of care for all its members, whether or not they have acted responsibly in the past. The theoretical debates on the one hand (How to understand justice, luck and responsibility in health care?) and the highly pragmatic challenges on the other hand (like the – eventually preventive and predictive – treatment of patients with genetic diseases, dementia, etc.) make us all aware that we have to move forward: to create a more "just" world for all human beings.

Far too long, bioethicists have neglected the duty to situate highly personalized responsibilities and challenges in the context of national and international health care systems and health care policies. I still remember my first years in the field of bioethics (from 1982 onwards): only a small part of our time was devoted to the societal aspects of the topics we discussed (like reproductive technologies, medical decisions at the end of life, etc.). Gradually, however, bioethicists started taking a look outside of their "micro-context" and integrating societal challenges in their ethical reasoning and advice: No one lives merely on his own. No one is born with a purely white page. We are all situated human beings.

In their reflections and discussions of issues like abortion, reproductive technologies, human genetics, medical decisions concerning the end of life, treatment of severely demented patients, bioethicists have to integrate the societal, generational and human environment. This is unavoidable.

P. Schotsmans (✉)
Centre for Biomedical Ethics and Law, Catholic University of Leuven,
Kapucijnenvoer 35, box 7001, 3000 Leuven, Belgium

Y. Denier et al. (eds.), *Justice, Luck & Responsibility in Health Care*,
Library of Ethics and Applied Philosophy 30, DOI 10.1007/978-94-007-5335-8,

This growing societal awareness at the same time makes clear that times are changing quickly. Sometimes, it looks as if medicine and health care are no longer about healing, but about consuming and providing, as Hartzband and Groopman make clear:

> We are in the midst of an economic crisis, and efforts to reform the health care system have centered on controlling spiraling costs. To that end, many economists and policy planners have proposed that patient care should be industrialized and standardized (2011, p. 1372).

Both authors attract our attention to the danger: using terminology like consumers and providers might be a reductionist view on medicine and health care. It ignores the psychological, spiritual and humanistic dimensions of health care. These observations illustrate that it will not be an easy task to combine personal responsibility, economic welfare and just allocation of health care resources. Nevertheless, in our focus on the patient, who we should care for and care about, societal justifications should never lead to reducing the patient to a mere consumer.

This publication enters fully in the debate on the mixture of personal responsibility, economic progress or crisis, social ethics and value orientations. The authors clarify how complex the mechanisms might be to situate individual choices in an historical, societal and international context.

I am convinced that this is the future of bioethics. Without socializing the debates (even on seemingly purely private choices), we are acting as if we are supernatural human beings. Putting our choices and responsibilities into context makes them real and do "incarnate" the fundamental theories we are sometimes highly attached to.

Let us indeed move on and forward. Ethical reasoning and deliberation may contribute to a greater awareness of our duties to each other, and to a larger societal integration of our reflections. Finally however, we all might become sick and dependent ourselves. Therefore our reflection and inquiries must end in a better health care at the bedside of the patient. Only then, we might say that real progress has been made.

References

Prah Ruger, J. 2010. *Health and social justice*. Oxford: University Press.

Hartzband, P., and J. Groopman. 2011. The new language of medicine. *New England Journal of Medicine* 365: 1372–1373.

Personalia

Herman De Dijn Herman De Dijn (1943) is professor emeritus at the KU Leuven. He obtained his PhD in Philosophy at the Institute of Philosophy (KU Leuven). He was a postdoctoral researcher at St. Edmund's College, Cambridge (UK). He became full professor in Leuven in 1977.

His academic teaching and research was situated in the domain of Modern Philosophy (especially Spinoza and Hume). He spent periods of research and lecturing in Great Britain (Cambridge and Edinburgh), Mexico, Japan, China, South Africa and the USA. He occupied the Belgian Francqui Chair in Philosophy in Louvain-la-Neuve in 2001, the Spinoza Chair at the University of Amsterdam (spring 2007) and held the Erasmus Lectureship in Harvard (spring 2009). He is a member of the Royal Academy of Belgium, and was vice-rector for the Humanities at the KU Leuven from 1995 till 2000.

Apart from Spinoza and Hume, his thought is influenced mainly by the philosophy of Ludwig Wittgenstein. Most of De Dijn's academic publications are on the philosophy of Spinoza and Hume. He published *Spinoza. The Way to Wisdom* (Purdue University Press 1996), *Modernité et tradition* (Peeters/Vrin 2004) and together with his colleague Arnold Burms a collection of essays on bio-ethics *De sacraliteit van leven en dood. Voor een brede bio-ethiek* (Klement/Pelckmans 2001).

Yvonne Denier Yvonne Denier (1976) studied Philosophy and Applied Ethics at the KU Leuven. In 2005, she obtained a Doctoral Degree in Philosophy with a study on justice in health care (published by Springer in 2007).

She has been visiting researcher at the *Internationales Zentrum für Ethik in den Wissenschaften* in Tübingen (2001–2002), and at the *Hastings Center* in New York (2006). She is Ethical Advisor of *Zorgnet Vlaanderen*, an umbrella organization for over 500 health care institutions (hospitals, nursing homes and organizations in mental health care) in Flanders (Belgium). She is also Assistant Professor of Health Care Ethics at the *Centre for Biomedical Ethics and Law* (Faculty of Medicine, KU Leuven).

Her research focuses on health care ethics, organizational ethics, end-of-life care ethics, and theories of distributive justice and resource allocation. She teaches on these subjects, has given over 50 lectures in national and international conferences,

Y. Denier et al. (eds.), *Justice, Luck & Responsibility in Health Care*, Library of Ethics and Applied Philosophy 30, DOI 10.1007/978-94-007-5335-8, and has published in several internationally peer-reviewed journals. She also participates as an ethicist in various ethics committees on local and community level in Flanders. She is a member of the Belgian Advisory Committee on Bioethics, which advises the Federal Government in Belgium.

Govert den Hartogh Govert den Hartogh (1943) studied theology in Kampen and philosophy in Leiden and Oxford. From 1974 until 2008 he has taught moral, political and legal philosophy and medical ethics, as an Assistant, Associate and Full Professor, in the Department of Philosophy and the Faculties of Law and Medicine of the University of Amsterdam.

He has been the first director of the Netherlands School for Research in Practical Philosophy (1993–1998). As professor emeritus he still directs some research projects, including a project on indirect paternalism in the professional ethics of doctors. He has been a member of one of the Dutch regional review committees for euthanasia from 1998 to 2010, and is a member of the Dutch Health Council.

He is the editor of *The Good Life as a Public Good* (2000) and the author of *Mutual Expectations: a Conventionalist Theory of Law* (2002). Recently, he published widely about philosophical issues concerning organ procurement and concerning death and the right to life. He is working on books on both subjects. His paper "The regulation of euthanasia: how successful is the Dutch system?" will shortly be published in: Gerrit Kimsma & Stuart Youngner (eds.) *Physician-Assisted Death in Perspective* (Cambridge University Press).

Chris Gastmans Chris Gastmans (1966) started his academic career in 1990 at the Centre for Biomedical Ethics and Law, Faculty of Medicine, KU Leuven. He has a Doctoral Degree in Theology, KU Leuven (1995). His doctoral dissertation is a critical study of the historical, anthropological and moral theological foundations of nursing ethics, conceptualized as an ethics of care. He received the position of Full Professor of Medical Ethics in the Faculty of Medicine, KU Leuven. Since 2002, he is member of the Bureau of the European Association of Centres of Medical Ethics (EACME).

He teaches Medical Ethics, Nursing Ethics and Ethics of Care. He serves as an ethicist in several ethics committees. He is member of the Editorial Board of the international journals *Nursing Ethics* (SAGE, London) and *Nursing Philosophy* (Blackwell, Oxford). His most important books are *Between Technology and Humanity* (Leuven University Press 2002) and *New Pathways for European Bioethics* (Intersentia 2007). He published over 100 articles in international journals and books on end-of-life care ethics, elderly care ethics, empirical ethics, care ethics, and nursing ethics.

Martin Gunderson Martin Gunderson is DeWitt Wallace Professor of Philosophy at Macalester College. He received his Ph.D. in philosophy from Cornell University and his J.D. from the University of Minnesota. For the past two decades he has been interested in areas where healthcare, civil liberties and philosophy overlap. He has published on informed consent, physician-assisted death, suicide, medical privacy, confidentiality, and human rights. He is co-author of *AIDS: Testing and Privacy*, and his articles have appeared in a variety of journals including *The Hastings Center*

Report, *The Kennedy Institute of Ethics Journal*, the *Journal of Social Philosophy*, *Public Affairs Quarterly*, and *Philosophy and Medicine*.

He is currently working on human rights, especially as they apply to issues in healthcare. His recent work on human rights includes 'Human Rights, Dignity, and the Science of Genetic Engineering' (*Social Philosophy Today* 2007), 'Enhancing Human Rights: How the Use of Human Rights Treaties to Prohibit Genetic Engineering Weakens Human Rights' (*Journal of Evolution and Technology* 2008), and 'Does the Right to Health Lack Content' (*Social Philosophy Today* forthcoming).

John Hardwig John Hardwig is professor emeritus of Philosophy at the University of Tennessee. He did his undergraduate work at Yale and earned his Ph.D. at the University of Texas at Austin. He taught philosophy at Wellesley College, the University of Tennessee, Humboldt State University, Maryville College, and East Tennessee State University before coming back to UT in the Fall of 2000. He served as head of the Philosophy Department at Tennessee from 2000 until he retired in August, 2010.

Research interests in bioethics include the place of the family in medical treatment decisions and end-of-life issues. Publications relevant to the themes of this book include: 'Going to Meet Death; The Art of Dying in the Early Years of the 21st Century' (*Hastings Center Report* 2009), 'Families and Futility – Forestalling Demands for Futile Treatment' (*Journal of Clinical Ethics* 2005), 'Spiritual Issues at the End of Life: A Call for Discussion' (*Hastings Center Report* 2000), 'Is There a Duty to Die? (*Hastings Center Report* 1997), 'SUPPORT and the Invisible Family' (*Hastings Center Report* 1995), 'The Problem of Proxies With Interests of Their Own' (*Journal of Clinical Ethics* 1993). Some of these papers in bioethics were collected in *Is There a Duty to Die and Other Essays in Bioethics* (Routledge 2000).

Daniel M. Hausman Daniel M. Hausman is the Herbert A. Simon Professor of Philosophy at the University of Wisconsin-Madison. He was educated at Harvard and Cambridge Universities and received his Ph.D. in 1978 from Columbia University. He has taught at the University of Maryland at College Park, Carnegie Mellon University, and he has visited at the Institute for Advanced Studies and the London School of Economics.

His research has centered on epistemological, metaphysical, and ethical issues at the boundaries between economics and philosophy. He co-founded the journal, *Economics and Philosophy*, and co-edited it from 1984 to 1994. He is the editor of *The Philosophy of Economics: An Anthology* (3rd edition 2007) and author of *Capital, Profits, and Prices* (1981), *The Inexact and Separate Science of Economics* (1992), *Causal Asymmetries* (1998) and *Economic Analysis, Moral Philosophy, and Public Policy* (2006, with Michael McPherson) and more than 130 essays. His most recent book, *Preference, Value, Choice and Welfare* will be published this year by Cambridge University Press. In 2009, Hausman was elected to the American Academy of Arts and Sciences.

Jeroen Luyten Jeroen Luyten is a doctoral student at the Centre for Health Economics Research and Modeling Infectious Diseases of the University of Antwerp and visiting researcher at the Institute of Philosophy of the Catholic University of Leuven.

His PhD-research focuses on ethical aspects of infectious disease prevention. He obtained a Master degree in economics at the University of Antwerp (2005) and a Master degree in philosophy at the Catholic University of Leuven (2009). He has published papers about ethical challenges in vaccination policy (forthcoming in *Public Health Ethics*) about Quality-Adjusted Life Years (*Value in Health* 2011) and about the economic impact of infectious disease outbreaks (*Pharmacoeconomics* 2009). He also collaborated on a health economic evaluation of hepatitis A vaccination for the Belgian Health Care Knowledge Centre (*KCE reports* 98A).

Thomas R.V. Nys Thomas R.V. Nys (1978) is Assistant Professor at the University of Amsterdam. He studied Philosophy and Applied Economics at the KU Leuven and obtained his doctoral degree in Philosophy with a study on the meaning and value of 'Autonomy' in 2006.

His research interests are at the intersection of ethics, political philosophy and philosophical anthropology. He has published several articles on a variety of subjects, ranging from political philosophy to ethics and philosophical anthropology. He is author of, among others, 'Psychiatry under Pressure' (*Medicine, Health Care, and Philosophy* 2006) and 'Paternalism in Public Health Care' (*Public Health Ethics* 2008). Together with Yvonne Denier and Antoon Vandevelde he is co-editor of *Autonomy and Paternalism: Reflections on the Theory and Practice of Health Care*, (Peeters 2007). Recently, he co-edited a volume with Katrien Schaubroeck on the philosophy of Harry Frankfurt (in Dutch): *Vrijheid, noodzaak en liefde* (Pelckmans 2011).

Shlomi Segall Shlomi Segall is a Senior Lecturer at the Department of Political Science at the Hebrew University of Jerusalem, and the head of the Integrative Program in Politics, Philosophy, and Economics (PPE) there. He holds a DPhil in Political Philosophy from Oxford, and has held a research position at the Harvard Program in Ethics & Health.

His recent publications include 'What's So Bad about Discrimination' (*Utilitas* forthcoming); 'Why Egalitarians Should not Care about Equality' (*Ethical Theory and Moral Practice* 2011); and 'Is Health (Really) Special? Between Rawlsian and Luck Egalitarian Justice in Health' (*Journal of Applied Philosophy* 2010).

He is the author, most recently, of *Health, Luck, and Justice* (Princeton University Press 2010). He is currently completing a book manuscript titled *Equality and Opportunity*.

Paul Schotsmans Paul Schotsmans (1950) is professor of medical ethics in the Faculty of Medicine, KU Leuven. He is co-chair of the Belgian Federal Advisory Committee on Bioethics. He is member of the Belgian Transplantation Council. He is past vice dean of the Faculty of Medicine (2005–2011) and past president of the European Association of Centers of Medical Ethics (EACME) (1998–2002).

He was board member of the International Association of Bioethics, president of the ethics committee of Eurotransplant as well as member of several local and international ethics committees. His research interest is mainly medical ethics and the integration of Personalism as an ethical model in the bio-ethical debate. He is the author and co-editor of several books in bioethics and papers in leading journals.

Antoon Vandevelde Antoon Vandevelde studied economics and philosophy. He graduated in 1986 with a PhD on Exchange and Recognition. Currently, he is Full Professor at the Centre for Economics and Ethics and Dean of the Institute of Philosophy of KU Leuven. Formerly he was teaching for a long time at the universities of Antwerp and Rotterdam.

He published many articles, mainly in the field of economic ethics and political philosophy, particularly on themes such as philosophy of social security, migration policy, responsibility for future generations, altruism and the logic of the gift, liberalism and communitarianism.

He also edited several books: (together with Guido Erreygers) *Is Inheritance Legitimate? – Ethical and Economic Aspects of Wealth Transfer* (Springer 1997), *Gifts and Interests* (Peeters 2000), and (together with Thomas Nys en Yvonne Denier) *Autonomy and Paternalism – Reflections on the Theory and Practice of Health Care* (Peeters 2007).

Index

Y. Denier et al. (eds.), *Justice, Luck & Responsibility in Health Care*, Library of Ethics and Applied Philosophy 30, DOI 10.1007/978-94-007-5335-8,

Q

R

S

MIX
Papier aus verantwortungsvollen Quellen
Paper from responsible sources
FSC® C105338

If you have any concerns about our products, you can contact us on
ProductSafety@springernature.com

In case Publisher is established outside the EU, the EU authorized representative is:
Springer Nature Customer Service Center GmbH
Europaplatz 3, 69115 Heidelberg, Germany

Printed by Libri Plureos GmbH
in Hamburg, Germany